THE ETHICAL ASPECTS OF EVOLUTION

BY
JOHN C. KIMBALL

BOSTON
AMERICAN UNITARIAN ASSOCIATION
1913

171.7
K49e

PREFACE

A volume entitled "The Romance of Evolution," and containing Mr. Kimball's essays upon the contact of the philosophy of evolution with the religious traditions and sentiments, has recently been published with a brief memorial preface which need not be repeated here. Mr. Kimball believed that evolution was the friend and ally of religion and not its enemy, that while it had overthrown an outgrown theology, it had opened the way for more rational and ethical interpretations of religion. He held that it had removed the foundations of religion from the quicksands of external authority and of supernaturalism to the solid basis of reason and experience.

The present volume contains some of Mr. Kimball's most characteristic lectures upon the relation of the doctrine of evolution to the ethical questions of his generation. Many of them were delivered before the Brooklyn Ethical Society and, in some cases, originally bore slightly different titles. Mr. Kimball believed in democracy and in human brotherhood. He believed in equality of privilege for every one.

PREFACE

He was a friend of peace, of justice, of liberty and of fraternity. He thought deeply and spoke forcibly on all such matters.

Appended to the lectures are six sermons preached in the course of a long and fruitful ministry. The concluding sermons are those in which Mr. Kimball bade farewell to his congregations in Hartford, Conn., and Sharon, Mass.

All who knew Mr. Kimball recognized the wide range of his knowledge, the freshness and independence of his thought, his keen sympathy with all who suffered injustice or wrong, his chivalry in taking up the cause of the weak and the unbefriended, his fund of humor, his sincerity and warm-heartedness. These addresses and sermons declare what manner of man he was and set forth his matured convictions upon many timely and important themes.

CONTENTS

THE ETHICAL ASPECTS OF EVOLUTION

		PAGE
I	The Ethics of Evolution	1
II	Evolution and Animal Life	52
III	Evolution and War	94
IV	Evolution and Politics	145
V	Evolution and Progress	201
VI	Evolution and Christianity	224
VII	Immortal Youth	260

SERMONS

I	Childhood—A Christmas Sermon	281
II	Stand-bys	297
III	Liberal Christianity and Liberal Orthodoxy	313
IV	A Dedication Sermon, Omaha, 1871	338
V	A Minister's Ideal	363
VI	The Humanitarian Side of Religion	389

THE
ETHICAL ASPECTS
OF
EVOLUTION

THE ETHICAL ASPECTS OF EVOLUTION

I

THE ETHICS OF EVOLUTION

The subject of this book is distinctively the Ethics of Evolution, not the Evolution of Ethics — in other words, the kind of ethics to which man is logically brought by the process of evolution, and not the process itself by which the results are brought about. Nevertheless, as there are differences of view among evolutionists with regard to the exact nature of the process, and as the results reached depend for their certainty somewhat on the view taken of how they are reached, I want, as a preliminary, to review the process part of the matter, and to state what is special in my own conception of its nature.

First, while accepting in general the revised utilitarian theory that ethics is the outcome under evolution of the accumulated experiences of our race with regard to what is fittest in conduct, consolidated into intuitions and transmitted from generation to generation by heredity, the theory so brilliantly set forth by Mr. Spencer and his disciples, I cannot go with them in the prominence they give to pleasure and pain as the chief things for which these experiences have been useful, or in holding, as they state it, that " acts are good or bad according as their aggregate effects increase men's happiness or increase their misery."

Utilitarianism is not necessarily confined to utility for happiness. To get at nature's form of it we must get at what nature wants things to be useful for, that is, at what nature in evolution is trying to bring about. What is it? Plainly, not pleasure alone, or pleasure even in the form of happiness, but growth, fuller and finer life, an ever better state of things alike in the universe at large and in its individual parts. As Longfellow has truly put it:

> " Not enjoyment and not sorrow
> Is our destined end or way,
> But to act that each to-morrow
> Finds us farther than to-day."

And the word utility, therefore, fairly includes everything which goes to promote this object. Pleasure is only one of these things, is a means and not an end, the guide and not the goal, the feather with which nature tips the arrow of conduct to send it the straighter to its mark, and not the mark itself. And even allowing it is an infallible guide, even allowing, what is undoubtedly true, that all good conduct tends in the end to happiness, and all bad conduct to misery, it surely is a mistake to put the means of a thing in the place of its end as constituting its distinctive character.

Compare conduct in this respect with the eating and drinking of food. These acts are pleasant, and the pleasure of them is beyond question the immediate motive which prompts them; and normally, food is good or bad according as it is agreeable or disagreeable to the taste. But nature's object in having us eat and drink is not the pleasure of eating and drinking, but growth, health, efficiency for work; and her supreme test as to whether food and drink are good or bad is whether they build us up as men and women and enable us the better to do our work in the world.

So with what is the food and drink of humanity's larger body. The hedonist is right in saying that its goodness and pleasantness must in the long run go together — is restating only the old Scripture doctrine that " wisdom's ways are ways of pleasantness." But its goodness does not consist in its pleasantness, but in its being morally nutritious, and so promotive of the doer's inner health and strength. Mr. Spencer himself has places in which he recognizes this to be the real criterion, as where he says, "Evolution becomes highest when the conduct simultaneously achieves the greatest totality of life in self, in offspring, and in fellow men."

There is one word in our language which expresses grandly all these ends, a word which includes happiness, yet is beset with none of its objectionable implications, the word "welfare." And I should define good conduct as the conduct voluntarily adopted which has been found by the accumulated experiences of mankind, consolidated into intuitions and transmitted by heredity, to be most conducive to the welfare of the individual and of the race, and say its rightness has come from its being in harmony with natural laws; and bad conduct as that which has been found in the same way to be conducive to the ill-being of the individual and of the race, and as getting its wrongness from its being in violation of natural laws.

Briefly stated, ethics is humanity's hygiene.

But while utility is thus the test objectively of all conduct as to its goodness or badness, whatever its source may be, it seems to me, yet farther, that to give any form of it subjectively an ethical character, its motive, purpose, cost of effort, ought to be made more prominent than they have been thus far by evolutionists.

ETHICS OF EVOLUTION

I cannot indeed go with those who would make the motive everything in determining the moral value of an act, for the world is full of cases in which the most outrageous deeds have had behind them motives which in themselves were sincerely good. It is not only hell down below, but some of the darkest, direst hells up here on earth which are paved with good intentions. It was a good intention which introduced slavery into America, kindled the fires of Smithfield, ordered the massacre of St. Bartholomew, beheaded Sir Henry Vane, burned Joan of Arc, crucified Jesus Christ, and, indeed, if the Bible account is to be trusted, it was a good intention which at first introduced into the world " sin and all our woe."

But, on the other hand, if outward utility is made the sole test, some of the grandest deeds humanity has ever risen to — liberty's ten thousand defeated battle-fields, religion's long list of martyrs whose blood never became the seed of any church, reforms which perished in dungeon cells, and the vast army of seekers after scientific truth who found only error or failure — all these will have to be set down as ethically bad; while at the same time not a few deeds whose prompting was the meanest and sometimes the wickedest motives, but which unexpectedly turned out well, as, for instance, the stealing of negroes from Africa, England's persecution of our Puritan ancestors, the slaveholders' rebellion, Joseph's being sold by his brethren into Egypt, and even the old serpent's tempting of Adam and Eve into sin, must be regarded as good conduct. Last summer a dog on the St. Lawrence River leaped bravely into the water and rescued from drowning a child that had fallen from the wharf. Of course everybody praised and petted and daintily fed him for the act; and the next day, wanting more of such treatment, and no child falling in to afford him the means of meriting it, the hedonistically philosophic animal deliberately pushed a nice little girl overboard and again plunged in for her rescue, evidently very much puzzled at the apparent inconsistency of ethics, when, on bringing her ashore, instead of caresses he received kicks. And if outward acts alone are to be considered, who shall say the dog did not have some reason for his disappointment, the deed itself in each case being the same.

Evidently, the only way of avoiding such inconsistency is to recognize both factors, the motive and the result, as contributing to render conduct ethical; and it is a recognition which has the fullest sanction of evolution. For all motives, whether they lead outwardly to failure or to success, have a reflex action inwardly on their subjects, which must be taken into the account. If they are mean and bad, no matter how helpful to the world's welfare their outcome may be, they make the man himself mean and bad; if noble and good, no matter how utter their outward failure, they give him within a nobler and better soul. And this inner growth transmitted by heredity and consolidated into character becomes in after generations as truly a part of the world's ethical possessions as anything which results outwardly from conduct.

Instead of its being true, therefore, that " some rise by sin, and some by virtue fall," the truth is that goodness, though often mistaken in its action and leading in some things to harm, never wholly fails; and evil, though sometimes acting rightly and leading to some forms of benefit, never wholly succeeds. Though out of Spanish lust for gold came the discovery and exploration of this New World, all the same out of it came Spain's own decay. The cruelty which wrenched from Indian hands " the pearl of the Antilles " secreted in its own blood the acid which all these later years has been dissolving it in the conqueror's very grasp. The valor of Naseby and Marston Moor, of Yorktown and Appomattox Court House, was the reflex action of liberty's ten thousand defeated battle-fields; and the martyrs' blood in religion which was never the seed of any church became the seed not less surely of the whole coming man.

"The aim, if reached or not, makes grand the life."

Again, as regards the altruistic element in ethics, I can but think that evolutionists, in taking a fully developed egoism as its starting point, have mistaken the process of its origin, and thereby have made for themselves a very needless difficulty. We all remember Pope's famous lines:

" Self love but serves the virtuous mind to wake,
As the small pebble stirs the peaceful lake,
The center moved, a circle straight succeeds,
Another still and still another spreads.
Friend, parent, neighbor first it will embrace,
His country next, and next the human race."

But ontologically it is vastly more probable that the real order was exactly the other way, the wider circle coming first, or, rather, it is probable that evolution followed here the same order as everywhere else, differentiated the various forms of love altogether out of one original homogeneity of feeling in which they all existed only as undeveloped possibilities, just as in astronomy nature did not make the planets, the satellites, and the sun all complete and then unite them in the solar system, but started them as one common nebulous mist, and evolved at the same time the system and its members. The ego and the alter are thus not father and child, but twin brothers,—

"Self love and social at one birth began,"—

it being philosophically just as impossible to develop the one without the other as in magnetism to get a north pole without getting equally a south pole. In the lower forms of life the two are only partially differentiated even now, their communities having a common gregarious self in which the individual selves are hardly more distinct than are those of its cells in an animal body. Years ago, before I had learned my wider ethical relations, and so, though ordained to be a fisher of men, used occasionally in the summer to indulge in being a fisher of fish, I have been in a line of boats off the Beverly shore half a mile long, pulling in mackerel as fast as the hook could be thrown, when suddenly, though the water remained full of them, they would cease biting with me and at the same time with every boat in the line. Then after half an hour or so, just as my ministerial conscience was regaining its sway, and about to send me home to my proper vocation, my hook would be seized, and instantly I would hear the captives flapping into boats the whole length of the line, evidently as much the result of one impulse as if they had been a single fish.

Wordsworth with his close observation of nature noticed the same trait long ago in a herd of cattle:

> " The cattle are grazing, their heads never raising,
> There are forty feeding as one."

Haeckel somewhere describes a creature named the flimmer-ball, whose parts some of the time swim about as independently as a shoal of minnows, but which, when frightened, unite again and move as one organic mass. Bees in a swarm are but a single body. And among human beings the same all-embracing tribal self is to be seen in the sway of fashion, in all boyhood's simultaneously bringing out its marbles with the first warm days of spring, and in the uniformity with which Easter bonnets appear as a part of Easter religion on the heads of all women, and summer hats disappear about the tenth of September, as by a common inner breeze, from the heads of all men. Especially is it seen in all panics, as at the battle of Chancellorsville, when the whole Eleventh Army Corps, with eyes bulging and hair on end, came rushing back pell mell on the very bayonets of the corps behind them, a vast shoal of human beings turned into a gigantic flimmer-ball in which all individual selves reverted to the common animal self out of which they had been evolved.

With this homogeneity of the ego and alter to start with, corresponding with what in paleontology is called " a prophetic type," it is easy to see that as it differentiated into distinct individuals, each individual must have inherited and developed in itself some share of what was in the original common stock, regard for self and regard for the whole, so that the command of Jesus, " Thou shalt love thy neighbor as thyself," that is, as being thy larger self, is not a mere arbitrary precept, but an ethic of evolution which has behind it the foundation principle of all society.

It is a process which is still going on, integration, the third great stage of evolution, being the phase of it which is now most in evidence; and as in astronomy when the separating planets were organized into the solar system, the gravity which had made them originally one nebulous mass was not lost, but became the force which is now holding them organically together and keeping them forever acting on each other, so by the same beautiful law, as fast as the units of our race are integrated in their social system, the regard for the common homogeneous self which they had at first, becomes the affection which holds them in altruistic relations, and makes each of them still interested in the welfare of the whole, so that as Pope says:

"There's not a blessing individuals find
But somehow leans and harkens to mankind."

Again, as regards the origin of that mysterious feeling in ethics which is ordinarily denoted by the little word "ought," or, when we want to talk Kant, by the big words, "categorical imperative," it seems to me that evolutionists, in trying to derive it from the inherited teachings of those in authority, from the dread of punishment, from the reasoning that to get rights ourselves we must give them to others, and the like, have justly exposed their efforts to the criticisms of unbelievers, and have failed to use one of the most fundamental and far-reaching of their own principles, the natural tendency of things to vary; a principle set forth so clearly by Mr. Darwin in his great work on the "Origin of Species," and one which exists not only in all forms of outward life, but in all parts of our inward being. Oughtness, obligation, is indeed, as all the intuitional opponents of ethical evolution insist, a new species of feeling; but there is no reason to suppose that it did not originate, like all other new species of things, simply as a variation by minute changes from an older and more primitive species. It was probably at first the simple compulsion to get food and to do the other immediate visible things which were found by experience to be necessary for the continuance of life; then in the course of ages, it varied with men into the abstract feeling of compulsion to do whatever the inherited experiences of the race had shown to be essential for its welfare, those that had the variations and acted upon them surviving and leaving descendants, those that had them not inevitably dying out. Must,— that is the missing link in the chain between appetite and oughtness; duty — that the Messiah which came to men, as Jesus did, that they might have life and have it more abundantly. A rudimentary indication of its humble origin still remains in the very words of the beatitude which is its highest expression, "Blessed are they which do hunger and thirst after righteousness, for they shall be filled." And thus, instead of the moral law's being dragged down by evolution, as Mr. Balfour sneers, from the sublimity of the starry heavens to the ingenuity of the protective blotches on a beetle's wing, is not its real grandeur increased by its being made by it, like gravity,— rather, like Deity, a power which holds both the starry heavens and the humblest dust all in one comprehensive grasp?

Beyond oughtness, and as a crown to all the other factors concerned in ethical evolution, I have to recognize that of free will, not free will of the illusive nature that many evolutionists have made it, that is, freedom to will what one pleases, what pleases being as fixed in its action as what forces, nor yet free will as itself a cause and originator of force,—I cannot follow Dr. Martineau in that conception,— but free will as a self-determining faculty, able to choose which among pleasing things shall be its motive, and a director of causes and forces, — the free will which makes with heredity and environment the three great factors of all conduct. I know well the difficulties such a free will involves as regards law and motive and the chain of cause and effect, and that the exact process of its origin under evolution has never been explained. But it is no harder to deal with in this respect than life, or self-consciousness, or any of man's higher spiritual faculties,— is simply one round more of a ladder, each of which, though taking us into a world which is outside of all previous science, is found ultimately to take us to one which is inside of a yet larger science. It is what we are as directly conscious of as we are of existence itself; and the recognition of its reality is the only thing which can save evolution from the charge of a fraud at the very foundation of man's moral nature, the only thing which can give ethics its supremely distinctive character over all other conduct, or make it otherwise than a very delicate kind of mechanism, the only thing out of which it can get honestly its feelings of responsibility, remorse and self-approval. So I say with Emerson:

> Nor pauses in his plan,
> "For he who worketh high and wise,
> Will take the sun out of the skies
> Ere freedom out of man."

Passing now from these special points in the process of ethical evolution, to the results of the process, the first thing to be noticed is that ethical evolution does not exclude those results which have been arrived at by other systems, but includes alike them and their explanations,— differing in this respect from all other systems. The others are like the medical student at an emergency hospital where a good deal of rivalry existed to see which of the young men, when a call came to them for the ambulance, would get to the injured man first and bring him in. Having a very slow horse, this student was for a long while the last at the accident, and returning so often empty-wagoned, he was a good deal jeered at by his comrades for his ill success. By and by a change occurred by which he got a fresh young horse, and the very next day came in ahead of all the rest with four wounded men. The question at once arose of how he had done it. "Oh," said he, gleefully, "I drove full speed with my new horse to the one knocked-down man I was called to, and in galloping back I knocked down myself three more men and brought them along also." That is exactly what ethics hitherto has done,— in getting to its operating room any one of the world's four great systems, the theological, the legal, the intuitional and the utilitarian, it has had to knock down each of the other three and has brought in their shattered remains also.

Ethical evolution on the other hand is like the well-known Irish soldier with the group of prisoners he one day captured and brought into camp. Instead of knocking down either theology, law, utility or intuitionalism, it has captured them all without a bruise or a blow, as he did, by simply " surrounding them."

It is this which is the distinguishing mark of all great truths, their reconciling and including on a higher plane what lower down were only antagonistic half truths; and I know of nothing in the history of human thought which has done this so completely and beautifully, and with such a wealth of far-reaching suggestions as Herbert Spencer's " Data of Ethics." Somebody has called it his weakest book. But to my mind it is his strongest and most original, not excepting even his " Psychology,"— the Columbus discovery of a new continent on the globe of truth. Its hedonism is only the mistake of

ETHICS OF EVOLUTION 17

supposing its new world to be the old Indias, not affecting seriously its real grandeur. And, if he had written nothing else, this alone would have made him what I believe the future will write him, the leading mind of the nineteenth century.

Equally, evolution includes and justifies the various practical ethics of all nations, races and ages. Take the great central ones now held by all civilized people as the highest to which the human mind has come,— temperance, chastity, honesty, veracity, benevolence, self-sacrifice, good citizenship, reverence and the like,— evolution does not with its moving into its ethical house propose to store them all away, like old furniture, into the garret of the past, and put brand new ones in their place, any more than the nebular hypothesis proposes to change the stars, or geology to re-make the strata of the earth. It recognizes that like the stars and the earth they may in the course of ages be modified and have new relations, but it will be with no shock, no interregnum of virtue and duty. All evolution is in its very nature conservative. It points out how everything which is has a tap-root reaching down the eons into the world's primal dust,— shows how its future will have to come, not by any fiat of religion, or science, or legislation, but as the slow outgrowth of the present and the past. And, pre-eminently, it does so with regard to our age's great central virtues and duties,— traces them from their far-off beginnings, shows that though often poorly kept, they have survived, according to its own principles, only because in their struggle for existence they have been found the fittest for men to live by, and emphasizes that by its own definition of ethics as that conduct which is most conducive to human welfare, they are the ethics of evolution.

Look at the history of one of them which many persons have thought to be the most incapable of originating and flourishing and being sanctioned under the doctrine of utility, that of self-sacrifice. How, it is asked, can a kind of conduct which consists in the individual's giving up his own life, and a nation's giving up the lives of its noblest and best citizens, be conducive, in this world at any rate, to either individual or social welfare?

Well, to get at its root we must go back far beyond humanity into that homogeneousness of tribal life and care, out of which egoism and altruism have alike come. When a flock of grasshoppers out on the prairie meets a line of burning grass, its foremost ranks do not turn back, as a single grasshopper would, but unhesitatingly plunge in, and the rest do the same, and so on, each perishing till the fire is extinguished and a bridge formed over which the main body, or, perhaps, as the only ones left, the rear ranks, pass on. It looks at first like a magnificent example of self-sacrifice away down in the lower parts of the animal kingdom, something which could not originate in any evolutionized love of life, or in anything but a Heaven-implanted altruism. But really the swarm is only one large, loosely-jointed body, a part of which dies to save the other part, and is precisely what every individual animal does with the cells of which it is made up when it wants to rush through fire, is precisely what the most selfish person does when about to fall,— flings out his hands to get bruised rather than have his whole body harmed, — is done from the love of their common life. And when this common life with its common love develops, as it does in man, into individual lives with their individual wills and selves, how natural it is that the instinctive impulse to their common preservation, sacrificing a part to save the whole, should develop with them into that grand voluntary altruism which can sing that

"Whether on the scaffold high,
 Or in the battle's van
The noblest place for man to die
 Is where he dies for man."

How inevitable is it also, that those tribes of animals and those nations of men which have the most of such individuals ready to sacrifice themselves in battle and in danger for the common good, should survive, while those which have them not, or have the fewest of them, must inevitably in the struggle for existence be overwhelmed and perish, the evolutionary fulfilment of Jesus' words, "He that findeth his life, shall lose it,"— lose it in the dying out of his tribe; "and he that loseth his life for my sake shall find it again,"— find it in the larger life of his nation and his race. And who shall say that the fagots around the martyr's stake are any the less ethical because they are thus only at the upper end of a long line of fires at whose other extreme a flock of grasshoppers died; or that the cross on which Jesus hung, "towering o'er the wrecks of time," loses any of its moral grandeur because its foot rests in the ashes of earth's unnumbered animal myriads that gave their little undivided shares of life in order that the world's great whole might live; or that Mr. Kidd is not most profoundly mistaken when he declares in his "Social Evolution," that there is nothing in nature which can prompt a man to sacrifice his present good for the good of posterity, and that we must go to a heavenly religion to get what is thus rooted at the beginning in every phase of earthly life and without which no earthly life could ever be?

But, while the ethics of evolution thus includes the highest existing ethics and those of the highest races, it includes, also, just as certainly, those of the lowest character, alike in the present and the past, and of the lowest races, even the most savage and uncivilized ones. And how is it possible for any set of things grouped under the same name to be more utterly different from each other than many of these are? Look at a few specimens. The Ashantee girl who, when she wants to be very dressy, ties a twig to her back hair,— puts on this and nothing more,— is morally shocked at the English girl who is so ashamed of her natural charms that she covers them up with yards of cloth. A man with only one wife is despised for his selfishness by the Mokololo women exactly as an old bachelor without any wife is by all self-respecting Christian women. Filial duty among the Fijians is performed by a son's tenderly burying his old mother alive. Honesty is practised among the tribes of the Philippine Islands by their keeping a careful debit and credit account of each other's cut-off heads — tribes that some of our statesmen to-day are anxious to make our fellow American citizens. A Mayoruma man's great objection to becoming a Christian was that if killed in battle he was liable to be buried and eaten up by worms, instead of being broiled and consumed by human beings. An Asiatic chief in his last sickness, being urged by a missionary to forgive his enemies as a preparation for dying, answered with the most self-righteous complacency that he hadn't any,— he had already killed them all. And generally the graces and good deeds by which a savage expects to be saved are the number of lives he has taken, the extent to which he has hated his foes, the amount of property he has stolen, and the success with which he has lied.

It is a difference which no other ethical system has been able to explain, except as the work of an evil spirit or of man's inherent depravity, but which under evolution becomes perfectly explicable as the prompting of his inherent goodness, each form of it being the kind of ethics which the people producing it have found to be in their circumstances and for their stage of development most conducive to their preservation and welfare.

Look at one of its apparently worst manifestations, that of children's putting their parents to death as soon as they arrive at old age, so different from the civilized one of caring for them then as the most delightful of duties. It has been explained as the prompting of a religious belief that as people die, mature and strong, or old and weak, so in the future they will always be. But its origin is really ethical. Among tribes liable at any moment to be attacked by foes, and always living on the narrowest margin of food, the old are a burden whose keeping or removal makes all the difference between extinction or survival. Those tribes which kept them alive were starved and defeated; those which killed them became strong and victorious. The killing proved to be the conduct most conducive to the common welfare; and just as the Russian mother in her sleigh pursued by wolves, flung to them a part of her children to save the rest, so these poor savages, pursued by the wolves of famine and war, threw over from their life-carriage those who had come to their second childhood, rather than see their whole tribe perish. Friends, let us thank God we are living in a social state where such things are no longer needed; but let us not talk of total depravity, and of no ethics at all among those,— our own ancestors probably doing the same thing,— who by such acts have brought us safely through the wilds of time to our civilized home. Their deeds are but side blossoms on that one great tree of sacrifice, flowering with so many yellow and crimson petals, on whose topmost bough is the blossom that all Christendom honors to-day as ethics' highest reach.

It is this necessary relativity of conduct to a people's social condition which explains the degradation of their life which civilization so often carries to the barbarous races. Because the higher ethics are good for Christian lands, it does not follow that they are necessarily good for some far-off isle of the sea just emerging from savagery, or from some nearer new state out West like prize-ring Nevada, just sinking back into brutality. The story is told of an old farmer who, having a two-year-old colt he wished to train not to shy at every unexpected sight and sound, mounted him one morning and ordered his young son to hide behind the fence at the end of the lane and "boo" at him as he came along. Down the lane they went, the animal with his ears erect and his head alert, ready with the first appearance of a foe to take the alarm; and at the appointed place out rushed the boy flinging up his hat and at the top of his voice shouting "Boo-oo!" Instantly up in the air went the colt's heels and flat on the ground went his rider's body. "You young rascal, you!" exclaimed the irate old man, picking himself up and shaking his fist at the boy, "what did you frighten that horse for?" "Why, father," replied the young hopeful, "you told me to run out and say 'boo.'" "Well," answered the sire, cooling down, but still somewhat severely, "it was altogether too big a boo for such a small horse." So with the exalted Christian morality that our young missionaries have shouted to the world's old heathen tribes mounted on their half-tamed social state, it has been "altogether too big a boo for such a small horse," and the result has been, as in the Sandwich Islands, their prostration physically and morally to the earth.

On the other hand, we have in our modern civilization not a few ethical principles and ethical practices which are the outcome of evolution and entirely appropriate to a savage and half-civilized state, but whose requisite environment the world has outgrown, and that are as harmful and incongruous now as those of civilization are to savagery. Just as in the human body there are rudimentary organs like the cœcal sac of the intestines, the thyroid gland of the throat, the muscles of the scalp, the frontal sinus of the brain, and the air passages between the mouth and the ear, which are the shriveled and often harmful remnants of devices that were large and valuable in the animals from which the human body came, so in humanity's social body we have the same phenomena, ethics which in our animal and savage ancestry were all right, but which in its civilized state have only the place and are doing only the mischief of rudimentary organs. A while ago one of the dime museums over in Boston had on exhibition an orang-outang named Joe, that his captors had dressed up in gentlemen's clothes, and taught to eat with a knife and fork, drink out of a glass, hold receptions, and even write on a card. But his anatomy and brain and all his own natural actions were those still of a wild man of the woods. Well, what are the ethics of our newspapers, our congresses, our pugilistic encounters, our tariff laws and our Bradley-Martin balls but moral Joe Outangs — practices evolved in the woods and well enough there, but which are now only dressed up in civilized clothes, taught the outside rules of etiquette, and enabled to hold receptions, wield a pen, write articles and sometimes sermons, and that are fit only to be shown in dime museums?

Nor is the contrast that of ludicrousness alone. All savages in the midst of their ferocity have some regard for children as conducive to the tribal welfare; and one day out in Borneo, a Dyak warrior was seen running through a captured village, holding tenderly under one arm a little infant, and grasping under the other the gory head of its slain father. We are horrified at the thought of such an act in a savage; but what is all our civilization as yet but the mingling of the ethics which on the one side holds orphan children in its asylum arms, and on the other builds battleships and raises vast armies with which to grasp in war the gory heads by the hundred thousand of the children's slain fathers — what all our Jingo statesmen but would be Dyak savages?

It is this which is the real ethical character of all modern war, a mixing up of methods and virtues which were once vital elements in the world's great struggle for existence, but which it has now largely outgrown, with the finer and often directly antagonistic ones that are the special feature of our own later time.

The fact is, war is a rudimentary organ in the body of our modern civilization, — our thirty-feet-thirteen-inch cannon, with all their hugeness, but the vermiform appendix to the ethics of evolution; and however useful such an organ may have been in digesting the crude moral food of our wilder state, it is not strange that its presence now should result in cases of national appendicitis.

With the rudimentary ethics of the past, now antiquated and dying out, evolution has also what may be called its embryonic, or growing ethics, which, though the very opposite of the other in its own youth, is nevertheless equally the product of a by-gone age. It is a well known fact of biology that each animal, including even man, has in its growth to pass through all the ancestral forms from the amœba up, out of which its race has been evolved. A similar thing takes place in a man's moral growth, his passing through all the various forms of it from that of the savage up, which society has ever known, only here it occurs after his physical birth. It is thus that we have infant ethics, schoolboy ethics, football ethics, politician ethics, sportsman ethics and courtship ethics, all mixed in with our civilized Christian ethics, and gradually leading up out of themselves into its higher form.

Many a poor mother does not understand the necessity of these lower stages, and so when she sees her darling boy begin his moral life by telling lies, killing cats, swearing oaths, stealing tarts, fighting other boys, domineering over his little sister, and similar undeveloped ethical performances, she is in despair, fears the gallows is the only moral agency which will ever lift him up, and wonders how civilized people like herself and his father could ever have given birth to such a savage,— has his actions pointed to, perhaps, by her minister as evidences of his inborn total depravity.

Let her not be alarmed. They are only the inevitable rounds of the moral ladder he is climbing over into his ethical manhood. Give

ETHICS OF EVOLUTION

him plenty of good bread and butter and play and parental love, and a modicum of minister and Sunday-school, and unless he is a case of arrested development, some of which, alas, the highest evolution does now and then show, she will see him rise out of all which is thus embryonic into an adult ethics which is all that even a mother's prayers have ever asked for.

Then, as accounting for another part of the mixed morality which under evolution we find in the world, is the necessity nature is under, when she wants to make some very great improvement in society,— change it, say, from a military to an industrial state, or from savagery into civilization,— the necessity of tearing up and rendering useless much of what was once her very precious work. If anybody thinks evolution is all plain sailing, either physically or morally,— thinks that nature never has any perplexities and hard problems to solve and to hesitate over, he is woefully mistaken. Some of us passing through Boston a few years ago, while its great subway was being built, had an opportunity to notice the awful havoc that had to be made with the city's past conveniences, and the awful condition of the old streets which resulted,— indeed the Hub people are not yet over feeling sore at what they suffered during the insertion of this new spoke in their wheel.

But no engineer tunneling a subway through Boston ever came across so many sacred graveyards, networks of gas pipe and water pipe, involving now and then a terrible explosion, foundations of old churches, concealed cesspools and venerable Sam Adams monuments, which he had to cut through and push aside, as evolution does every time it opens a way into any new part of its domains.

See how it has been in securing man's physical rectitude. The animal body from which the human one was derived, going as it did on all fours, had the valves of its veins, the ligaments which support its embryo young, and the lenses and muscles of its eyes, all admirably adjusted to its horizontal position. But when nature wanted to set the animal upright and make a man's body out of it, all these arrangements contrived and fixed with such ages of care became wrong in their position, and no longer of any use, the valves in the horizontal veins where they are not needed instead of in the perpendicular one where they are needed, the ligaments at the side of their burden instead of under it, and the optic lenses and muscles usable only by a strain out of their natural position, so that not a few of the weaknesses, sicknesses and imperfections of the human body, including its spectacle-wearing, have arisen inevitably from its being set physically upright.

ETHICS OF EVOLUTION 31

So when nature set man morally upright, it involved a similar undoing of his old ethics: the checks and supports provided for his animal estate became useless, his appetites and instincts tending one way, his aspirations and intuitions another, while to see duty clearly, he had to get artificial helps. And now, every time a great reform is introduced into society, that is, the giving of it more uprightness, it involves inevitably a disturbance of the old safeguards, a breaking up of the old associations, and the making of it for awhile an ethical, subway-building Boston.

Coming in part under this same head is the confusion of duties which arises in a transition state from the necessity not of suppressing all at once a lower set of principles to make way for a higher set, but of keeping for awhile both of them in active operation. Nature in evolution does not bring one stage of progress sharply to an end before beginning another, but splices them together by letting the old run taperingly on side by side with the enlarging new, till the new is strong enough in itself and in its environment to act alone. While the ethics of the world's past, and especially of its animal past, has been the survival of the fittest and the killing of the unfit, that is of those who relatively were weak and poor and unadapted to their surroundings, the coming human ethics is the preservation of the unfit by the fittest, the ethics that is especially the teaching of Christianity. But to carry out the higher principle all at once would crowd the world with invalids, idiots, criminals, tramps and barbarians, and would undo all that nature for ages at such an enormous cost has been trying to do. So for the present we are acting and are obliged to act in part under each of these two ethical systems, our churches and charitable societies and a few advanced individuals doing all they can to save the weak and poor, and our governments and business institutions and society at large all they can to crowd them, if not out of existence, yet down to an ever lower place; and it is from the need of using both of what are such opposite principles that arise not a few of the great problems of our modern civilization,— our Indian question, our country's Philippine policy, the morality of England's South African War, the imposing of tariffs, how to deal with trusts, and, towering above all else, the world's Chinese problem.

Yet, while evolution thus sanctions the use of both principles, the proportion in which they shall be used is left to statesmanship and to humanity as their grand opportunity, and its lesson for them is that stress ought to be laid ever more and more on the side of the weak and the poor and physically unfit, those alike among

ETHICS OF EVOLUTION 33

individuals, nations and races,— ought to be in the direction of their survival and of their development each after its own type. By a beautiful law of nature their care lifts the fit up into a higher kind of fitness, that which can be reached in no other way; and in the world at large, while it will prevent its exclusive possession by the highest race of the highest religion, highest government, highest civilization, it will result in a fitness which is vastly better than that of the best alone,— in a variety of race, religion, government and civilization where, as in the human body, the humblest organs will have their special place and work and will unite with the highest in producing a richer life and completer form than the highest could without their help.

Periodicity, or what Mr. Spencer calls rhythm, is another element which has to be considered in accounting for the ethics of evolution. Nothing in nature moves forward, or by the very constitution of nature can move forward, with even pace. There is first an advance; then a rest, or perhaps retreat; then an advance again a little further; then another rest or retreat and advance, and so on, like the coming and going of the waves on the sea-shore in what as a whole is a rising tide. Some of these periods, as with the waves of light, are only the millionth part of a second apart; some, as with religion and business prosperity, stretch over twenty or thirty years; and some, as with the evolution of the different forms of life on the earth, are eons in length.

The development of ethics follows this same law of rhythm. Just now the world is in the midst of a retreating wave, is losing apparently much of what we hoped it had permanently gained. Wars are raging far and wide over the earth. Nations which took part in its great Peace Congress are among the first to rush to arms. The world's foremost republic is lapsing into imperialism. The grand principles of liberty, self-government and equality of rights, set forth in our Declaration of Independence, after a hundred years of reverence are being laughed to scorn. Even the teachings of the Sermon on the Mount are denied, that, too, by some of its own preachers. The class distinctions of birth have given place to the class distinctions of wealth. The question with regard to the half civilized nations of the earth is which of the civilized ones in dividing them up shall get the largest slice of their territory. And everywhere the ape and tiger in man, which seemed to be dying out, have sprung up again into new life.

It is a going back which apparently justifies pessimism and is filling many good people with

ETHICS OF EVOLUTION

despair,— is something which here and there is even ascribed to evolution as its cause. Evolution is its cause, not the doctrine of evolution, however, but evolution itself. It is one of its great laws of progress, is a retreat which is the necessary preparation for another advance, is a going backward of the jumper only that he may leap a higher fence and reach a farther mark. Geology has had its times, one of them especially at the close of what is called the Permian Era, when the whole physical world appeared to have reached its climax, and all its life alike animal and vegetable to be either dying out or sinking to a lower type; and the finite observer looking then over its condition, would equally have despaired of its future. But, as the geologist can now see, it was only one of the stages preceding its great human era, was a sinking and dying, out of which have come the rising and living of the better and fairer world which is ours to-day. So with this Permian moral era. Peace will spring with new beauty from the fields which are being fertilized with war. America will return with fresh loyalty to its Declaration of Independence, the pulpit with revived ardor to preaching the Sermon on the Mount. The jingo politician will be assigned to his true place as an ethic fossil. And the door of the East, which cannon can only smash, will be found to open wide to the touch of him who said of old, "I stand at the door and knock."

Then, beyond this, there is under evolution a relativity even of the highest virtues to each other and to their environment which makes them vary with circumstances as to the imperativeness of their use. As Mr. Spencer has well said, "Absolute ethics are possible only in an absolutely perfect social state." Some of them, to be sure, as those of honesty, veracity, justice, fidelity, kindness, self-sacrifice and the like, have been shown by such ages of human experience to be safest for man's welfare as to have in them for all ordinary cases the force of intrinsic rightness, and he must be a very bold man who would dare depart from their dictates.

But the world has found that all rules, even moral rules, have their exceptions, and that all stars, even the starry virtues, differ from one another in the degrees of their brightness. Situations arise now and then in which it is impossible to be faithful to the one without being false to the other. There are conflicts of ethical as well as legislative laws; kings in the realms of duty as well as of state between whose claims occasionally we have to choose. And much as we may condemn the principle in its Jesuistic shape of doing evil that good may come, we have out of our very love of right to

ETHICS OF EVOLUTION 37

say that when two evils are presented as alternatives, duty prompts, evil though it be, the doing of the least. Veracity is one of the manliest of virtues, lying one of the meanest vices; yet, if the cherry-tree cut down is that of a patriot army's movements, and the issue between a truth and an untruth that of a country's liberty, where is the George Washington fit to be its leader who will not say, " I did *not* do it with my little hatchet." When Booth was trying to escape after the murder of Lincoln, was it right to give him food and shelter, that food and shelter which in any ordinary case it would have been a sin to have refused? Who to save his wife and children from outrage does not feel that he ought to deceive and maim, and if need be, kill their assailant? What are all wars, defensive as well as offensive, but a legalized cheating, wounding, pilfering and destroying of the foe, a direct violation right through from opening shot to closing shout, of religion's Golden Rule? And, indeed, what is self-sacrifice itself, the highest virtue, but a deliberate choice between two wrongs, the wrong of allowing one's own life to be destroyed, which, if a man can prevent it, is suicide, or the wrong of seeing one's country, or cause, or fellow creatures, destroyed, which, if he can prevent it, is murder?

These are not questions merely of scholastic

casuistry, but of actual life, specimens of what every man, consciously or unconsciously, has daily to meet; and the difficulties they involve are not peculiar to the ethics of evolution, but are what all ethics have to deal with. There is no system which can make right in spite of its etymology, otherwise than sometimes a very crooked line; none which can have its higher without having also its lower law; none which on a revolving earth can make its moral, any more than its mathematical perpendicular, always lie in the same direction as regards absolute space.

The advantage of evolution over other systems is that it provides at its very core a principle for dealing consistently with such difficulties, and that is the principle which makes the question, which of them is conducive to the highest welfare, the supreme test of their rightness. It is no Greek grammar which after giving a rule has to give it a long list of exceptions more difficult to learn than the rule itself; no martinet soldier to enforce routines without regard to results; no ship's captain with the motto, " Obey orders, even if you break owners." It makes every man a part owner in the world's great ship, puts the port of a common well-being before him and says, While you use compass and stars and chart and all the experiences of the past as your help, use also your own brains, use also that force of evolution which is working in you not less than in all the past, and subordinate everything else, subordinate even compass and chart, if need be, to the one grand duty of reaching the port,— would say, were the alternative presented, Let the heavens stay up even though justice fall. And what is this after all, wicked as it may sound in the phrases of evolution, but the great Christian doctrine, so precious to us in its Scripture words, that love is the fulfilling of the law, that each man is to judge for himself what is right, and that it is the spirit in which a thing is done, not obedience to its letter, which giveth life?

In thus making duties relative to each other and dependent on their environment for their imperativeness, the ethics of evolution is of necessity intensely practical. It would not indeed go to the extent of the Honduras woman Mr. Spencer speaks of, who refused to kill a hen for her sick husband, because, as she said, " her husband might die and then she would lose him and the hen, too "— would not refuse to follow blindly sometimes a generous impulse. But on the whole, it does not believe much in pursuing virtue for its own sake, " in scorn of consequence," especially when it is others who are involved in the consequence.

Before it can say whether a thing is good, it wants to know what it is good for. Art, poetry, music, religion, beauty in all its forms are not despised by it, for it recognizes that they are all possible ministers to the world's well-being, but when they palpably fail of such use and are only corrupting and degrading, it has no toleration for the reverence of art, " for art's sake," or of " beauty as its own excuse for being," but joins with the most rigid iconoclast in its readiness to stamp them out. Deformity, poverty, pain, discord, ugliness in all its forms, likewise, are looked upon by it leniently as transition states and as possible means of discipline to man's higher nature, but never as objects to be sought after for what they are in themselves. Miss Frances Power Cobbe, while visiting a hospital of incurables in Rome, filled with wretches who had so little in the way of food that they fairly screamed to her for bread, asked an attendant, " Are there no charitable people in Rome to come and see them? " " Oh, yes," the sister replied, " there are the Princess So-and-so, and the Countess Blank-and-blank, saintly ladies, who come once a week." " And don't they provide them with food? " " No, signora, they don't do such things as that for them." " Then in Heaven's name what do they do? " " Oh, they comb their hair," hair filled with filth and vermin; and these great ladies took upon themselves the task not to relieve the sufferers, but as a work of the greater merit in saving their own souls because of its disgustingness. Evolutionary ethics has no place for such merits. It is very suspicious of any salvation which is to be realized away off in some other world. It believes in direct, outward salvation as the first thing to be sought, the salvation of the sufferers rather than of the saviors. Its method is to get rid of poverty and pain and ugliness, not to idealize them; to feed the hungry and clothe the naked and clean the filthy, not to comb their hair. It is no anchorite, but a strong, well-fed, well-clothed, business-like man, most glad when it can do both things at once, make a dollar for the world and make a dollar for itself. And while in case of need it is ready to sacrifice everything it has, even life itself, for the common good, it believes that when the same thing can be accomplished without self-sacrifice, to do it without is the greater virtue and ought to be chosen.

Again, if evolution takes off something from the rigid peaks of virtue, it adds vastly more to its breadth and depth. Every act which bears on welfare, and not what are called the intrinsic duties alone, is endowed by it with moral significance, the digging of a sewer more so at times than the preaching of a sermon, going to a political meeting than going to a church,— our eating and drinking, as Paul says, can be done to the glory of God. And it includes logically our conduct to animals as well as to all classes of men, for it recognizes them all as the unfolding of one life-principle, and all as having their well-being as a means and part of the world's well-being. Indeed, there is nothing in the universe so trivial and minute that under such ethics its bettering may not become a duty. Hitherto, as you know, the germ theory of disease has been that human ills are caused by too active microbes, and that the way to cure men was to kill microbes; but now, with more recent discoveries, it begins to look as if the cause of diseases is further back,— that it is only sick microbes which make sick men, and that to cure the men we need first to cure the microbes. So with humanity's larger moral body, to make sure of curing all its sicknesses, we must make healthy all its atoms.

"From nature's chain whatever link you strike,
Tenth or ten-thousandth, breaks the chain alike,"

and to have virtue wholly divine, it will have to be like the Deity himself

"As perfect in a hair as in a heart."

ETHICS OF EVOLUTION

Moreover, with all the flexibility of its application and all the indistinctness of its outlines, the ethics of evolution is very far from being, as so many even scholars have feared, without its solid foundation of everlasting principles. The two things are not by any means inconsistent with each other. Everybody knows how it is with the outward rules of hygiene,— that what is one man's meat is proverbially another man's poison, that clothing worn with comfort in summer would to the same individual be fatal in winter, and that the out-of-door, all-weather exercise which makes the strong man stronger, takes away from the poor invalid what little strength he has. Yet who denies from such facts that there are great fundamental hygienic principles, imbedded in our very nature, which, if we are going to live at all, we have got to live by?

It is the same with moral health. Intuitional ethics says its rules exist in the nature of things and are to be acted upon without regard to expediency by all people in all weathers. Evolutionary ethics avoids the expression "nature of things" because in it nature does not mean real nature, or things actual things; but it says instead that its laws exist in the constitution of the universe, must have been there from the very start, at least in the germ, otherwise how could they ever have been evolved; are the laws

of human conduct which are in harmony with
the laws of the world's conduct; and that in
being flexible to reason and common sense they
are only on a par with all other natural laws.
"*Suaviter in modo, fortiter in re,*" is its
motto;

> "All the forms are fugitive,
> All the substances survive,"

is its song. And when it suspends any law, it
is, as when those of gravity yield to those of
chemistry and those of chemistry to those of
vitality, not to make any interregnum of
morals, but only to have a mightier law take
its place, only because it would not have the
letter which killeth supreme over the spirit
which giveth life.

Who shall say that such freedom of choice
among principles makes them any the less fundamental?
Can there be anything in the metaphysician's outside-of-the-world nature-of-things more safe and solid on which to base
conduct than this inside constitution of the universe?
And if the evolutionist is accused of
having only the changing winds of expediency
to live by, can he not truthfully answer,—

"The winds that o'er my ocean run,
Reach thro' all heavens beyond the sun;
Thro' life, thro' death, thro' fate, thro' time,
Grand breaths of God they sweep sublime."

ETHICS OF EVOLUTION

Equally fixed and certain under evolution are the rewards and punishments of conduct. Instead of being arbitrary, loose and dependent for their enforcement on an external divine will, its very definition of good conduct as that which tends to promote welfare, and bad conduct as that which tends to promote harm, puts it under its own laws and makes it its own executor. It agrees with the Bible that " as righteousness tendeth to life, so he that pursueth evil, pursueth it to his own death "; that " whatsoever a man soweth that shall he also reap," natural good from natural seeds, spiritual fruit from spiritual sowing; and that though justice sometimes is long delayed, yet " sin when it is finished, bringeth forth death," and well-doing, in due time, that is, when it has had time to ripen, its harvest of good.

> " It knows the seed lies safe below
> The fires which blast and burn,
> And that for all in tears we sow,
> There waits a glad return."

It has before it, just as truly as religion has, a kingdom of heaven, a kingdom whose beginning, at least, is to be on earth. The striving, self-sacrifice and even the sense of oughtness which it now has, are from their very nature not to last forever, not, at any rate, as the necessities of any one of its fields. What is striven for is to be attained. Private and public welfare are to be so adjusted to each other that self-seeking will do the work of self-sacrifice, egoism of altruism,—

"All true self love and social be the same."

And with each repetition of a duty, tending, as we know it now does, to make its performance easier, how can it be otherwise than that the most difficult ones shall at last become habits, like the beating of the heart and the breathing of the lungs, carried on without effort and without consciousness, a realization, so far at least as they are concerned, of the old Buddhist Nirvana, and of what in Christianity is called "that peace of God which passeth understanding and which the world can neither give nor take away."

Yet with all this, and all its utilitarianism, practicality and rootedness in the earth, the ethics of evolution is not without its ideality, its mystery, its poetry and its possibilities of infinite progress,— is very far from being a system under which, as Mr. Balfour says, "in becoming perfectly good we shall all become perfectly idiotic." Who has ever measured the length and breadth and height of that human welfare which is its ideal? As with Whittier's waterfall,—

"Somewhere it laughs and sings, somewhere
Whirls in mad dance its misty hair:
But who hath raised its veil, or seen
The rainbow skirts of that Undine?"

What opportunities are there for skill, courage, consecration, heroism, all that is noblest in man, to bring up the world, even as it now is, to its highest ethical standard,— unite the nations in peace, level up and level down society's horrible class inequalities, abolish vice and wrong and ignorance, make the "concert of Europe" something else than a symphony of battle guns, fill Turkish hearts with Armenian love, take the last stolen dollar out of man's hand, the last murdered bird off from woman's head, and teach countries that to knock their weaker brethren down on battle-fields and rob them of their colonies is no more Christian than for highwaymen to knock travelers down in streets and rob them of their cash.

Then, with each new social state, each larger and complexer environment, something which is sure to come with evolution, how inevitably must there be a larger and complexer ethics for the promotion of its welfare. Said a fond mother looking down at her puling, squalling baby, "He is only eleven days old yet, and of course has some failings, but"— turning to the visitor —"I think he gives promise already of being at least a very truthful man." Humanity now, as compared with its mighty future, is little more than eleven days old, but to the fond eyes of evolutionary ethics it gives promise amid all, even of its puling and crying infancy, of a manhood, how large and true. Read Lecky's "History of European Morals" as some hint of the ethical progress, not only in virtues but in ideals of virtue, that we can fairly look for in the eighteen hundred years to come. Scientifically, as well as poetically, does earth have before it

> "A dream of man and woman
> Diviner but still human,
> Solving the riddle old,
> Shaping the age of gold."

And beyond earth, who can doubt that ethics with its new spiritual environment will have new heights to climb, new realms to enter upon, and that what here had to include the welfare of every hovel and every savage will have finally to include the welfare of every hell and every soul?

It is in this possibility that the peace of Christianity differs from the Nirvana of Buddhism. As fast as one faculty, one virtue, one part of our nature attains it, the vitality released from the need of struggling for its attainment goes into the unfolding of another, and then another, just as it does now; and thus it becomes possible for the soul to go on climbing up forever the stairway of Jesus' command, " Be ye therefore perfect even as your Father which is in heaven is perfect."

It is an ethics which in thus throwing its light forward, throws it backward,— gives the whole universe, even its darkest parts, a moral meaning. When we want to know whether a tree is good or bad, we do not use its roots, or trunk, or limbs or leaves as a criterion, much less its spines and bark, but its fruit; and, if this is sweet and wholesome and what all the other parts have tended to produce, even though it is only a small part of its whole bulk, and appears only after many years of its life, we call the whole tree, including its darkest root and its sharpest spine, a good tree.

Why should we not apply the same principle to our judgment of the universe, fruiting little by little in a moral man,— recognize it all through from nebulous root to the bark and spine of human cruelty and ignorance and sin as a moral universe? According to the fundamental principles of evolution, all that will be in it at its highest reach of ethical attainment must have been as a possibility in its original fire mist. Matter is moral, gravity virtuous; the dragons of far-off geologic ages

"That tore each other in their slime"

were a part of the violent who with their violence were taking the kingdom of heaven. The roots of mercy are in the earthquake; the seeds of love in the thunderbolt. Even sin has its side of saintliness; even wrong its work for right. They are all the stages of an evolving universe, all a part of the things that are working together for good. And justly they must all share in the character of its final outcome — the Satans of nature not less than of Job report at last as sons of God in the court of their common Lord.

Viewed thus, how rich is the subject, not only in philosophic interest but in its satisfaction to one of man's deepest heart wants. Cold as the word morality is sometimes thought to be, all our hopes, all our happiness, all our safeguards, all the best parts even of love, are bound up with what it represents. Without an ethical element at the world's core, how little could the splendor of its skies, the grandeur of its mountains and seas, the abundance of its physical comforts, and its manifestations of majesty and might make it a really desirable dwelling place for beings like man,— as little so as a magnificent city in which was no provision, outward or inward, for enforcing what is

ETHICS OF EVOLUTION

right. And it was the feeling that evolution did away with this element — deprived the world of a lawgiver, and so necessarily of a moral law, which prompted at first religion's opposition to Spencer and Darwin. How baseless the fear! Their teaching has revealed under the broken tables of Sinai the unbreakable tables of the soul, made the Sermon on the Mount a part of the sermon of the universe, and in place of a policeman God armed with a club, walking the world's streets, has unveiled a Divine Principle in the world itself whose wand is simply welfare. Evolution has done many wonderful things intellectually for man. It has lighted up the dark caverns of the earth below and flooded with radiance its vast animal and vegetable kingdoms up above. History has under it a new meaning; society a key which unlocks not a few of its intricacies; religion the only lens which can focus again its broken lights. It has given to psychology the first glimmer of sense it ever had, and revealed in heredity marvels of the mind that render miracles commonplace. But its crowning gift, after all, tried alike by what it is and what it does, is — the Ethics of Evolution.

II

EVOLUTION AND ANIMAL LIFE

Man has always had a deep interest in animals. When he first woke to consciousness from the sleep of his own brute infancy in the early morning of the world's day, possibly its tertiary hour, he found them already risen before him, a habit of precedence they still keep up, crawling as insects over his face, singing as birds in his ear, sporting as quadrupeds at his side. The oldest works of art found on earth, Preraphaelite by at least two hundred thousand years, as well as in other qualities, are etchings of their forms on plates of reindeer horn exhumed from anteglacial caves; and the liking for them and for pictures and stories about them, and the aptness for getting acquainted with them which all children exhibit to-day, are but the individual child repeating in himself, according to a well-known law of evolution, the intimacy and wonder for them which he learned originally in his childhood as a race. How close ever since have been his relations with them, how impressive to him their instincts and intelligence, so like yet unlike his own, how many and varied their contributions to the beauty and glory of his dwelling-place and to the comfort and joy of himself! Beneath all outward differences they have been his fellow-citizens in the great kingdom of nature, his inevitable neighbors and associates, if not his recognized blood-relations, in the great family of life. Delegations of them have toiled with him at the plow, hunted with him in the chase, fed with him at the table, played with him at the fireside, traveled with him in the journey, fought with him on the battle-field. All the deeper experiences of his own existence — birth, growth, pain, pleasure, love's thrill, and death's agony — he has seen repeated in them. Language is filled with expressions for the qualities and activities they have in common — men, wolfish and foxy; bulls and bears in Wall Street; camels, "ships of the desert"; and ships in their turn "ocean greyhounds." Great nations have used them as the emblems of their power — made them play what a part in history as the Roman eagles, the British lion, and the Russian bear! Poetry has found in them some of its most suggestive themes, soaring with them how loftily in Bryant's Waterfowl, singing with them how sweetly in Shelley's Skylark, running with them how gracefully in Cowper's Hares, swinging with them how enchantingly in Lowell's June bird, " atilt like a blossom among the leaves," and galloping with them how gloriously in Sheridan's steed bearing its rider and victory to Cedar Creek and a flying army thirty miles away! Who would lose out of fiction Ulysses's faithful dog, or the lesson-teaching asses, apes, and foxes of Æsop's Fables, or Don Quixote's Rozinante, or the Cid's Bavieca, or Scott's Antlered Monarch of the Waste, or Dickens's Boxer and Jip, or Poe's croaking Raven, or, later, Mrs. Sewell's Black Beauty, or even Mary's Little Lamb? With what a wealth of vigor and grace they have lent themselves to painting in the canvas of Landseer and of Rosa Bonheur, and to sculpture in such marbles as the Plunging Horses and the Farnese Bull! Astronomy has taken them as its helper into the far-off skies, bidding the north forever know its place with a Great and Little Bear, covering the earth in its cool autumn nights with an Eagle's starry wings and establishing in the solemn heavens the never-stopping merry-go-round of its zodiacal Ram, Bull, Crab, Lion, Scorpion, Goat, and Fishes. And even in the midst of religion's grand service and majestic thoughts they have occupied how large a place both as the victims offered the gods and as the very gods they were offered to — even in our Christian faith have borne on their backs what mighty doctrines as the Serpent, the Worm, the Dove, the Lion of Judah, and the Lamb of God!

It is out of this great wonder realm of animal life, associated with man in so many ways and of which he himself is so vital a part, that zoölogy has arisen, seeking to arrange its objects, to discover their structure, relations, and laws, and to get at their cause and reason. There is no other branch of science which alike in its materials and in itself is so full of interest, no other which embodies so completely the great world-wide principles of evolution and on the field of which the battles against it have been so fierce and the victories for it so brilliant, no other which lets the student in so close to the very workshop and elbow of nature and so near to the great mystery of life, no other which opens so suggestively into the whole philosophy of man's own being, both physical and mental, individual and social, as this; and a lecture devoted not so much to its details, needing years of study, as to its growth and larger teachings and to its bearing on these other themes, may have its modest place, even when the lecturer's qualification for it is only a love about equally divided between its outside live objects and its inside live truths.

I. Looked at historically, the growth of the science itself has been along the direct lines not only of evolution, but of evolution in its Darwinian phase of mounting up from species to species through variation, modifying environment, a struggle for existence, and natural selection. In its beginnings and first forms, the same as with life itself, it was vague, nebulous, protoplasmic, consisting for ages of only such acquaintance with the habits and structure of animals as the hunter and the herdsman following them in the chase and the field, and the priest and the householder cutting them up for the altar and the table, would be likely to acquire, and of such accounts of them as wonder and amazement would be likely to suggest. Even after collections of their varieties began to be made it was as objects of curiosity and amusement rather than of study; and in regard to their very names, if it is not a puzzle as to how they were obtained from their more waspy, bearish, and uncommunicative owners, as it was to John Phoenix how astronomers ever got at those of the stars, it is one, certainly, as to which animals those used in its earlier books were really meant for, so loose is their description.

Aristotle (384–322 B. C.), that mountain mind which caught on its brow so many of the beams of wisdom's rising sun a thousand years before they touched the vales below, was the first observer to look on animals with the really scientific eye, describing minutely their wonderful varieties, and, by his divisions of them into oviparous, viviparous, and the like, recognizing the need, if not the method, of their classification. It was a work in which Alexander the Great was his friend and patron, putting at his service, it is said, millions of money and thousands of men, specimens also of all the new animals and plants found by him in the countries he ravaged; and it is an interesting fact that while the empires over men that the great Macedonian established have long since passed away, and the glory that he won as a warrior become only a blot on the page of history, the little he did among the brutes was the founding of a kingdom that has gone on to gather all lands into its sweep and is the sole thing remembered now to his credit.

But Aristotle, like advanced thinkers in all departments of life, even in religion itself, if a great help to progress, was also a great hindrance; if a mountain to catch long beforehand the beams of the rising sun, a mountain likewise to throw long afterward a deep darkness over the plain. For two thousand years men lingered in the shadow of his great name, studied what he had said about animals rather than animals themselves, and trembled lest in going beyond Aristotle they should go beyond truth. It was not till the seventeenth and eighteenth centuries, and with them the advent of Ray and Willoughby in England, Buffon in France, and preëminently Linnæus in Sweden, that the science resumed its growth, one of the many instances in known history of a leaping from mind to mind over whole centuries with hardly a connecting link between, which ought to remove all difficulty about missing links in the ages before history when in accordance with the same law the leap was from species to species and from form to form.

The great service of Linnæus (1707-1768) to zoölogy, the same as to botany, was his well-known twofold one of classification and of nomenclature. He was a new Adam in the Eden of science before whom each of its creatures passed again to be named, a scientific Napoleon in the kingdom of nature, who took its myriad inhabitants as a mob and organized them into the divisions, brigades, regiments, and companies of a vast army, each with its own distinctive uniform. And though his organization, while serving well on some fields, has proved inadequate for science's advancing needs, his system of double names — one for genus and the other for species — has been of immense permanent value, and illustrates strikingly the new power that words with fixed meanings have to make charges with, bayonet-like, in the battles of thought.

The work of Linnæus was taken up and carried on yet further by Cuvier (1769-1832), the third great name in zoölogy. A new and vastly improved system of classification, based on the structure of its objects as a whole, rather than on a single feature of them, was added by him to its growth. The idea of its kingdom as a regular series, *scala naturæ*, ascending from zoöphyte to man, which had hitherto prevailed, he supplanted with the conception of it as a tree-like structure, having four distinct branches — mollusc, radiate, articulate, and vertebrate — an immense gain. He was the first zoölogist to enter the great nature-built museum of the rocks and recognize the exceeding value of its fossil treasures as the antecedents of living forms; and his skill as a comparative anatomist is indicated by the fact that while his predecessors had mistaken the bones of creatures as wide apart as the elephant and the salamander for those of men, he out of a single tooth could reconstruct the whole body of an animal otherwise unknown.

It was under him that zoölogy reached the maturity of its second great form, that of organized knowledge, natural history; and who can compare it with what it was to begin with, a mere unassorted collection of strange stories about animals, and not see that it was as much a transmutation of species as any that the primitive amœba ever underwent in mounting up from its original protoplasm to be an organized mammal?

Side by side with this process of classification, however, another one still more striking had already begun — that of asking what was the origin and cause of classes, and of trying to get at the laws and forces by which they had naturally come. As far back as the time of Linnæus — not to go back to that of Hippocrates and Lucretius — Buffon (1707-1788) had given the question birth. He is usually ridiculed as a dreamer rather than a scientist, a man who in studying animals vivisected them unopened with his imagination as a scalpel, and arranged them unpunctured with his philosophy as a pin; and indeed as a dealer with facts he is not for a moment to be compared with Linnæus and Cuvier. But he got hold in his dreaming of some things in nature that they with their eyes wide open for facts were utterly blind to; he was a babe in zoölogy as compared with them, but, like the primitive anthropoid, the babe of a new species. He reached forward in fancy to almost the exact thing that Darwin later found in fact, expressing it, however, as he had to, in the subjunctive mood of church fear rather than with the indicative of scientific manhood. "If," he says, "we did not know the contrary to be the case by sure warrant, we might easily have concluded, so fallible is our reason, that animals always varied slightly, and that such variations, indefinitely accumulated, suffice to account for almost any amount of ultimate difference "— words that for delicate ingenuity in hinting a truth so as not to hurt a prejudice, serving God and yet not offending mammon, even a minister in the pulpit could hardly rival.

The new species of zoölogy thus feebly begun developed in the time of Cuvier into a great school of brilliant thinkers who in their aims and methods were widely differentiated from the old stock. On the side of the past were the patient observers and careful experimentalists who held to the traditional doctrine of species as the immediate work of the Creator, and believed in letting new theories about causes alone and in confining themselves to the collection and arrangement of facts. On the other side were the bold speculators and nature-philosophers who believed in studying the causes which underlie the facts, and in all species as originating through natural laws out of a primitive stock, a side which embraced such advocates as Erasmus Darwin (1731–1802), who believed in a slow inward variability as leading to their differences; Lamarck (1744–1829), who ascribed them to the efforts accumulating through inheritance of the animals themselves;

St.-Hilaire (1772–1844), who emphasized the action of the environment; Oken (1779–1851), who taught the doctrine of protoplasm and the cell; and Goethe (1749–1832), who explained the skull with all its wonders as only an enlargement of the upper spinal vertebra. The antagonism between the two schools widened gradually from word and work into feeling and friction; and at last, in 1830, it broke out on the floor of the French Academy in an open dispute, headed by Cuvier on the one side and St.-Hilaire on the other, which for violence and ferocity the beasts themselves could hardly have excelled, the famous dispute which Goethe at his home in Weimar looked upon as of so much more importance than the French Revolution breaking out at the same time, that he could hardly imagine how his friend, when he spoke to him of "this great event," could think he referred to the mere political outbreak.

Cuvier won the victory for the time in hand, nothing being able to withstand the torrent of facts that his brain, made on the mitrailleuse principle, was able to pour forth; and for thirty years he was the hero, the world over, of conservatism and the church. All the same, however, the new phase of the science kept on with its growth. Von Baer (1792–1876) opened and read the testimony of embryology; John Miller dissected and described, with an accuracy unknown before, the animal body; Richard Owen (1804-1892) pointed out the distinction of analogous and homologous members in comparative anatomy; Schwam (1810–1882) discovered with his miscroscope the starting-point in the cell of all animal life; and Herbert Spencer formulated the great principles of biology in his new synthetic philosophy. Then evolution, having done its work with observation and speculation, separated, took its next great step in order — that of integrating them in a man who, with a minuteness and accuracy of observation which place him at the head of all fact-gatherers, united a skill of interpretation and a boldness of generalization which place him at the forefront of all truth-finders — Charles Darwin, the fourth great name in zoölogy; and the result was the "Origin of Species," and the transmuting of what with others had been a brilliant guess into a statement of the very laws and principles by which as a fact it had been brought about. It was itself another phase of its own doctrine — raised zoölogy to be a new species of science as distinct from those which had gone before it as ever man was from monkey. In its first form it was natural knowledge, in its second natural history, in its third natural science; in its first fact, in its second order, in its third truth; in its first an unorganized amœba, in its second a vertebrated animal, and in its third an intelligent man. It exists in all three of those forms to-day, just as other derived species do; has its museum and picture-book species, its cabinet and school-book species, and its ethical-society and philosophical-lecture species; and people are interested sometimes in one, sometimes in another, and now and then in all three.

With the proclamation of its new truth there came in natural order its struggle for existence, the world's modern thirty years' war. Against it have been brought to bear all the thunderbolts of theology, all the flippancies and squibs of the newspaper, all the stupidities and timidities of society at large, and all the arguments the conservative side of science could find in its arsenal. Agassiz's great work on " Classification," the crowning effort of zoölogy's old dispensation, was published by a striking coincidence the same year that gave to the animal world its new evangel; and even he had to say " Darwinism is a burlesque of facts," and " science would renounce the claim which it has hitherto possessed to the confidence of earnest minds if such sketches were to be accepted as indications of true progress "— words that evince how distinctly a man may see facts and yet how utterly blind he may be to truths, how accurately know the trees of the forest and yet how ignorant be of the forest itself.

On the other side have stood from the start such names as those of Wallace, Spencer, Tyndall, Huxley, Haeckel, themselves masters in the realms of thought. Little by little Cuvier's great victory on the floor of the French Academy, gloried in for thirty years as the triumph of fact over theory, observation over speculation, has been turned to defeat. The facts themselves, whole regiments of them, enlisted so carefully under the banners of observation, some the very ones that Agassiz himself gathered, have mutinied against their own leaders and have put in their sturdiest blows in behalf of theory. Darwin's doctrine, whether or not it is regarded as the whole truth about descent, is held, almost without exception, to be a large piece of it, the grandest generalization yet reached in zoölogical progress. And Darwin himself stands forth to-day a testimony forever to the value of the speculative reason, as well as of the plodding, practical, fact-gathering senses, as an agency in winning victories even on the fields of material science.

But while recognizing thus the inward growing force of zoölogy's great names and the struggle for existence it went through, there is another element of evolution working with them in producing its changes, which is not to be forgotten — that of its environment and of the world's general unfolding knowledge. Meat-eating, and with it the need of cutting creatures up, making in every butcher's shop a dissecting-room; medicine, and with it the study of man's structure; vatication, and with it the inspection of animal bodies, each of these must have contributed largely at the start to its knowledge of facts. The discovery and exploration of America in the fifteenth, sixteenth, and seventeenth centuries, bringing to its hands a multitude of new animals, brought about almost as a necessity the classificatory stage into which it then developed. And geology, revealing a score of other new worlds with their missing links under the old one's feet; the microscope, revealing still another score in the old one's every drop of water; astronomy, explaining with its nebular hypothesis the origin of a myriad worlds from one primal mist; chemistry, explaining with its atomic theory the origin of a myriad substances from possibly one primal element; Lyell, explaining with his uniformatory doctrine the production of all the varieties of rock from one central mass; Harvey, explaining with his circulation of the blood the moving of a thousand little drops from one common fountain of life; and Herbert Spencer, explaining with his grand synthetic philosophy the evolution of the universe as a whole from one starting-point of matter and force, all sweeping along in the same path of a single natural cause for a series of widely different results — all surrounded zoölogy with an atmosphere which inevitably helped to sweep its thinkers on to Darwin's like new truth.

Even the changing climate of the religious world was not without its modifying effect. The zoölogical mind, the same as the thinking mind everywhere, felt the inspiring warmth of the new summer, the delicious trouble in the moral ground, that with the Reformation began coming to the world of men. Ideas that Buffon could only hint in the cellar, Darwin could proclaim unhindered on the house-top. The scepticism of religion became the faith of science. And just in proportion as the Church got rid of its doctrine that man had gone down from his primitive perfection to being " a worm of the dust," it became possible for the lecture-room to show that his being a worm was the very condition from which he had come up.

Nor were humbler agencies lacking as contributors to the grand result. Darwin notoriously was started on the track of his doctrine of how species originate by what he found in the farmyard and the garden. The experience of breeders down through long ages had accumulated a vast fund of practical knowledge on the subject, overlooked by other scientists, that he was not ashamed to sit at their feet and learn. Hodge was found not to have raised his pigs through so many generations only for pork. The story of the crafty Jacob in the sheepfolds of old Laban was discovered to have a truth in it beyond anything the most inveterate believer in biblical infallibility had ever dreamed of. Doves, drawing of old the chariot of Venus, drew for him the fairer one of wisdom. Mares bred to win prizes at the Derby were taught under his touch to win them on the race-course of science. And while other men had sought truth by converse with the gods, and thought of it as too holy a thing to be enshrined in aught but learned tongues, its nineteenth-century disciple found it, like the Magi of old, cradled in a stable and uttering itself in that most despised of all things, " horse talk," illustrating anew Emerson's words:

" 'Tis not in the high stars alone,
   Nor in the cups of budding flowers,
Nor in the redbreast's mellow tone,
   Nor in the bow that smiles thro' showers,
But in the mud and scum of things
   That alway, alway something sings!"

II. Passing now from what zoölogy has been historically as an embodiment of evolution to what it is scientifically as a field for it, how widely already has it opened its gate for its entrance! It is not indeed the whole of its sphere.

The starry heavens, the rock-ribbed earth, the chemical elements, the vast realm of botany, and who shall say how largely the kingdom of mind, are other rooms in its great house. But it is one of its most important departments — one that, with the great mystery of life already its occupant, it seemed beforehand almost impossible for it to enter. All its great fundamental principles — homogeneousness at the start, differentiation, rhythmic movement, the multiplication of effects, integration, and then dissolution and the use of its materials over again in a new series — all these, with some others, as natural selection, peculiar to its own realm, it illustrates with marvelous beauty alike in the individual and the race, evinces it as holding good in the realms of flesh and life as well as in those of matter and force, shows that what made the star made the soul, that what organized the earth organized its inhabitants, and that the highway of creation trod out of primal fire-mist over whirling atom, tenuous nebula and blazing sun, over cooling planet, heaving continent and quaking rock, was not ended or interrupted when it came to man and mind. It is not strange that to the world at large Darwinism means the same thing as evolution. Without the "Origin of Species" to lead the way it is doubtful whether the "First Principles of a New Philosophy" would ever have got beyond the scholar's study. It was its victory on the field of zoölogy that forced it into the ears and faith of the general public. With the citadel of life carried by its logic and the myriad armies of the animal world made its captives, it was felt that the whole vast fort of the universe might as well be surrendered to it at once as wait for an assault it now became certain nothing could resist.

What a field, too, it affords for its further progress! Darwin's discovery, with all it did for it, was but a stage along its way, not by any means its goal. It gives us the doctrine of animal descent, starts the student on the right track for all coming investigation; but the actual lines of their descent, the ages and order in which their different classes, families, genera, and species have branched off from the common stock and from each other; in short, the construction of that vast genealogical tree, world-wide and ages high, on which each member of the animal family shall have its place marked — that, except it be in Haeckel's imperfect outlines and with a few ancestors of the horse, is as yet hardly touched. Departments for its study that were thought of old to be outside of zoölogy are brought by the "Origin of Species" directly within its sphere. Ontogeny, the science of the individual, is made by its principles as much a part of it as is phylogeny, the science of the race. Embryology, once regarded as hardly a fly-leaf in its mighty volume, is found under it to be a most precious table of contents, repeating with the child in a few months what it took ages to accomplish with its parents, and giving in its summary whole chapters again, ages long, which in the book itself earthquakes have blotted out and oceans covered up, opening, therefore, what a new world for evolutionary eyes! Morphology, the science of structure, the study of the origin of the organs inside of the body — as much species as the animals which are outside of it — what made them vary from their original homogeneous protoplasm into all the complexities of their present condition, three hundred thousand fibers, for instance, in a single optic nerve, and why is it that each animal and each species has the exact size and shape and number of limbs and of senses that it does — all as much a matter of law as the shape of crystals or the orbit of planets — all this is legitimately within its zoölogical sphere. Then, with man as an animal, sociology, the study of the laws and forces which evolve society, is surely as much a part of it as is the study of those which gather the bee in hives and the ant in hills; and especially comparative sociology, an investigation of the common elements which run through all collections of animals from those of the insect up, how much has it got here to learn — what a help, also, we find from it in solving some of the social problems that we are vainly now seeking wisdom for among ourselves, giving a new point to old Solomon's words, " Go to the ant, thou sluggard, consider her ways and be wise." And, crowning all, psychology, the marvels of mind and soul, the wonder that fills and overflows this wonder of body — consciousness, love, thought, aspiration — how they unfolded out of protoplasm with the body, what they root in and what they lead to, all these have got to be studied henceforth in connection with animals — are for some future Darwin to make discoveries in as much beyond the " Origin of Species " as the " Origin of Species " is beyond the animal pictures that the old troglodytes drew on their half-eaten bones in the caves of Dordogne and La Madelaine.

III. Proceeding from the historic and scientific aspects of the subject, we find it unfolding into still another species of truth, one which in some respects is the most interesting and important of all. Evolution is not only a history and a science. It is also a philosophy. It embraces not only facts and causes, but with them reasons — asks not only what and how, but, likewise, why. And after giving us in its department of zoölogy the natural history

EVOLUTION AND ANIMAL LIFE 73

of animals and the methods and causes of their origin as species and individuals one from another, it is met at once with the further question of why their existence and descent in this way, what the object of the myriads of them that lived and struggled and died before men came on earth, as well as of the myriads that are doing it now — a page of nature written how deep in blood — what the philosophy of their different forms, many of them so repulsive and monstrous, and of man's being born out of their loins, as Darwin represents, instead of his coming up directly out of the dust and with a human shape to start with, as theology so long has taught.

There is doubtless a sense in which animals are their own end, a side of philosophy which must recognize that, like beauty and the multiplication table and man himself, the ugliest beast and the humblest worm are their "own excuse for being."

"Know Nature's children all divide her care;
The fur that warms a monarch warmed a bear.
While man exclaims, ' See all things for my use.'
' See man for mine,' replies the pampered goose."

And yet it is not the less true that a secondary purpose, a vein, if not of the old, Paley, watchmaker teleology, yet of practical good sense and of a reason for things, does run everywhere through nature. And it is this that evolution finds shining out as a vein of gold from the dark strata of paleontology and from the forms even of the most monster-like brutes.

Not to dwell on their work in making the earth's continents and soils, and in elaborating its crude inorganic elements into nourishing foods, the why of their existence, of their forms in the past, and of the whole process of their growth from monad up to man, is to be found in Darwin's doctrines of variation and heredity — in their acquisition of organs and qualities by variation step by step in the only environment that was fitted for their production, and then in the transmission of them by inheritance from species to species up into higher surroundings and finer shapes, and at last into their existing completeness. Animals have been not merely the lineal ancestors, but beyond this the necessary makers of humanity, the only possible builders not only of man's dwelling place and man's food, but of man himself. Nature's method of phylogenic growth, made inevitable apparently by her own inherent laws, has been herself to push forward an organ a little way, and then to set its recipients to using it with their own will-power over and over, till at last, like the beating of our hearts, it unconsciously did itself, and then to employ her vitality, released from this work, in pushing out still another organ on which the process was repeated; and so on, the gain of one generation being transferred by inheritance to the next, a thing impossible, you see, under the old idea of species as independent creations. The uniting of its four great elements, in some respects the most refractory of nature, into the original protoplasmic mortar out of which all animals are built up, had probably to be done millions of times by its low amœbic forms before they got the habit of staying united; and every step of the wonderful organization and functioning to which it has now arrived in humanity has been taken by having myriads of animals along the way go through with its various operations of digestion, respiration, nerve-action, sense-perception, blood-circulation and the like, again and again till what at first was direct effort — done by giving their minds to it — became at last involuntary action, done without a thought. Man is indeed a bundle of habits, and a bundle formed not only by himself, but by all the multitudes of creatures that are in the lines of his descent back to the first amœba that ever ate its bit of brother slime. A few years ago, as a German naturalist was watching the hatching of an egg, he noticed that after the shell had broken apart, and while the chick was yet in one side of it, a fly lighted on the other. Instantly the little creature, not wholly hatched as yet, darted its bill out for the fly and caught it and ate it up; and in doing so, the naturalist reckoned that it must have made, bodily and mentally, at least three thousand co-ordinated motions, each one of them absolutely perfect. Where did it get its skill? "Instinct," said old ignorance. " Inherited habit," says new evolution. Millions of mature chickens in the generations before it had spent their lives in catching flies, and the skill they had acquired came down to their descendant in its blood. So with man in his facility for catching flies, whether they be in the shape of milk on his mother's breast, or of base-ball on the playground, or, further along, of crinkled lightning on the breast of earth, it comes how largely from the skill of muscle trained into him by the brutes. We live not only outwardly on strata of rock filled with their bones, but inwardly on strata of flesh filled with their deeds. The whole marvelous story of paleontology is recapitulated in every babe that creeps, the four-footed ways of its fossils in the very creeping itself. Honestly indeed, as the saying is, do boys come by the monkey tricks and the habits of sliding down banisters and climbing up trees, reckless of clothes, they are so notorious for, acquired in far-off tropic forests when literally it was "Rock-a-by, baby, in the tree-top,"

EVOLUTION AND ANIMAL LIFE

and when the only nursery tales they had to amuse themselves with were what they carried appended to their own bodies, and the only pantaloons to tear, those which their mother nature had made. Primeval heats, which blotted all traces of the Eozoon out of Laurentian limestone, left the marks of it cindered on the inner, more imperishable bed-rock of the geologist himself who goes out in its search. And live men are not only " dead men warmed over," as Holmes has expressed it, but with them dead animals warmed over, whose subtler selves, never dying, still wriggle and crawl and climb in our every bone and nerve.

The value of the unconscious automatic functioning thus established in the human body it is hardly possible to overestimate. Suppose that man had to superintend and execute each act of his physical living by the direct conscious exercise of his own will; suppose the sailor, reefing the topgallant sails of his ship in a tornado, with the masts swinging through the air like whips and the lightnings jabbing through it like bayonets, had at the same time to keep the pumps going of his own heart; or that the orator, while filling his audience with inspiring thoughts, had with every respiration to give part of his mind to the filling of his own lungs with breath; or that the poet, right in the midst of his subtle fancies and revelings in the ideal world, had ever and anon to turn his eye in a fine frenzy rolling down on to his liver to keep it from idling, or in along his digestive apparatus to make sure its thousand little nutrients were not sending his nourishment off to the wrong places — what power or time would they have left for success in their immediate human work? More to us than any outward legacies from human parents are those inherited habits within that we are all born to from our animal progenitors. It is because they used their volitions and vitality so well in the establishment of such physical ones that we are able to go on and use ours for the establishment of those that are intellectual and moral. Out of their awful conflicts in the long past, seemingly the expressions only of ferocity and cruelty have come to us for use in the mighty moral conflicts of civilization.

"The wrestling thews that throw the world."

"Thirty centuries look down upon you," said Napoleon to his soldiers as they went forth to the battle of the Pyramids. Thirty eons look down upon — nay, join you and fight with you — evolution says to every man who goes forth to the battle of life. And with such an inheritance from the brutes is it a thing very discreditable to us that we have had them as our ancestors — a philosophy wholly without significance which shows thus the reason for nature's method of human descent?

It is a philosophy, moreover, which holds good not only with reference to those species of animals which are in the direct line of man's origin, but in some measure of all the side ones, also, that have branched off from it and ended only in themselves. Mr. Dawson urges it as an argument against Darwinian evolution that the trilobite, after existing all through the Silurian and Devonian ages, finally died out without giving rise to any new forms of life. It is a kind of reasoning which hardly looks further than their own stony eyes. The trilobites did their work and answered the why of their existence by the nutriment they afforded the surviving main stock of animal life. It is a part of the magnificent economy of nature, one of the reconciling features in its horrible system of having animals eat each other up, that its very failures are used thereby to make its successes — its creatures that perish in their struggle for existence are made to live and triumph in those which survive. The distinction between eater and eaten, as we go down the scale of being, grows continually less and less. Reproduction by nutrition is only the opposite side of reproduction by fission. When a big amœba eats a small one, the result is a new creature almost as much as when higher up the two parents unite their lives in that of a child. Indeed, there are some cases where the new food is a direct agent in producing a new species. Inheritance in nature is from branches as well as roots, from uncles and aunts as well as from fathers and mothers. The lower limbs of a forest tree are not the less necessary for its growth, nor the less represented in its final fruit, because its top boughs grow on it elsewhere, leaving the bottom ones to be overshadowed and die. And whole species of animals have done the same thing for man's stock in the past that individual animals and plants are doing now — elaborated its food and food qualities out of coarse, inorganic elements up into what was most akin to its own flesh and blood.

Of course the process has been a very slow one — myriads of animals to establish a single habit, ages of time to deposit a single organ. But time with those animal antediluvians was of no especial value, a million years but as a watch in the night, and a small eternity but as yesterday when it was passed. It was the one thing and the only thing that in those days they had to do; and it was what right in the midst of their frolicking and fighting and eating each other up they could go on doing just as well. And here again is where nature's economy comes in and the reason comes out why the originators of man were brutes instead of higher beings and why he was not set to build himself. It was as brutes with brute shapes and brute tastes that they could best make what is animal in man. It was protoplasm alone that was plastic enough to begin with, protoplasm alone that could be the flask in which life could imprison the four great genii of matter. Rough claws shaped parts of man grandly where fine fingers would have miserably failed. And what would have been the sense of having a creature with fifty ounces of brain in his skull at work generation after generation on the stomach, lungs, heart, and eye just to establish in them the habit of involuntary action, when a ganoid fish with a pennyweight of skull-stuff, or a megalosaur reptile with all the cycles of Cathay at his command, could do it vastly better? I have a young friend, a machinist, who keeps a few barn-yard fowls for his amusement, and who, like most amateurs in that line, became fascinated one year with the idea of raising young spring chickens ahead of nature by means of an incubator. So one Sunday morning, disregarding the remonstrances of mother, wife, and sister, he went to consult a friend in the city who already had one on his hands. His friend showed him his instrument, its spirit-lamps and steam-pipes and hundred eggs in their compartments, and then told him how careful he had to be in its management, sitting up all night to watch the thermometer and feed the lamps and to keep everything right, and then took him solemnly out into the back yard where were two other sets of a hundred eggs all spoiled, one because he had left the apparatus fifteen minutes in the care of a small boy who had let them roast, and the other because he himself had gone to sleep a moment or two the twentieth night and let them chill. "Now, Joe," said he, with a melancholy air, "if you will take the benefit of my experience, so long as your time as a machinist is worth more than that of an old setting hen as an incubator, I should advise you to stick to your lathe and let the old setting hen hatch the chickens." And that is what nature did in hatching the chicken qualities of her myriad creatures in the early spring of life — used not her thinking man, but her brooding hens to be their incubator. And slow and muddle-headed as they were, how grand is the resulting body which has come out of their nest! How supple and varied its powers, how marvelous its organization! What a strain it has stood of battle-fields and long abuses and accidents by field and flood, what a foundation proved on which to build the enormous structure of mind, what a new significance given to the pious

hymn of good old Dr. Watts that alike saint
and scientist can for once unite in singing —

> " Fearful and wondrous is the skill that molds
>   Our body's vital plan,
> And from the first dim hidden germ unfolds
>   The perfect limbs of man!"

And with all the work there is still before it as
the agent of mind, all the business cares and
social problems and weights of philosophy and
science, all the marvels of our coming civilization,
that are yet to be piled up on its brain,
who shall say it is a particle too strong, who
feel that those old brutes with their myriad
years took for its building one hour too much,
who not fear, with it breaking down so often
even now, that the future may show that those
tertiary anthropoids who put on it its final
touches before the superstructure of reason
was begun, hurried up their part of the work
a little too fast?

Nor is it body alone that man owes to the
brutes. In them, too, were laid all the great
foundation stones of mind, heart, and soul!
And how far back in their blood do some of
the qualities reach which seem now to be most
distinctively the badges of human superiority!
Little did that old amphibian think, when he
saw under far Devonian skies the fish-fins with
which he had come out of the water separate

into the ten phalanges of his fore limbs, that
he was laying the foundations of an arithmetic
that was to count at last the stars of heaven
with its digits and measure the distances of
Sirius and the nebulæ with its multiple; little
those " dragons of the prime that tare each
other in their slime " imagine that out of their
conflicts they were storing up in their blood a
courage, energy, and pluck that were to fight
the great battles of liberty when bayonets
were to be the claws and steam rams the tusks,
and win victories for truth when ideas should
be the horns, and arguments the jaws; little
that early batrachian, who called his mate to
him with a croak, foresee that his vocal faculty
was to go on developing itself through human
voices till it broke forth in the eloquence of a
Demosthenes, drove reform to its mark in the
sarcasm of a Phillips, and went up to heaven in
a song the angels might hush their own to
hear of a Nilsson and an Abbott. Love, with
its mother tenderness and its sex-passion
climbing in humanity to what splendors of
poetry and romance, has its root down how far
amid the tenants of the rocks. Society and its
duties, and that " social contract " about which
philosophers have had so much to say, were
made for man by the Rousseaus and St. Simons
of an ancestry that went on all fours — had
already been in existence millions of years at

the period when the great Frenchman thought of them as being formed, and can no more be overturned now than our human nature itself. A large part of our moral uprightness antedates our walking physically upright. A few years ago a family on the Hudson, going away for their summer vacation, left in their cellar a piece of meat which they showed their pet dog as the food he was to live on in their absence. The dog, however, mistook their gestures and supposed it was food he was meant to guard. Three weeks afterward, the family returning, found the faithful creature's starved bones beside the untouched meat. Who does not wish that at least an equal share of the fidelity which had thus come down to the little dog out of his brute ancestry had descended to some of the bank presidents and insurance-company trustees that are set to watch people's financial meat? Even as regards religion, not from the lips of angels, but very possibly from the insight of animals, did its first knowledge come. The terror they manifest in the presence of objects which to them are uncanny, as when a horse shies at a bit of whirling paper or at anything in motion whose propelling power he does not see, in spite of the other explanations given of it, is impressively like the dread which lies at the base of all savage worship and which civilized man, his children especially, who repeat in so many ways their far-off ancestral experience, feels in the dark and at the hearing of strange sounds. It suggests, how inevitably, their common origin in a four-footed worshiper who was their common progenitor — is " a fear of the Lord" starting in the awful shadow of primeval woods that was the beginning of a wisdom which is to sing and soar at last in what splendors of Christian day! And with such inheritances, bodily and mental, received from animals, is it not about time that the words brutal, beastly, and the like, as designating what is worst in man, should have a rest? The really brutal and beastly qualities we have derived from them are often a hundredfold more and better than the human ones that the persons thus described have added to them since. Our animal infancy as a race is just as honorable to us and just as worthy of being referred to with tender regard as our animal infancy as individuals, the two being exactly of a piece. And instead of making it our aim, " working out the beast, to let the ape and tiger die," ought we not rather to keep them in us tamed and civilized as the beasts of burden to carry us on their backs, as no outward ones can, in the long, long way our human nature is yet to travel?

IV. It is a question which opens up into the last and crowning phase that zoölogy as interpreted by Darwin has entered upon, and that is a morality that shall include animals as well as men among its objects and a religion that shall save civilized brutes from the hell so many of them are now in as well as savage heathen from the one they are threatened with by and by. What hitherto has been only a kindly sentiment warring against the wretched cruelty that in so many forms they have been subject to is based by the " Origin of Species " and the " Descent of Man " on a solid foundation of science. Sharing with them the membership of one larger animal body, we inevitably share with them also the great divine law, alike natural and scriptural, that " if one member suffer, all the members suffer with it, and if one member be honored, then all the members rejoice with it." A lady, on getting a kitten for her little boy to play with, told him as a means of keeping him from doing it harm that only half of it — the hind half — was his, and that she was going to keep the other half — its head — as hers. The next day, sitting in the parlor, she overheard a terrible cry of animal pain coming from the play-room, and exclaimed: " O Tommy, Tommy! what are you doing to my end of the kitten? " " I ain't doing nothing to your end," was the answer. "I only pinched my end, and it was your end that squawked." And that is what Darwin has taught us with regard to the whole animal kingdom, man included, that it is only a larger kitten, and that cruelty can not pinch the meanest worm at its tail without having its farthest human end squawk, can not do any part of it needless harm without having it react through nerves subtler than those of flesh, and harm the harmer also — the frightened calf poison its eater, and the whip that scars the horse's flesh at one end ply an unseen lash at the other, scarring with its every stroke the driver's soul. Revealing our origin from a common stock, it is not only the good Samaritan, but his good ass also that is made by it our neighbor; not only the savage man, but the savage beast that is our brother; not only at the tomb of Adam in Palestine, but at the tomb of the eozoön, nature-built, in the primeval rock, that we can stand, weeping, if we will, and say, "A distant relative to be sure, and yet a relative." And all the reasons that ethics can show based on self-interest, gratitude, blood connection, and the mystery of a common life-tie for the exercise of justice, kindness, and the Golden Rule toward the lowest man, it shows hold equally good for their exercise toward the humblest brute. Philanthropy is widened by it into zoöphily; humanitarianism into panzoism; altruism between man and man into altruism between man and all that lives. It completes the great circle that theology has traveled from its finding of Deity at first in animals out in its search for him into the infinite, and then back through man to its finding of him in their life again — makes it the word of science as well as poetry that

> "He prayeth well who loveth well
> Both man and bird and beast."

And though its practical influence in doing away with cruelty is yet only partially felt, it has the potency in it of truth, and it is as sure at last to bring about a reform in their treatment as Christianity is in that of human beings. Darwin was the Apostle to the Gentiles of the forest, field, and flood; the Light of Asia to the darkened world of the brute; and as he "passed on" to his great discovery it is not difficult imagining their myriads as doing for him what Arnold represents them as doing for Siddârtha of old:

> "Large wondering eyes
> Of woodland creatures — panther, boar, and deer —
> At peace that eve gazed on his face benign
> From cave and thicket. Bright butterflies
> Fluttered their vans, azure and green and gold,
> To be his fan-bearers. The doves flocked round,

And e'en the creeping things were 'ware and glad.
Voices of earth and air joined in one song
Which unto ears that hear said, ' Lord and Friend,
This is the night the ages waited for.' "

And now, under the reign of these new influences in their behalf, what does evolution point to as likely to be the whole final outcome to animals from their long struggle for existence, what their own place at last on the great life-tree they have done so much to nourish — a look into their future which surely may not unfitly close our look into their long past? Philosophers are not wanting who have held that, sharers of man's mortality here, they will be sharers of whatever immortality awaits him in the realms beyond. Mourners of household pets have easily agreed with the poor Indian

"Who thinks, admitted to that equal sky,
His faithful dog will bear him company."

And there are some sportsmen, I verily believe, animated with a somewhat different shade of interest, to whom heaven would lose half its attraction if they thought its river of life was to have no speckled trout in its waters waiting to be caught, its tree of life no robins and squirrels among its branches placed there to be shot at, its New Jerusalem no blooded trotters on its golden pave to be bet upon, and its fields of amaranth and asphodel no flying fox and hunting hounds to gallop over in the merry chase.

But without speculating on their condition beyond the realms of time, we can reasonably look forward, under the light of evolution, to their developing side by side with man in the long future which is before him on earth, and to their sharing with him — at least their more saintly representatives — that ideal state, the golden age of heathendom and the millennium of Christianity, which beyond question our existing world is to ripen into before it passes on to its final stage. Mosquitoes may not tune their voices in its dewy airs, nor rattlesnakes join their harps in its choral song, but it is hard to think of a perfect earth, even with its silver questions all settled and its social problems all solved, that is not to be musical with the song of birds, graceful with the forms of quadrupeds, and alive with myriads of the happy things which have labored so long to build it up — as hard as it is to think of a flower, however fair, that is not the fairer when encircled with its chaplet of leaves. Its poisonous reptiles, its pestiferous insects, and its more ravenous and untamable beasts, unrepenting sinners of the swamp and fen, will doubtless die out, for universal salvation, however true it may be of man, and even of the old theological serpent, can hardly be stretched out wide enough, even by its most determined advocate, to cover the snake in the grass and the worm in the flesh — killed off not so much by human hands as by the earth's changing clime. But with these gone it will be all the easier for its better ones to survive, preserved alike by nature's softened laws and man's co-operating care. Its woods will still be merry with the frisky squirrel and its airs sweet with the song of birds; its brooks still alive with the silver gleam of scales and its meadows with their painted butterflies and golden-trousered bees; its tropics still have their winged rainbows and feathered gems; and its mountain thrones and courts of snow their eagle kings and nature-ermined lords. The same principle of ripened stock, better living, and more mental activity that operates among men to lay the Marthusian specter of over-population some philosophers are now troubled with, will obtain among animals to keep their numbers from ever crowding the earth. Death will round off their old age with its sleep the same as it will that of human beings even in their perfect state — a death as painless as that which the cells of our bodies in passing from living tissue to waste matter already every day undergo. With the earth's grains and fruits perfected and the chemical means discovered of producing artificial nitrogenous foods, all need of their slaughter and all taste for their flesh will have passed away.

And at last, with the material world all perfected, as some day it must be, and our human world all freed from its sins and shames and wrongs, as some day it shall be —

> "Every tiger madness muzzled, every serpent passion killed,
> Every grim ravine a garden, every blazing desert tilled,"

love shall have in the animal world all forms of life as its own;

> "The spirit of the Lord
> Lie potent upon man and beast and bird";

and in no small degree literally as well as figuratively, old Isaiah's prophetic vision shall be fulfilled: "The lion shall eat straw like the ox; the wolf shall dwell with the lamb, and the leopard shall lie down with the kid, and the fatling and the young lion together, and a little child shall lead them, and they shall not hurt nor destroy in all my holy mountain, saith the Lord."

III

EVOLUTION AND WAR

It is a well proclaimed, though not always a well practised maxim of good citizenship, that the legislator, the reformer, the political economist, the voter, everybody who is to have anything to do with discussing and directing the affairs of society and the State, ought to have, as a preparation for it, a knowledge of history,— that is, of what other men in other days have done and have tried to do in the same great fields. Equally important is it, also, as we are now beginning to see, that such persons should have, as a requisite for their fullest intelligent action, a like acquaintance with science, and especially with those departments of science, as zoölogy and paleontology, which relate to what animals and plants have done, and with their great interpreter, evolution. Human history is but the last chapter in a vast volume, many chaptered, of the world's transactions, impossible to be understood without reading in its preceding ones what our ancestors older than man have been doing; human society, as Mr. Spencer has so admirably shown in his "Principles of Sociology," is but the enlargement and further development of organisms spread all through the animal and vegetable kingdoms, on which nature has been at work for millions of years. The root and germ not only of man's body, as seen in the oldest vertebrate fossils, but of man's mind, and of all that mind does and can do both individually and socially, have existed in the world's great life-tree from the start,— must have done so, according to evolution,— and have been continually unfolding themselves, if not at first as flower and fruit, yet long ago as shoot and stalk. There is hardly an experiment humanity is now trying in mechanics, art, government, labor, capital, education, sociology, and even ecclesiasticism,— some of them with its own children as the materials,— that nature has not already tried at least the principles of, over and over, in the cruder forms of matter, and with the cheaper materials of animal and vegetable structure. And, such being the case, who cannot see that to study these, — which have succeeded and which have failed, and what have been the causes of their successes and failures, and what the philosophy is which lies behind them,— would save the statesman, the reformer and the citizen many a costly experiment on human beings, and would open the way for the intelligent choice of many an agency and path of progress now lying, it may be, right before their eyes, but which, as things are, they are groping for in utter blindness, or trampling down in utter contempt?

One of the great questions that is before our country to-day, and that every country has to meet,— one that involves millions of dollars and the principles, to some extent, on which is to turn the whole future of its civilization, and which in many respects is the most difficult that statesmanship has to deal with,— is what its people shall do in the way of arms and armor for their protection and defense. And it is a problem, too, that nature, not less imperatively than nations, has had to deal with all through the past. War and the wager of battle, weapons and the wounds of conflict, are not the accident and disease of her original economy, not a human lapse and folly, but a constituent element in her very system of things. The moment she set her creatures on earth, even in their lowest forms, exposed to the elements and compelled to get their own living, most of them, by preying on each other, it became necessary, if their lives were not at once to be extinguished, to provide them with some means on the one hand of assault, and on the other of defense,— a necessity which is bound up inseparably with those two great principles on which all organic evolution is based, the struggle for existence and the survival of the fittest. Devices to meet it have played a part in her economy second only to those for alimentation itself; are a field in which she, too, as much as any statesman, has had to tax all her resources and lay under tribute all her skill. The rocks below the earth's surface are a vast gallery in which, while the muscles, stomachs and brains of her children have perished, the arms and armor with which they fought have for ages been preserved, as in our museums above its surface are the swords, shields and coats-of-mail that our human ancestors, now dust, wore to battle in their brave days of old. And the result of these long experiments as to what are fittest, and have helped their users to be fittest also, is not only of itself one of the most beautiful chapters in the Book of Evolution, but one that pours a great flood of practical wisdom on the problems of our time as to the true principles to be followed in securing national, social and even religious survival and supremacy.

The first effort of her Vulcan fingers was in the line of protective armor pure and simple, the encasement of animals and plants in a mere hard outside covering. It is what the exposure alone of their original protoplasm to water, sun and air, aided by the secretion of mineral matter on the surface, and intensified by the survival and reproduction of the animals and plants which had it most, would tend naturally, in strict accordance with Darwin's laws, to produce; and it is now seen to advantage in the sea-urchin and star-fish among radiates, in the oyster and clam among molluscs, in the turtle and alligator among vertebrates, in the eggs of birds, and, to some extent, in the skin and hair of all animals.

It was a form, however, to which nature could not confine herself, especially in the animal kingdom. If live things were to live, either on each other or on vegetables, they obviously must have some means of breaking through each other's hard covers and getting at their inside meat. The means came to them in the form of cilia, tentacles, suckers, claws, mouths, horns, jaws, tails, tusks, teeth, beginning, perhaps, in such mere thread-like extensions of the inner protoplasm as are now seen in the rhizopods and culminating in the apparatus of such magnificent vertebrate carnivora as the lion and the tiger.

But such weapons alone, with only the old protoplasmic bodies to wield them, would not have been enough; would indeed have been of

EVOLUTION AND WAR

less value to them than even their old outside covering. To have them of any real use nature had to develop, along with them, bones, muscles, nerves, senses, brains; and, in some of their owners, the habit and power of association,— all that constitutes a highly organized internal structure. These were organs and faculties which became, in their turn, a new species of armor still more interior; became at any rate what had the same use as armor,— the quickness of eye that could discern the foe, the activity of limb that could fly to it, from it and around it, the shrewdness of mind that could observe its habits and select the best points for its attack, and the instinct of co-operation that could join forces in coping with it, differing only in their fineness from the sharpness of the tooth and the strength of the claw. And thus were introduced the two great principles that nature has used in all her arming, and that have played and are still playing a most tremendous part in her economy,— their distinction being not exactly that of defensive and offensive weapons, for both, when need required, could be used defensively, but that the one had its chief value in its own outside strength, while the other depended for its efficacy on qualities connected with its possessor's inside development.

Equipped from her arsenal with the varied

arms and armor which embodied, some of them one of these principles almost exclusively, and some a mingling of the two, nature sent forth her myriad creatures into their great life-battle, world-wide in its field, where the issue has been not only which of themselves, but which of their weapons and of the principles on which their weapons were made, would prove the fittest, and best help their users to survive. During the long geologic ages they were all, and especially the outward kinds, enormously developed both in size and strength, and their underlying philosophy was tested in the severest way by contests alike with each other and with the world's equally ferocious natural elements. The orthoceras, a huge cephaloid mollusc of the lower Silurian rocks, had a thick, hard, cylindrical covering, twelve to eighteen feet long and at its base a foot in diameter. The dinichthys, a Devonian ganoid fish some thirty feet long, was protected about its head with a suit of massive articulated armor that a cannon-ball could hardly have crushed. Among the famous reptiles of the jurassic and cretaceous ages,— the ichthyosaur, megalosaur, mosasaur, iguanodon and others,— some were fifty, sixty, and a hundred feet long, plated over with thick scales for defense, and armed for attack with claws hooked back like sickles, with long projecting tusks that shut down by each other like clasped fingers, and with sharp, glistening saber-like teeth, sometimes four rows of them, and two hundred in number,— indeed "monstrous and prodigious things worse than fables yet have feigned." And the age of mammals had its mastodon with tusks twelve and fourteen feet long, its glyptodon with a solidified bony armor on its back nine feet across and weighing nearly four thousand pounds, its megatherium with clawed feet a yard in length, and its machairodus, a tiger whose open mouth was an arsenal set with natural swords.

How terrible must have been the contests of such monsters with each other, and the slaughter made by them on their weaker and less protected neighbors,— most truly "Nature red in tooth and claw with ravin"! How different the scenes of their world from the peace and repose that Miltonic poets have loved to picture as the condition of the earth "before the advent of man and sin"! The sea was alive with animal frigates, the land with self-moving Krupp cannon, the sky with literally "flying artillery." The modern question between steel plate and steel shot, tried of late by the *Merrimac* and the *Monitor*, was tried of old as a principle between ivory tooth and horny scale by many a megalosaur and mosasaur, carnivore and pachyderm, each increasing, as now, the force and size of the assailing weapon, as the other increased the thickness and strength of the defensive plate. The physical stuff of which a Nelson and a Napoleon, a Paul Jones and a Farragut, were afterwards made, cruised, perhaps, around the headlands of England, and marched, perhaps, across the wilds of Europe and America, ages before their day, as dinichthys and dinosaur, machairodus and megathere. Battles of Trafalgar and the Nile, of Marathon and Waterloo, deciding the fate of great animal kingdoms, were fought, to begin with, under far-off triassic and mesozoic skies. And whether or not Tennyson's lines are true of the future,—

"And there rained a ghastly dew
From the nations' airy navies grappling in the central blue,"

they have been true of the past, the "airy navies" being those of such great reptile birds as the pteranodon and pterodactyl, the latter with a wing-spread of twenty-five feet.

What has been the result of this long, ferocious war, as related to the various kinds of armor used by its combatants? The records of the rocks conclusively answer. It has been the overwhelming of nearly all the races and orders that were provided with its massive outside varieties, and the survival and supremacy of those that have been equipped with its inner and finer forms. Orthoceras and dinichthys, megalosaur and megathere, ichthyosaur and iguanodon, monsters armed with shell and scale, tooth and claw, enormous and terrible, have all without exception gone down in the great life-battle; while those whose weapons were the finer skeleton, the keener sense, the quicker nerve, the larger brain and the stronger social instinct, faculties good for peace as well as war, — and some that apparently have had no outward fighting-apparatus at all, nothing but inner shrewdness and wisdom,— are the races that have been victorious, and survived. Even the armed ones whose descendants are still on the field, as the lion and the tiger, the eagle and the shark, have evidently held on by virtue of their quickened inner powers, rather than through their outward strength; or else, as with the oyster and the clam by reason of their insignificance and unprogressiveness, rather than because of their hardened shells. And man, the one that has progressed most of all, that has become the head of the animal kingdom and the lord and master of the earth,— he is the one that, outwardly, is the most unweaponed and defenseless of all; the one whose claws are taper fingers, whose skin every mosquito can puncture, and whose armor of thought has no size or weight whatever.

What is the reason of this result, what the underlying causes why inward development should thus prove itself more effective in the struggle for life than outside strength? They are not hard to find. To begin with, the animals that trusted to exterior arms and armor were less able to adapt themselves to the ever-changing conditions of the earth and of food supply, than those whose weapons were within. The very things which protected them against one set of elements made them often the more exposed to be overcome by another set,— as the heavy fur, so warm for winter, becomes an intolerable burden under the heats of summer. The endowments that were efficient against one set of enemies, by reason of their bulk, were inefficient against another set by reason of their unwieldiness,— as the huge frigates, so powerful against each other broadside to, are helpless against the lively little ram that rakes them turning round. And as the struggle went on between thicker plates on the one side and more formidable jaws, claws, teeth and limbs on the other, their weight and size became of themselves in time their owners' worst foes, sinking them in morasses, stranding them on bars, exposing them to be overwhelmed with sudden floods, and at last bearing them down to earth and to extinction by simply their own hugeness. On the other hand, with some disadvantages, the development of the animal's inner powers and parts had, in all these directions, a corresponding gain. When nature invented her backbone, and put her limbs, flesh, senses, and so many of her soft and vulnerable parts, on its outside, it looked at first like a great military mistake,— like the building of a fort and the putting of its garrison outside of its walls rather than within their protection. But what a tremendous part this very arrangement of it has acted in all her subsequent operations. The mineral matter its possessors needed to carry about was, in proportion to their size, greatly reduced by it, alike in weight and bulk. How flexible it has proved in the line of adaptations,— ranging all the way from the fish in the sea to the bird in the air, from the snake that crawls to the man that walks, and from the uses of war to the needs of peace. What beauty and dignity it has gathered around it in man's kingly stature and in woman's queenly grace; and how fitly, in the higher conflicts of civilization, it has become the symbol of the statesman's crowning attribute,— his "having backbone." So with each of nature's other steps in the same direction. What was the sharp tooth as a help, either in defense or attack, as compared with the sharp eye? What the huge limb, clumsily brought down on its object, in contrast with the quickened nerve which, in the same time, with a smaller limb, could rain a score of blows against the selected weak parts of its victim? What the chance of the creature with the strongest claw and the widest range of wood and sea, in its contest with hunger and cold, as measured against one with the hand and mind to weave every fiber that grows into robes of warmth, turn every force of nature into weapons of war, and lay every land that blooms under contribution for food? If the inner development lost sometimes in its direct fitness for fighting, it made up for it a thousandfold by its larger fitness for peace; and as peace, even in the wildest nature, is at least one of its normal conditions,— is the time, even among beasts, in which to prepare for war,— it is not strange that what was fitted in part for each of these states should have proved, as a whole, the fittest to survive.

Beyond this, just in proportion as a live thing was protected by outward armor, either against the elements or against its foes, the stimulus for its interior development was taken away, the nourishing qualities of its food went to its outside parts, and the freedom of its circulatory system, always needed in the making of a highly differentiated organism, was sacrificed in the interest of its harder shell. It is not improbable that the starting-point of the whole divergence between the animal and vegetable kingdoms, now so broad, was that the original protistic protoplasm out of which they both came, identical in all other respects, was a little more solidified in the one case than in the other, as it still is in their germs,— that early outside protection being fatal to all animal-life development. And when nature surrounds any creature at its birth with an encasement that is a guard without effort on its own part from all harm, as with the snail, oyster and clam, or develops its teeth, claws and bulk so enormously by inheritance that their mere display protects it from all ordinary assaults, what inducement does the creature have for interior growth, and what sustenance have left for it even should the need arise? It is the animals whose very existence depends on the completeness and activity of their internal equipment,— on their quickness of motion, keenness of sense, and cunning of brain, rather than on their outside covering,—it is these that will necessarily make the most of every variation in the direction of such powers, using them more and more, and be the ones to mount up at last from monad into man. Historically, in the animal kingdom, it is out of the bodily weakest that have come the mentally strongest. Lacking talons, they have developed talents; unable to throttle, they have learned to think. Danger has been their school; difficulty their teacher; and, instead of yielding to the arsenal of outward weapons arrayed against them, they have turned them into helpers,— sharpened their wits against the very teeth of tigers, made the ferocity of the hyena and bear contribute to their fineness of nerve and sense, and the portion of nature's goods that megalosaur and megathere consumed with riotous living in the making of brawn, they have used with economy in the making of brain.

Then, too, the imperfection of their outward armor must have had a very important influence in driving the weak into that mightiest of all military arts, mightier than any tusk or claw or individual accouterment,— co-operative effort. All animals even of the same species, organized to prey on each other, would naturally be foes at first, and inclined to live apart. Outward shelter meant only the continuance of this separation. What society could the oyster and the clam have with each other? What need of mutual assistance, the ichthyosaur and megalosaur, fifty or a hundred feet long, and panoplied all over with thick plates? It was only the unprotected that would be under the necessity of overcoming their individual enmities and combining against their protected foes; only the outwardly weak who would be apt learners of the lesson that union is strength. Once learned it became not only a mighty weapon of attack and defense, but the teacher of innumerable other things. The association it involved was a powerful stimulus to mind-development. Liking its benefits, they grew inevitably to like the benefit-givers,— that is, their associates. And thus, under the wonderful alchemy of evolution, out of the crucible of animal hate in this seething world of ours, stirred with tusk and claw, has come, as much as there is of it, the fine gold of brotherly love, the protective arms into which all weapons are at last to merge.

As plants, in their relation to the world's great food-question, are necessarily the assailed rather than the assailants, being the prey of animals, but made to get their own living chiefly from unobjecting inorganic matter, their armor for the most part is naturally outward and protective rather than inward and offensive. It is what is found in the bark of trees, the rind of fruits, the shell of nuts, the beard of grains, the spines and thorns of many shrubs, and in the roughness and hardness of nearly all vegetation in its native state. And yet plants are not by any means entirely destitute of what may be called offensive arms, or wholly incapable, when assailed, of assailing in return. Species of them are found, here and there, like the sun-dew, the pitcher-plant, and the Venus fly-trap, which completely turn the tables on the animal kingdom, and, instead of being the eaten, are themselves the eaters,— catching their insect-victims with sticky fluids, spring-traps and imprisoning doors, the ingenuity of which the best patent, corner-grocery fly-destroyer might well emulate. Anybody who has ever tried to work himself imperiously through a tangled thicket, or to rob a blackberry-bush of its shining progeny, or to climb a pear-tree for its juicy products, will be a not very incredulous sceptic as to the capacity of at least some plants for offensive warfare. When a forest has been cut down and a multitude of new shoots are springing up, and one of them gets a little the start of the others, no human being in the arena of politics or society or trade ever used his faculties more combatively, to elbow out and kick out all competitors, than such a vegetable upstart does its limbs and roots to shade out and starve out its vegetable brethren. The forest and the swamp have their leafy denizens that are weaponed as effectively with deadly poisons, offensive odors and biting flavors as any in the animal kingdom that wear scales and furs, or in society that wear tongues and clothes. And the small boy who has assailed the green-apple tree has, in his doubling up from it during the night afterwards, an evidence which neither he nor his mother will dispute, that the assailed orchard is not inferior to the assailed pugilist in its skill to strike back at its antagonist's most sensitive parts.

There is the same difference, also, as to the fineness, beauty and organic rank of the weapons used in the vegetable kingdom, that is found in the animal world, and the same rivalry as to which will prove the most effective in its struggle for existence. Their coarsest and ugliest forms were the ones with which nature necessarily began. During the vast periods of paleontology the monsters of scale and claw were fully matched by those of leaf and bark. Trees were the grass on which fed iguanodon and dinocere; tree-tops the grain that was reaped by hadrosaur and dinothere. Reeds grew to be sticks of timber, and club-mosses to be forests in size. With flowers not yet come at all, and the true woods only in a limited degree, the world's plant-forces went forth for ages to their life-battles under the hueless cryptogams as their banners and with the savage stigmaria and sigillaria trees as their lances and clubs,— fought them too, amid the thunder of volcanoes, the rising and falling of continents and the fierceness of tropic suns as we never know them now. And the coal-measures of to-day, their ancient battle-grounds, heaped thousands of feet thick with their dead remains, testify to the ferocity of their conflicts and to the grossness and strangeness of their weapons. The weeds of our own time, rough, tough, unsightly and bitter, are looked upon as the special enemies of man's race, a part of the earth's curse for his primal sin, and as exercising their disagreeable qualities out of mere deviltry and love of mischief; and are warred against with all the unpitying sharpness of the farmer's hoe and the gardener's hate. But weeds to begin with were the special friends of agriculture and man, the vegetable aborigines of the land, and pioneers of civilization, and were armed thus with special reference to their work. When our modern earth was yet a wilderness built over the graves of its extinct geological vegetation, and incapable of nourishing any cultivated fruits, the "weeds" settled down on its great glacial furrows just plowed up, and began battling with its crude, inorganic elements to work them over through their own veins into fruitful soils. Go out on the edge of any desert to-day, and you will see some of their tribe still engaged in their old pristine war, throwing out their advanced guards and establishing their slender outposts each year a little further into the waste, too poor as yet to hoist over them the banner even of a flower, but winning what at last will wave with all springtime's streamers and autumn's signal-hues. And who does not see that their roughness, toughness and acrid-ness are the only possible weapons with which they could have withstood the parching drouths, elemental starvations, and fierce animal hungers, of those elder days and outer realms, and so have won for their kingdom the first stages of its struggle for life? Who, in remembrance of what they have done, and as a foregleam of that philophyty into which mankind is some day to broaden out, will not forgive them the stained fingers and smarting palms with which, in garden and field, they resist being torn from what is so truly their own hard-won soil?

Mingled, however, with these rough and repellent weapons of the vegetable world, its finer qualities of color, form and flavor have gradually come in,— flowers on bush and tree, arching limbs and drooping boughs out in the stately woods, sweet and nourishing pulps in and around the seeds, and fragrant odors wafted on the evening gale; — these, moreover, not merely as ornaments to themselves or as foods for other creatures, but as forces, also, which primarily they all are, in their own struggle for life,— arms and armor in the same way as are the senses and the higher faculties that have played such an important part in the battles of the animal kingdom.

With the finer qualities themselves, an ingenuity and skill have also been developed in their use and application, which seem sometimes to be almost human. Not a few of the arts and devices of mimicry, that are so wonderful among animals, have their counterparts in plants. How they huddle together in glorious companionship for defense against heat and cold. With what architectural wisdom they send out their roots and build up and balance their branches so as to hold and fortify their positions against gravity and wind. With what shrewdness, while some of them hide from animals and men, others find their protection by following in their steps. And when domesticated and hedged in with fences, and defended with hoes, how winningly for more of such armor, do they, as flowers, put on their brightest colors, and as fruits clothe themselves in their richest pulps.

Especially do their wisdom and care, not to say love, come out in what they do for their young. All plants, the same as all animals, seem to reach the best they are capable of in their position as parents,— sonship, being apparently the axil out of which branches all good, vegetable, animal, human, and, if Christianity be true, even divine. Unable to protect their fruit with claws and wings, like beasts and birds they do so, while it is immature, by making its color green, like that of their leaves, so as to hide it from view, and its taste sour and bitter, so that no ordinary creature would think of putting it into its stomach. But when it is ripe, and there is need of its being scattered away from its parent stalk to find room and warmth for its own further growth, they put on it, in direct contrast with their leaves, all the bright colors of the cherry, berry, apple, peach and pear, so as to attract the attention of passers-by, and make its outside luscious and sweet as an inducement for them to eat of it and carry it off,— at the same time wrapping its inside germ, and that germ's own special nutriment, in an armor which is proof against the digestive assaults of even a wild animal's stomach. How much is all this like the human mother keeping her darling boy inconspicuous at home during the first years of his life, but who, when the time comes for sending him out into the world to get his own living, takes off his old homespun, dresses him up in his best clothes, and puts a little money in his pocket, the sinews of war with which he is to pay his way to a new home and begin his battle of life, and beneath this, right around his heart, the armor of a Bible, or of principles and good advice, to keep him in his inexperience from being at once the world's prey. Fruits like those of the hickorytree, whose sweetness is wholly in their meat, are provided with a bitter outside covering, which, instead of growing bright and eatable with their ripening, simply opens, when, in the frosty autumn they drop from their parent tree, exposing a white inside shell very conspicuous for boys and squirrels to see and gather, but at the same time a veritable fort, built with all manner of intricate casements, salient angles, and retreating walls, that only nutcrackers and the sharpest teeth can storm and break through. The cocoa-tree, having a large heavy nut whose hard shell would be liable to crack open in falling from its high limbs to the ground, wraps it up beforehand in a soft cushion-like matting, as its defense against the hard earth. And more ingenious still, the cashew-nut, growing in tropical climates and much loved by monkeys, has in its immediate covering a pungent, acrid acid, which, touched, burns not only their tongues but also even their paws, so that not even a hungry monkey, after one experience with its armor, can be tempted to fool with it again; but, as an allurement to secure their aid in its dispersion, it has at the end of its stalk, and independent of the nut itself, a most delicious edible tuber, which they can have and do have at the cost only of giving the real fruit a chance to grow,— a contrivance equal to that of the old lady who presented the boy, whose integrity she was not quite ready to trust, with a roll of candy for carrying her package of sweet cakes safe to a neighbor, but at the same time wrote on its cover, " Wallop him well if you find it opened."

What is the result of nature's experiment here as to the two ways of arming her creatures? As told in the broad pages of paleontology, it is the same as in her animal kingdom, — the gradual evolution of its inner and finer forms out of and over those which are outward and coarse; the weapons of sweetness, beauty, grace and use, above those of hardness, hugeness, acrid juices, and outside strength. The flowering plants have more and more come to the front,— the white lily and the fragrant rose left far behind, in their struggle for existence, the old hueless, odorless cryptogams. The grains, with their great heads, have grown up over the graves of the gymnosperms, with their great bodies. The apple-trees, the pear-trees, and the peach-trees, with their rich fruit, have elbowed out the seal-tree and the scale-tree with their tough skins. And the graceful elm towering up over the cottage roof, looks down the chimney out of which curls up to it, as if in homage, the smoke of the carboniferous pale-oxon and the old hirsute neuropteris. It is a struggle, to be sure, that is not yet over, a war whose wilder participants are very far yet from being all subdued. But the master forces, and the qualities and reasons which make them masters, are plainly to be seen. The industrial age of vegetation has come in. The work of doing something for others has been found even among trees and shrubs a mightier weapon than any art of mere individual defense. Plants have learned, whole species of them, that it is cheaper to hire other tribes to wage their wars than it is to train up themselves to do it; learned that vegetable gold, heaped up in the orchard and the field, will turn the edge of vegetable iron hammered out in the jungle and the fen. The honey that attracts the insect-tribes has done for the flowering shrub, in its struggle for existence, what no hardness, driving them away, ever did; and the luscious outside of the fruit which feeds the birds has secured them against foes more effectually than any bitter rind that repelled them had the power to do. What does the cherry-tree want of a gun of its own, when it has made it for the interest of the small boy to sit patiently with one all day keeping off the too eager robins, by giving him at night a quart or two of the red balls that it spends its own energies in ripening by the thousand? What need does the wheat-field have of building fences against encroaching cattle, when it has allied itself with almost omnipotent corporations to surround its millions of acres with barbed wires, and secured dignified legislatures to build insurmountable legal posts

to hold them up! How vain is it for the potato
to distill a poison of its own against bugs, when
out of its rich tubers it can pay patient human
fingers to feed them day after day with imported
Paris-green? And how smilingly the
serried ranks of the corn-field can straighten up
their own spines and use their green blades only
to parry the sunshine, while the farmer and his
boy bend their aching backs and ply their sharp
hoes at their roots to drive away and put to
death, as no skill in themselves could, their thousand
weed-foes?

Ascending now into the kingdom of man himself,
the evolution of what has played such an
important part in the animal and vegetable
worlds has certainly not been less prominent or
less interesting in that of their head, and in his
struggle for life. "*Arma virumque cano*,"—
not unnaturally did the old Latin poet put the
two together as themes to be unitedly sung; the
arma perhaps logically first, as something without
which man, surrounded with the savage wild,
and so weak in himself, never could have been
man. His earliest weapons may indeed have
been the nature-given ones that he had in his
brute-estate, fists, nails and teeth,— the ones
that, in all emergencies, he falls back upon still,
— mingled perhaps with the bare sticks and
stones that he picked up in the woods,—

"*Arma antiqua manus, ungues, dentesque fuere
Et lapides et item silvarum fragmina, rami,*"

as wise Lucretius has it. But when, as our great anthropoid ancestor, he came down out of his tree-life, he had, in his fingers able to grasp a club,— the fingers which his forelimbs, in grasping the tree, had developed into,— something far better with which to meet his foes than the claws with which he went up into it; and he has not been slow to use his new powers. From grasping clubs and stones he has gone on to grasping repeating-rifles and dynamite-shells. There is no chapter of human progress more interesting and impressive than that of its arms-making, unless it be that of its arms-using. All the resources of art, all the illuminations of science, have for ages been brought to bear upon it. Some of the most honored names of antiquity, though forgotten now, as those of Luno, Galen, and Andrea Ferrara, were the names of sword-makers and armorers. It was an occupation not considered unworthy of an Olympian god; and one of the most brilliant pages of Homer is the description of a shield, as one of the most graphic in Walter Scott is that of a sword. Kings sat at its followers' feet; the fate of empires turned on their skill; civilization in its onward march kept time with the rise and fall of their hammers. And, though stained with blood and smoke and hate, their products have been plumed also with some of the noblest deeds of chivalry, honor, courage, self-sacrifice and manly devotion that human nature has ever reached.

But amid all their multiplied devices as to form and mechanism, the two methods, the two principles which ran so conspicuously through the animal and vegetable kingdoms, have been equally kept up in that of man,— on the one side a stronger outside covering, whose efficacy was chiefly in itself, as the thick garment, the bull's-hide buckler, the brazen shield, the visored helmet, the plated greaves, the glittering coat-of-mail, the massive fort, the turreted monitor, and the steel-clad ship; and on the other, something which involved, more directly, inward skill and power, as the club, the spear, the sword, the cross-bow, the catapult, the matchlock-gun, the rifle, the cannon, the ram, the torpedo, and behind them all the cunning, the courage and the union instinct of man himself. And in the struggle between them here, the same as among the plants and the brutes, the result has been the supremacy of the inward over the outward, and a progress ever more towards their finer and more inward forms as the ones on which at last wholly to rely. The old Bible story of Goliath and David,— the one a giant six cubits high, armed with a coat-of-mail of "five thousand shekels in weight," and a spear " like a weaver's beam," the other a ruddy youth armed only with a sling and five small stones out of the brook, and his own skill,— has been the story of the ages. The barbaric nations have always relied most on outward defenses, the civilized ones on those that require inward skill; and victory the world over has sided with the skill. The weapons with which the Roman soldier carved his way to universal empire against all the shields, greaves, breast-plates and forts of his foe, were the short two-edged broadsword, nineteen inches long, and the famous " pilum," four feet in length,— himself protected only by his own stout heart and a very light defensive armor. The slender spears of the ancient Greek infantry, twenty-four feet in length, and the lances at a later day of the old feudal cavalry, projecting ten feet beyond their horses' heads, again and again bore down in battle all the massive protective defenses that their opponents were panoplied with. The best steel-plate armor of the middle ages, forged with marvelous skill, and completely covering the person, was no match for the arrows, five feet long, of the English yeoman, hitting the target every time an eighth of a mile off, and on the victorious fields of Crecy, Poitiers and Agincourt shooting down their mailed opponents at the distance of two hundred yards "as readily as if they were naked men." If now and then the strength of the armor caught up with that of the arms, as at a battle in Italy during the latter part of the 15th century, where they were so nearly matched that the two opposing armies fought ferociously for seven hours without having a man killed or wounded on either side, it was only at the very next battle to have a new assailing weapon introduced to maintain the old supremacy,— as, in this case, musketry at the battle of Pavia, before which all the gorgeous panoply of chivalry went down as completely as the fields of bearded grain before the driving summer hail. Waterloo was the last great fight in which bodily armor was used, Napoleon's cavalry wearing it, and up to that time with some success; but in the charges there made, his iron-sheathed cuirassiers went down like rows of pins before the quick-moving English horse dashing in upon them with only naked swords and naked hands. The contest now is between massive forts and steel-clad ships, with ever thicker and thicker plates, on the one side, and mathematically-aimed mortars and steel-wrought rams and cannon, and projectiles themselves shot-loaded,— cannon fired from cannon,— with ever more and more size and force, on the other. But with mortars dropping shells from above at the rate of one a minute into forts three or four miles away, and torpedo-boats creeping under plated frigates from below as readily as eels under a plank, and projectiles driven with smokeless powder through five inches of steel backed with fifteen of oak as easily as a boy's teeth pass through slices of bread and butter, and dynamite-guns throwing from the shore at marks two miles off five-hundred-pound explosive-bombs that tear up the heart of old ocean itself for a hundred yards around, who can doubt the result?

It is a result, moreover, in all these cases, which has not stopped with teaching and helping on the superiority and evolution of an ever finer and finer weapon alone. It has taught and carried with it also the superiority and evolution, behind the weapon, of an ever finer and finer man. It has done it, first of all, in the artisan who makes the weapon. Rifles that shoot sixty balls a minute, and cannon that send hundred-pound shells through twenty inches of solid oak and steel, do not grow naturally, like teeth and nails, out of the soldier's own body. They have to be invented and wrought out by a man back of the soldier. They involve, in their maker, art and science, skill of hand and skill of brain,— immense amounts of them. And what is more, they involve in him honesty and truth. There is nothing which detects cheap workmanship and base alloys quicker than the acid of war. We tolerated shoddy in our shops, in our homes, in our churches, easily enough while peace reigned on our soil; but when it came to sending it to our soldiers on battle-fields, America's outcry of rage brought its dealers to a very sudden halt. Rotten timbers have small chance of passing the inspection-eyes that fifty-ton broadsides of iron direct against them. And when you touch off dynamite-guns, that exert a pressure of a hundred tons to the square inch, varnish and putty and the men who make them are apt to fly very high and very far, leaving back of the soldier only solid steel and solid workmen. Equally, too, finer armor has evolved, in the soldier himself, an ever finer and finer man. It is no longer, as it once was, physical strength alone that counts in war; no longer the more a brute the more a soldier. Gunpowder made bodies equal, and began the process of having battles turn on brains. It is a process that has never stopped. With rifles like those now made, as delicate in their machinery as chronometers, and with cannon that have to be aimed at foes as mathematically as telescopes at stars, it is obviously impossible to trust clod-hoppers with their use. New weapons involve precisely the same necessity for a more highly organized soldier that new teeth and new claws did of old for a more highly organized animal. It is not the fighter in the mass, as it was in ancient Greece and Rome, but the fighter in the man, that makes an army's strength. With each more intricate arm more responsibility rests on the individual soldier, not on his captain or his corps, for its efficiency; the more need, therefore, there is of his individual training. Bayonets have had to learn not only how to thrust but how to think. Battle-fields, which hitherto have been supposed to necessitate the most absolute despotism in command, and to be the last places where personal liberty could be allowed, are having the way opened through their new weapons to taste for themselves what they have won so long for peace. And the armor which began with a sharp animal spine is mounting up step by step to that quality in the soldier's soul which can say, in all its sharpness, the grand word I.

It is not only individuals and brute races, however, but tribes and nations also, that use arms and are combatants in the struggle for existence; and as such, they are going through the same experiments as to the best ways and means of doing it that animals and individuals have tried, only on a larger scale. Originally a tribe's entire corporate body was a soldier going out to battle as one man. Every male member of it was accustomed to the use of arms alike in war and the chase. Fighting was considered to be the only employment worthy of a man; and honor and leadership and wives, and the best of everything, waited on his courage and success. But gradually nations found that, to fight well, something more was needed than brute courage and the rude weapons that each man could make for himself. Food was needed, and finer weapons, and resources to fall back upon when the struggle was long, the tribes which had the most of these being the ones that finally survived. And so a differentiation took place, the inevitable process in all evolution,— some of the members devoting themselves exclusively to the raising of food and clothing, and others to the manufacture of arms, and with these, gradually, to all the employments needed for social nourishment, while a third part were trained specifically as soldiers. Thus inside the nation were started the soft industrial arts, the fluid, nutritive, growing, organizable parts of the body, and, on its outside, the hard military protective shell,— precisely the same state of things that existed in the earliest forms of individual life. And along these two lines, away up into the civilization of to-day, has been all national development,— these as methods of protection distinguishing countries in precisely the same way that they do animals and plants. On the one hand is outward military encasement, as with all the great nations of Europe,— orthocerates and glyptodons that stretch over vast territories; megalosaurs and machairoduses whose dimensions are those of States. Forts and frigates are their shells and scales; long rows of sharp sabers and glittering bayonets their teeth; vast armies their ponderous jaws; Krupp-cannon and Gatling-guns their talons and claws, and

" The bursting shell, the gateway rent asunder,
   The rolling musketry, the clashing blade,
And ever and anon in tones of thunder
   The diapason of the cannonade,"

the wild-beast cries with which they leap upon their foe. On the other hand is interior development, as, in some degree, with our own land,— the skeleton of a better social organization for the uniting and upholding of the body as a whole, the nerves and arteries of telegraphs and railroads for the quicker and closer communication of part with part, the muscles and ligaments of industry and business for the obtaining of better nourishment, and the eyes, ears and brain of more schools, more arts and sciences and more churches, for the gathering of knowledge and the growth of mind.

EVOLUTION AND WAR

Which of these methods is it the part of true statesmanship to emphasize and use? There is a tendency even in our own land to fall back on the method of outward force. We get alarmed ever and anon at what we call our defenseless condition,— at our small army, our rotting gun-boats, and our dilapidated forts. We picture to ourselves what a terrible thing it would be if some little country with a big cannon should declare war against us; and follow with boyish pride the excursions of our costly show-frigates into ports where our protective commercial policy has driven from the seas every flag of ours needing protection. And this very winter the proposition is before our Congress to vote the nation's money by the score of millions for the building of a steel-clad navy that shall match those of the old world.

But if there is anything to be learned from the long experience of the mighty past, alike animal and human, is not the question's true answer largely, if not entirely, the other way, — an answer that tells us to go on as we have in part begun, and as the real genius of our country prompts, letting Germany, Russia and France follow the lead of the dinichthys and the megalosaur in heaping up outward armor, while we seek to develop as the man-nation of the earth by unfolding from within? It is, indeed, true that the man-animal of the earth has been a fighter,— one of the worst; and that all the world's great historic nations have been fighters, and terrible ones, too; but the point to be remembered is that they have got their best means of fighting, got the real qualities which enabled them to come off victors in their fights, by cultivating the arts of peace rather than those of war. "A nation of shop-keepers!" exclaimed Napoleon, contemptuously, as he looked across the English Channel; but one day, in his dealings with the shop-keepers, he found, very uncomfortably, that among their wares they had a Waterloo. How was it in the recent struggle on our own soil between the North and the South? The South was the military part of the nation. It had the most accomplished generals. Its children had been trained from their youth up in the use of arms; and in courage and in direct fighting qualities it certainly was not inferior to the North. But the North had the freedom, the wealth, the inventive genius, the mental training, the higher interior development,— all those qualities which are the outgrowth of peace. It called them at once into action; — where it wanted a new rifle, new war-ship, new sanitary device, called on its rear guard, back of all other rear guards, to invent it. The rear guard never failed to do so; and the result was just as certain with the first gun at Sumter, as with the last at Appomattox Court House,— was wrought out by the school-mistress and the aproned mechanic quite as largely as by the brave general and the bannered soldier. It has been said that the nations which shorten their swords lengthen their borders,— historically a fact. But, ultimating the same principle, we are now learning that the nations which go still further, and shorten their swords into nothing at all, lengthen their borders still more,— and at the same time lengthen their lives. Wherein is the wisdom of voting millions of dollars for forts and frigates which in a few years will be as *passé* as cross-bows and coats-of-mail, and when the genius that, by its other, finer inventions, is to make them so, is growing of itself in our laboratories and workshops? It is the people hereafter who can raise Ericssons, not Napoleons, send to the field the best manhood, not the biggest mortars, boast the completest social, not soldierly organization, that can laugh at their foes. " Damn the torpedoes!" shouted the grim old naval hero of our Civil War, as he took his unarmored flagship into the hottest hell of the fight at Mobile Bay; and well the old *Hartford* might despise them, for within its wooden walls were iron-clad hearts, and above it waved Liberty's banner, and it was sheathed all over with a cause that gunpowder could as little blow up as it could omnipotence itself. And no matter though every sea were to be filled with explosives, and every bay with dynamite, let America carry stalwart manhood on her decks, and unfettered liberty at her masthead, and the sheathing of a righteous cause at her prow, and, if need demand, she can go into the hottest hell of the world's battle, exclaiming again, with the sacred profanity of her dear old Farragut, "Damn the torpedoes!"

Of course this does not mean that the country should rush all at once from its policy in the past over to the opposite extreme; does not mean that in the interests of peace it should wipe out the army and navy and beat into plowshares the swords it now has, or that it should abate in any degree its reverence for the brave soldiers on its own soil, and all through the ages, who by their use have filled history with heroisms and the world with salvations. For peace, when it comes, will be the result of evolution, not manufacture; and evolution here, as everywhere else, must have the root and stalk of the past on which and from which to unfold; and to cut down the armor-part of the past would be to cut down the very tree on which, as things look, its flower at last is to bloom. But it does mean that we should recognize what has been the bent and strain of

EVOLUTION AND WAR 133

nature in all her kingdoms and all her ages, and ourselves work with her in the same direction. It does mean that, without destroying what now is on her armor-tree, we should join with her, so far as we do anything, in cultivating its finer industrial branches, as good alike for peace or war,— not spend our millions in merely crowding it with bigger ones of the old type that will be of value for neither state.

It is in this way, by a simple and natural unfolding from the past, not cutting loose from it or sticking to it, that will come the supreme stage in the evolution of arms and armor,— that in which wars will be waged with no guns, no forts, no ships, no outward explosives at all; with no need, therefore, even of the arts that made them,— but with missiles only that are forged out of mind. So far as fighting of some kind is concerned it would indeed be a fool's security for humanity to suppose that its days are over, and that peace in the sense of harmony is close at hand. Problems are before it to-day more perplexing than any that the past has ever known; passions at work in it fiercer than ever fired hearts in the jungle with rage; interests at stake with it more conflicting than any that a Marathon or Waterloo decided,— and there is no possibility of settling them without contests. It is their very greatness and intricacy, however, that are going to make it all the more a matter not of sentimental choice but of military necessity, to meet them with weapons of a corresponding substance and temper. It is a process that has already begun, a new bud that, like all buds, is springing directly from the axil of the old war-tree. The best general, even now, is not he who fights the most battles with guns, but he who so manoeuvers his army as to win victories with the fewest actual conflicts; not he who, when a battle comes, takes part himself in the deadly charge, but he who sits quietly in his tent with a map before him, directing charges with a pencil's point, and neither sees nor sheds personally a drop of blood. Literature in all ages has had its words that were half-battles; eloquence its vibrations of air that have shaken the world wider than parks of artillery; religion its love-whispers that neither Greek phalanx nor Roman legion could withstand, and before which empires have tumbled down as readily as savages before canister and grape. Paws and claws, if not yet extinct, have climbed up from the feet into the forehead, and from weapons that scratch and tear into weapons that think and plan. It is brains to-day, behind the cannon, that are the world's real battle-fields; ideas that are battering down strongholds which shot and shell, armored ship and gaping mortar have knocked at in vain; ink that is solving questions of State that blood has only confused. And the process is bound to go on, till nations shall wage all their wars with logic and reason, diplomacy everywhere take the place of generalship, battles with powder and armies be as vulgar as those with teeth and fists are to-day, and civilized countries as little think of going about the world armed with forts, and showing off frigates, as civilized individuals do now of going about society with bowie-knives stuck in their belts and revolvers gleaming from their pockets. And this is what every citizen can help along; is what every soldier should rejoice in, as he does now in the introduction of every finer and more effective weapon; is what the great poet of England, who sang so grandly the Charge of the Light Brigade, has also sung as the charge of all the ages,—

"Move upward, working out the beast,
And let the ape and tiger die."

With it will come the world's real struggle to see which are its fittest nations to survive; a war more thrilling and with more chance for real heroism, generalship, and glory, than any ever waged with outer weapons and garments rolled in blood; and in it the great military nations of Europe are preparing to fail, through precisely the same causes that overthrew the monsters of the geologic ages and that have meant failure in all time. Their vitality and food-substance are going too largely to the outside shell. Internal social organization is being neglected. They are not keeping up with the world's changing intellectual climate. And, continually rivaling each other in the size and strength of their armaments, they will drop down at last in the fight like the iguanodon and glyptodon, overcome simply by their own enormous weight, leaving the great scientific, industrial and thought-using man-nations to examine their bones, organize over them the new civilization, in which " the war-drum throbs no longer," and hold the future.

> " Dream not that helm and harness
>   Are signs of valor true:
> Peace hath higher tests of manhood
>   Than battle ever knew.
>
> " Henceforth to Labor's chivalry
>   Be knightly honors paid;
> For nobler than the sword's shall be
>   The sickle's accolade."

The lesson, however, does not stop with statesmanship. Religion is a field where precisely the same principle is at issue. What are creeds, forms and great ecclesiastical systems but the outward armor in which men have sought to protect the inward spirit of religion? What are many of the churches and denominations of the past but monsters of the theologic ages, rivaling those of geology in their fierceness? What the rack, the stake, the thumbscrew, the inquisition, and, later, all the awful imagery of eternal suffering, but the teeth and claws and jaws of the old brute-world reappearing on earth in subtler and sharper forms? Their use has no doubt been honest and natural; their hardness and cruelty have been thought a necessary means of defending and perpetuating their inside truth. But how futile they have been! How many of the old dogmas are now as dead as the old brutes! How certain are all the institutions and all the churches, whose trust is in any outward letter or outward form, sooner or later also to go! And for the same reason,— the use of their vitality in the wrong direction; the impossibility of anything thus hardened to adjust itself to the world's ever-changing spiritual climate, and the pressure at last on their believers, under the effort to make them ever stronger and stronger against their foes, of their own dead weight. On the other hand Christianity itself lives, the great spirit of all religion lives, because an element within it has always acted on the other principle,— refused from the start, as with Jesus, to encase itself in any words or forms, used its divine food for inward growth, adapted itself to the world's progress, and relied, when assailed, for its real defense, on the inner weapons of reason, spiritual insight and the power of truth. When religion first started, ages since, from form to faith, from outward authority to inward insight, and from one vast body to a multitude of little sects, it did indeed seem, from the ecclesiastical standpoint, as great a mistake as when the animal kingdom branched off from a shell to a back-bone, and from a megalosaur to a microlestes. But the wisdom which has been vindicated of her children in the kingdom of animals will just as surely be vindicated of them in that of spirit. And if the friends of religion want to defend it most effectively of all, is it not plainly along the line of its interior development, rather than along that of building it into creeds and fortifying it with logic, that their work should be done?

> " Than tyrant's law or bigot's ban
>   More mighty is the simplest word,
>   The free heart of an honest man
>   Than crosier or the sword."

Going now a step further, does not the same principle hold good with regard to morals, right, reform, and that greatest of all organisms, society itself? These things are precious beyond all price, have grown up to their present condition through enormous toil and suffering,— would mean, in their loss, what never, perhaps, could be restored; and so it is not strange that men should seek to protect and promote them with rigid precepts, with stern prohibitory laws, with great bodies of police and with all the weapons of courts, jails, scaffolds and penal legislation. It may indeed be impossible yet to abolish such things altogether, as the safeguards of society. Nevertheless, even while using them, must it not be acknowledged that they belong to the triassic and mesozoic rather than to human social states; are nature's methods in the oyster and the clam, the lobster, and the lion, rather than in the man; are the use for defense, of shell and scale, tooth and claw, instead of sense and soul? Whatever the good they do, their defects are the same as have been found in all outside arms and armor, from the brutes up. The moral vitality, alike of the individual and of society, goes into their production and support, away from inward growth. The stronger and better they are made for any one period and condition of things, the less easy it is to adjust them to the world's changes, and the less fit they are for those which follow. What is the effort to put down increasing crime by increasing laws, an experiment that every unfolding social state goes through, but a renewal of the old contest between stronger scale and stronger claw, stouter iron-plate and stouter gun? It is a contest sure to result at last in a dead weight of legislation, too large for society to carry. Crime in it, as the assailing force, will continually get ahead, the same as in the struggle between tooth and scale in geology, between thieving and law in England a century ago, and between landlord-legislation and tenantry-violence in Ireland to-day. And even were such efforts successful,— were laws to be made so wise, and a police-force established for their enforcement so strong as to suppress absolutely, for the time being, all vice and all crime,— how inevitably would they lead to a reliance on these agencies alone, and to a relaxation of inward culture that in the end would stop growth and turn society back towards its mollusc-state. Take the use of prohibitory laws in behalf of temperance,— whatever their value, a real value in some respects, it must be confessed that just in proportion as they are enforced, the other and finer agencies of the cause, which should act on the drunkard's moral nature to strengthen that, are liable to be dropped, leaving him, while safe from drink simply because he cannot get it, a prey all the more to other, worse vices, whose means of indulgence no laws can stamp out. What children are the weakest and surest to fall when

EVOLUTION AND WAR 141

they grow up and go out into the temptations and trials of actual life? Those, notedly, who have been sheltered most carefully by home walls and parental care from all contact with evil, rather than those who have been strengthened inwardly, it may be in the very midst of temptation, to take care of themselves. What is the source of all Phariseeism, all hypocrisy, all obedience to the letter and not the spirit of right,— social states worse sometimes than open vice? It is the attempt to make people righteous by precepts rather than by principles; to protect virtue by an armor of rigid rules instead of by trusting to its own larger development; so that wisely did the old Apostle to the Gentiles exclaim: "The law worketh wrath." The truth is, there is only one sure way of arming either society or the soul against their foes,— the way taught by all the ages, from those of geology up,— that of completer inward equipment, putting nature's moral line into the back-bone of principle, rather than into the shell of statute-books; building more school-houses and more reformatories in the place of more scaffolds and more jails; developing more eyes and ears with which to see and hear the right, rather than more teeth and claws with which to put down the wrong, and organizing not so much a better police as a better people. It is this which is the fundamental idea of Christianity; this, what it means by its doctrine of faith as opposed to law; this, that it has come back to in all its great reformations, from that of Luther down; this, the goal at which it joins hands with science; this, very singularly, that is the real meaning to-day of a word almost too hateful for utterance,— the blossom in society of religion's most cherished teaching and the outcome in morals of nature's divinest struggle for life. Its shortest expression, "Right its own best weapon," is a Damascus-blade that what battle-fires have tempered and battle-blows hammered out! Not poetry alone, is it, but sober fact, that "thrice is he armed that hath his quarrel just." To put on "the breast-plate of righteousness," "the shield of faith," "the sword of the spirit" and "the whole armor of God," is the injunction of Hoplology not less than of Scripture. And it is as true of social safety, as of national defense, that

"Were half the power that fills the world with terror,
    Were half the wealth bestowed on camps and courts,
Given to redeem the human mind from error,
    There were no need of arsenals and forts."

The whole subject, thus looked at, is a good illustration of how, throughout the entire universe alike of matter and mind, and often amid the greatest apparent contradictions, it is possible that one increasing purpose runs. There is nothing in nature which at first sight is more disheartening than the awful warring of its creatures one against another, provided for, as it is, in their very structure; nothing which to many persons so militates against the idea of a loving God as the awful cruelties of that struggle for existence into which, with no choice of theirs, all organic beings are plunged; nothing which could seem less the purpose of things, especially while the monsters of the geologic ages were being brought forth ever more and more terrible, than that the meek and the righteous should inherit the earth. Yet with the points of tooth and claw, " red in ravin," as pens, and the blood of her myriad creatures dying in battle, as ink, she has been writing all the time the first pages of a philosophy under which of necessity all fighting must end; and at the very anvils of war, with her monsters, brute and human, as smiths, has been forging the weapons ever finer and finer that alone can overcome violence, and which only the righteous and the meek inheriting the earth can wield. And in all the marvels of eastern magic is there anything more wonderful, more unexpected, more beautiful, than the story that not on a tree transplanted out of Paradise, or from a seed sown in the gardens of sentiment and nourished in the hot-house of the church,— but on the rude stalk of war, rooted in the dust of slaughtered myriads, spined and petaled with the sharp points of tooth and claw, sword and bayonet, and budding in the red of battle-fields,— there should bloom at last, in the midst of a hushed and waiting earth, by strictly natural laws, the snow-white flower of universal peace?

IV

EVOLUTION AND POLITICS

While exploring with a party of friends several years ago one of the many crab-like arms with which Puget Sound crawls back from the sea up into the land, our boat anchored for the afternoon in a picturesque spot under the shadow of the Olympic mountains to allow the amateur artists on board — mostly ladies — to make a sketch of its beautiful scenery. Suddenly the silence of lead-pencils, which had been reigning supreme for an hour or more, was broken by the horrified exclamation of a feminine voice, "Oh! oh! oh! we are all adrift!" Its occasion was the tide, which, up there amid the innumerable inlets it has to visit, often gets bewildered and loses all sense of its obligations to the moon, sometimes piling itself up twenty-six hours and calling that a day's work, and four feet at once, sometimes rising or falling, sometimes running so long in one direction that, like a sentence many-phrased, it seems to have lost all connection with its starting point — the tide unexpectedly turned, that was bearing our boat its cable's length the other way from its anchor. On coming to a stand again, which it did in a moment or two, the scene we had been sketching, though itself the same as at first, was, in the aspect it presented to us, an almost entirely different thing. The white man's cabin, the Indian's tent, and the dog's humble kennel, before wide apart, were now in exact range with each other. The houses and hewn logs had made a complete swap in their visible sides and ends. A beautiful white cataract, concealed before in all except its music, had come plainly into sight; and even the great snow-peaked mountains, immovable as they were at their granite bases, were parallaxed against a stretch of blue sky quite different from the cloudy one against which at first they had seemed to lean. Most of the artists, recognizing the changed perspective, threw their old sketches aside and began wholly new ones from their new point of view. But some, hating to lose their work, went on and finished out what they had begun, a part by drawing the uncompleted things as they remembered them to have looked, and others by simply adding them on as they now appeared. At the close of the afternoon we organized an *extempore* art exhibition. The wholly new pictures, though somewhat hasty, were all well enough. But the others! Besides the mistakes of memory and the ludicrous results which had arisen from the mixing up of the two perspectives — the houses and logs with both ends visible, and the dog, the Indian, and the white man each with a double background — they all had a horrified jerk of the pencil where the exclamation "We're adrift!" had come in, exceedingly significant historically, but otherwise as unmeaning in art as the sudden quirk was in chirography that used to adorn our writing-books at the district school when the master came up from behind and rapped our knuckles with his ruler to keep us from making crooked lines. And, as we compared the two results, we all concluded that the best way to draw pictures when the tide has turned is to begin the whole thing anew and draw every object in them directly from its new point of view.

What took place with our tugboat on Puget Sound has taken place in our day with the bark of thought on the sea of life. Its tide has turned — the great tide of philosophy sweeping here and there in past ages through all manner of strange channels, turned at last in this bright afternoon of the nineteenth century to the side of evolution; and it has inevitably changed with it the point of view from which the whole universe is to be seen. It is a tremendous change. Not unnaturally, when first discovered, it wrung forth from timid lips

the ejaculation, "Oh! oh! oh! we're all adrift!"
And there are some even now who refuse to recognize in their work that anything has taken place; some who go on teaching and describing things from the old creation standpoint, just as they did before; and others — ministers, alas! — who do indeed recognize the new position, but who think the only safe way is to mix up the two in their views, look at nature and natural science from the standpoint of evolution, and at religion and ethics from that of creation, and who, with a miracle of perspective such as the devoutest saint-painter of the middle ages never dreamed of, represent the Bible, Jesus, Christianity, and our human nature as showing at the same time a natural and a supernatural origin and end. But the great body of thinking people are coming to see more and more clearly that if they would not make their work ridiculous, the only true way is to lay aside reverently all forms of it drawn from their old position, retaining only the ripened skill it gave them, and begin the whole thing over again from the standpoint of evolution. Religion, history, sociology, natural science, education, economics, even ethics, each has got to be entirely rewritten. The objects themselves which they deal with, these of course are the same; but their perspective, their relation to each other and to the eye which sees them,—

often a vastly more important element in the truth of things than any special facts about them — that is changed, that change that henceforth in any fair consideration of them must assuredly be taken into account.

What are the relations of evolution to politics? Here, at the very threshold of the subject, the world's changed perspective makes itself manifest. We all know what have hitherto been regarded as moral questions in politics. They have been questions about slavery, intemperance, gambling, the social evil, the treatment of criminals, the rights of women, and the like, as distinguished from questions that were simply sanitary, civil, economic, industrial, military, and the like; and their moral quality has been thought to consist, the same as with the individual, in their relation sometimes to utility, sometimes to happiness, sometimes to the Divine Will, and sometimes to an eternal distinction in the nature of things. But under evolution this old limitation with regard to them is largely wiped out. The scope of morality is made by it to be everything in man's conduct, both individual and social, physical and spiritual, which relates to his full development and well-being; or, as Spencer puts it, " the moral law is the law of the complete life, the law of the perfect man, the law of that state toward which creation tends." It does not exclude the idea of an eternal distinction in the nature of things between right and wrong, any more than counting on the fingers does the necessity that two and two would still make four even in a world which had no fingers to be counted on; does not deny that, so far as the individual is concerned, motive, volition, knowledge, capacity, are important elements in determining the moral character of an action; but it says that the only way in which we can know of the distinction is by the accumulated experience of the individual and the race with regard to their effects, and that so far as society is concerned it is the effects alone that are to be considered — the right being all those things which, taken as a rule, tend to promote the well-being of its members, no matter how material their form or lowly their motive; the wrong, all those which, taken as a rule, tend to prevent it, no matter how religious their garb or worthy their motive. And wherever it finds a question as to which of these two courses the community shall allow its members to enter upon or continue in, wherever a question of what will enable men in their relations with each other to best secure the great ends of life, whether it be that of freeing a street from filth or a race from bondage, there it finds what to society is a moral question.

It is the only definition which really covers the whole inner field even of recognized morality — is a theory which, instead of making ethics less rigorous and wide-reaching in forbidding robbery and murder and the like, as Mr. Huxley seems to fear, makes it a great deal more imperative and comprehensive. What are the worst crimes against life and property that society suffers from? Not those which are committed with the point of a pistol and the blow of a bludgeon, but often those which are committed with a point of law and a piece of financiering. Here is a factory whose agent insists against all remonstrance on keeping its windows closed because of the finer cloth he can thus make, out of which a girl is carried fainting who in three weeks dies. Out of a dwelling-house near by another girl is carried, stabbed, who in three weeks dies also. The one is called a murder, and its agent is hanged for it. The other is called a misfortune, and its agent gets a dividend of ten per cent for it and is admitted to the church. Is there any justice in such a distinction — any reason why all such cases should not be defined and dealt with as of the same moral character — anything in the philosophy which does it which lessens the stigma attaching to them as robbery and murder? What constitutes the real essence of slavery? Not alone the owning of a human being. When it began, as it did, in the sparing of a captive's life, it was a virtue. No; but the treating of a man as a thing, the supplanting of his own will with the will of another, one of the most deadly ways of interfering with his well-being. And wherever this is done, whether in a Southern cotton-field under a system of lashes, or in a Northern workshop under a system of wages, or in a Utopian government under a system of laws, why is not the question of how to prevent it as much in the one case as in the other a moral question — a widening, therefore, of the ethical field? What is the real difference between those matters which ordinarily are called economical and sanitary and those which ordinarily are catalogued as ethical and moral? How many are the instances in which it is only that of flower and fruit, cause and effect? What makes a man a drunkard? How often is it starvation wages! Where do filthy lives come from? How frequently from filthy lodgings! Debase the coin of a country, and how quickly will an alloy appear in its conscience! Put a tariff on its merchandise, and what is better proved by all experience than that it will pay a large part of it with its morals? And with such a relation between them is there any other consistent principle than to class them all together as parts more or less evolved of one moral species, steps higher up or lower down of one majestic ladder; anything in doing so that does not give duty a broader base and a wider sweep?

It is the only definition which affords a solid ground for the thorough scientific study and treatment of moral questions. The great difficulty with their investigation hitherto has been their wide separation as regards the origin of what is most distinctive in them from all the other departments of scientific inquiry — the doctrine that though their root was in the " nature of things," it was a " nature " that did not mean nature, and " things " that had nothing to do with things. Trying to trace their principles into it was like pursuing a defaulting cashier or a boodle alderman from the United States into Canada, an experience in which science came suddenly to a dividing line where its writs of observation and experiment were no longer of any authority, and where only the royal missives of intuition were recognized. And with such a difference of jurisdictions, in one of which were the deeds and in the other the doers, it is no wonder that their treatment has been haphazard and confused, an application of remedies to effects rather than to their cause. It is a difficulty that the evolutionary view of what constitutes their moral character entirely removes. The " nature of things " under which they are to be studied is real nature. And there is no longer any inconsistency in recognizing that the root of an evil may be in a sewer because its fruit is in a soul.

How are moral questions thus defined to be dealt with? Back of the inquiry as to whether it should be through politics is the more primitive one needing first to be settled as to whether it should be through any human agency at all, except as man is unconsciously the agent of the Power which has the universe in charge. There is a large school of thinkers who distrust all interference of the human will for moral ends with the processes of nature, and especially with its processes in other men. They are not only indignant, as the English girl was with the swimmer who ventured, without an introduction, to save her from drowning, but beyond this they deny the right of any man and of any body of men to save them or save society from anything without a direct request. Let things do themselves, is their motto. The mighty forces of evolution, which have shaped the physical universe so wonderful and fair, rounded out the earth with its marvelous adaptations of part to part, unfolded the animal and vegetable kingdoms to their perfection of form, and built up the human body into its splendid capacities of action, are not going to depend on man's puny aid, they say, for success, now that society is to be organized and morals evolved. The youth who took the place of Phœbus on the chariot of the Sun and attempted to drive its fiery steeds over the azure pave to their home in the West is to them modesty itself as compared with the man who would take the reins of nature in his hands and guide its forces to their moral goal. They find history filled with the mistakes and blunders of the world's would-be reformers. The objects that one age has labored for with all its ethical might have been, how often, the horror and curse of the next! Who would accept the ideals set forth in Plato's Republic, Sydney's Arcadia, and More's Utopia, as comparing for one moment with the realities that society has come to in the actual course of events? What is the source of nine-tenths of the tramps, drunkards, criminals, and good-for-nothings that society is afflicted with to-day? The mistaken Christian charity, it is answered, that for eighteen hundred years has been keeping alive a class of persons to perpetuate their stock that nature, let alone to execute her law providing for the survival only of the fittest, would long since have laid harmlessly away in graveyards. There are many evils, it is said, the same as there are many insects, which serve better than any human wisdom to keep each other

down —" Evil its errand hath as well as good "
— so that when one set is destroyed by man's
interference it only gives the others a better
chance to operate; many reforms, also, that
have a natural connection with each other and
with the world's physical progress, so that if
any one is artificially developed faster than its
fellows, no matter how good it may be in itself, it results, the same as with a flower pushed
ahead of the spring-time, or with one organ of
the body ahead of the rest, in a maladjustment
of the new good which in its effects is worse
tenfold than the old evil. And from such
facts it is argued that instead of trying to
guide nature's coach ourselves, either politically or otherwise, our true course is to sit
down very quietly at her side and leave its reins
very carefully in her hands.

Far be it from me to deny or undervalue in
any way the tremendous moral strain of nature's own work. There is no other standpoint
that mind can take from which it looms up so
conspicuous and so undeniable as from that of
evolution. It is the great mountain stream
rising in the far-off cloudy peaks of the world's
nebulous state, and flowing down with ever-
increasing volume through its starry gorges,
its bent and distorted geological strata, and its
monstrous animal forms into the regions of its
civilized life, the stream on the banks of which

all human moralities are built, and by the force of which all human reforms are carried on. The universe itself all through is a moral agent, not of the kind perhaps always that would win the prize at a Sunday-school, or get its practitioner admitted into good society as a model of deportment, but one that has been true to its great principle of doing what would conduce best to the ever higher well-being of itself and its creatures; one that has come up from the wild orgies of its saurian youth into the decencies of a nineteenth-century manhood, and from its myriad bloody-nosed rounds of fisticuff with savages and barbarians to the battlefields of civilized industry and to the victories of enlightened peace. If its contests at first were only those of brute strength and brute cunning, and its survivals the survivals only of those that were physically fittest, it was simply to lay the foundations of its final moral structure the more solid and secure, simply because the root of moral right, as we now know, is in a right physical soil. And the lily and the lark have not more surely come out of the awful struggles for existence of the vegetable and animal worlds than love's flower and religion's song have from the wars of hate and from the grovelings of passion in the moral world.

But this recognition of nature's inherent moral strain, instead of doing away with the need of man's voluntary effort in the same direction, is a stimulus all the more to its use. The human will is not a separate thing from nature any more than the human body is, but is a part of nature — one of its grandest parts. The daring injunction of the old apostle Paul, "Work out your own salvation with fear and trembling, for it is God that worketh in you both to will and to do," expresses the true relation of the two agents. And it is because of this mighty power working within us, because our little human wheel is belted to the great driving-wheel of the universe, that we can take hold of moral questions with some hope of being an aid in their solution.

The right to do so, and especially the right of the individual to help in the solution of those matters which concern other individuals, is based on the fact that man is not a unit separate from all other units, but a member with them of an organism in whose welfare his own well-being is vitally bound up, and for whose conduct he shares with them the responsibility. There is indeed a sphere in which the individual is supreme, and into which no other man and no body of men have the right without his consent to intrude — a sphere in which he must be good or bad, saved or lost by and for himself alone. Its existence is one of the grandest and most distinctive facts of our humanity. It is a realm in which the poorest beggar is monarch; a plantation on which the most abject slave is master; a castle in which, more truly than in his home, every Englishman and every man is lord. And any social system that would take it away or narrow its bounds, whatever compensation of other blessings it may promise, is to be fought against as man's bitterest foe. Not less true is it, however, that there are other relations in which the individual is only one part of a larger unit, one state of a grander kingdom, and in which he normally both controls and is controlled by its other members. It is these two organisms, each legitimate, each the product of nature, each vibrating rhythmically back and forth into the other, that make humanity. All the great questions between individualism and socialism turn on the extent to which their existence is recognized, one party going to the extreme of making the individual the all in all, the other to the extreme of subordinating everything to the control of society. Evolution recognizes them both in its principles of differentiation and integration; Christianity both in its command, Thou shalt love thy neighbor as thyself — words which mean not as much as thyself, but as being a part of thy larger self. And just precisely as the individual has the right to answer alone all moral questions in the realm where he alone is concerned, on precisely the same ground he has the right to join with others in answering all those in the sphere where he has with them a common interest.

Then as to the wisdom and policy of attempting to guide nature's forces to their moral goal — are they not as pronounced here as in the use of the human will anywhere? Men do not act on the *laissez-faire* doctrine in the other relations of life — do not let the fields alone to give them only their native fruits, or the winds and waves alone to toss them where they please, or diseases and sickness alone to kill them in their own good time, or the lightnings and the cataract and the expansive power of steam alone to advance society after their own slow fashion. No; they mix them up with humanity; they bit their wild mouths; they harness their mighty forces; they mount the box behind their swift heels; they guide them, loaded with ten thousand human interests, to goals that by themselves alone they would never reach. What is all civilization as compared with barbarism, what is America to-day, jeweled with cities, laced with railroads, waving with wheat-fields, rich with thought, as compared with America three centuries ago, a howling wilderness, but the refusal of men in other

EVOLUTION AND POLITICS 161

things to act on the let-alone principle? Why now should they act on it in the moral world? Why not join hands with nature in curing the diseases of the social body, raising richer virtues in the field of the soul, utilizing with temperance factories the eternal power that makes for righteousness, steaming labor on to justice, and making a trolley-system by which right's lightning shall hasten humanity's plodding feet on to its goal? With nature's force the same eternal mystery everywhere, is there any more immodesty in seeking to drive it with one rein than with another, any more impudence in guiding its stream of righteousness than in guiding its stream of life, any more absurdity in using it to improve a virtue than in using it to improve a vine? What if mistakes are made? They are not made in morals any oftener than they are in art and science and philosophy, and in everything else with which man has to deal — are a part of the food on which here, as everywhere else, man grows up into success. What if reforms do need to move on together, so that a good one pushed ahead of the others becomes an evil? There is just about as much danger of mankind's making the earth wobble on its axis by their all crowding into its one good country as there is of their disturbing its moral balance by their all uniting in one reform. Taste averages here as safely as in all other things. And just as the same swing of the earth along its orbit that brings the bobolink to his northern home in springtime, brings him the green meadows to sing in, just so the same eternal spirit, in its larger orbit that inspires the reformer to utter his song, operates to make the field ready in which it is to be sung, and to make spring also in all its surrounding fields.

How has the world's moral progress thus far been carried on? Just as certainly by the action of human wills as by the great working force of nature. The crown and climax of the universe's moral force, the last and finest form in which it ultimates itself, is mankind's volition. Other things are used to make its trunk and limbs, but it blossoms only in souls, and fruits itself only through wills.

More important still, it is man's personal effort in moral questions that is the source of that best of all results that comes out of them, his own moral character. If nature did all, and man was only the recipient, reforms might indeed be conducted as well as, perhaps better than, they are now; but they would not and could not have that wonderful flavor about them which makes them distinctively moral. It is the giver, not receiver, that in the struggles of humanity upward gets the greater blessing.

"Not the grapes of Canaan that repay,
But the high faith that failed not on the way."

What was the most precious outcome of the anti-slavery struggle and our Civil War? Not the freedom of the slave, or the salvation of the Union, or the new life it gave to liberty beyond the seas. No; but the new manhood into which it lifted up ourselves, the finer quality of union that it brought to our whole land, North and South. It is this kind of success that always comes in all moral struggles, however much they fail outwardly — this the laurel that the vanquished equally with the victors all win in the battles that are fought for human rights.

So I say in answer to this part of the inquiry that it is a strict deduction from the principles of evolution that men are to take an active part in dealing with the world's moral issues. I saw a coachman a while ago with his chubby two-year-old boy on the seat in front of him driving a spirited pair of horses. " He is young yet," said he, " and I keep a good grip on the reins back of him; but he'll come to it himself with a little practice by and by. He's got the blood of six generations of coachmen in him, and blood tells the same here as everywhere. Why," he continued, "we're all of us born into the world with a twist in our wrists for holding the ribbons; and I am going to train him so that when I am old and decrepit I can sit on the back seat feeling safe and let him do all the driving." So with nature. Yes; ridiculous as it has been thought to be, she has taken her boy, Man, with her up on the great coach of the universe and has given him its reins. He is young yet, and she keeps a good grip on them herself at the same time. But he has got her stock in him for sixty thousand generations, and she knows that such stock in the end will tell. He, too, is born every time with a twist in his soul-wrists for moral driving. And in the long eons yet to come, when her form outwardly has grown old and decrepit, she too, perhaps, expects to sit on the back seat of the spiritual universe and let him do all the driving.

The settling of this point, however, does not by any means settle the whole subject. There are two ways of driving, two methods in morals of helping things along. One is with politics, State authority, and the whip and spur of law; the other with inward principle, voluntary association, and the voice and rein of reason. And the question yet to be answered is, Which of these does evolution lead up to and sanction?

The great nations of antiquity, as is well known, placed their chief reliance on the first of these methods. The words of Pliny, *Non est princeps supra leges, sed leges supra principem* — principle is not above laws, but laws are above principle — and of Aristotle, that the State exists before the individual, and not the individual before the State, expressed the almost universal sentiment. What the world in its early days wanted beyond everything else, wanted with an intensity we can hardly realize now, was stability, a condition of things fixed against change, violence, disorder; and this it had in the State, this the origin and meaning of its name. Its form at first was naturally imperialism — that of the one strong man who could suppress disorder. He was its government; his will its law; obedience to him its morals. The oft-quoted saying of Louis XIV, "I am the State," was what all kings believed; the pious sentiment of the Bishop of Rheims, "When God had made Napoleon he rested from his labors," an expression of the reverence for great leaders as the greatest of divine gifts that all people felt. But kings were not always kingly or rulers always righteous; and little by little, each step a battle, each line a revolution, legalism took the place of imperialism, the people's law of the prince's will. Frederick the Great, wishing a windmill removed from before his palace that its owner would not sell, threatened to have it taken away by force. "There is a supreme court at Berlin," answered the miller; and the windmill stands before the palace to this day, a monument to the might of law against the might even of kings. But amid all these changes of form the State itself remained, the center of men's hopes, the object of their devotion, as honored under law as leader, demon as despot. The habit acquired through long ages of reverencing it as the source of all public order and the means of all public good had become a part of our very nature. And so it was almost inevitable when men in the progress of modern civilization came to have great moral questions to deal with that they should look to politics and political action as the chief, if not the only means by which they could be satisfactorily settled.

Evolution, however, has so sooner built up anything, even a sentiment, than it begins either to tear it down or to shape it over into something else. Gradually in our time a change is taking place in not a few minds with regard to the value of law and the State as the means of promoting any of man's interests. Emerson's words —" We are kept by better gods than the will of magistrates "; " good men must not obey the laws too well "; " to educate the wise man the State exists, and with the appearance of the wise man the State expires "— express a wide-

EVOLUTION AND POLITICS 167

spread feeling not among cranks and bomb-throwers merely, but among sober, orderly, peaceful thinkers. It is the same kind of sociological change, only a stage farther along, as that by which imperialism gave way to constitutionalism and the potentate to the politician — a change by which now legalism is giving way to individualism, law to liberty, politics to principle. The old order which put the State above the citizen, the laws above principles, has been already entirely reversed. Governments are being remanded, if not into the rubbish heap of the world's back yard, yet into a secondary and subordinate place. And whereas men have relied in the past on the sovereign and the statute book for order, safety, property, happiness, they are now fast coming to rely for them simply on themselves.

It is a change which has preëminently made itself felt in the estimate of politics as a means of dealing with moral questions. The very names of the two things have come to have a natural incongruity with each other. As Emerson says, "What satire on government can equal the word politic, which for ages has signified cunning, intimating that the State is a trick?"

Who are chosen to act as our legislators? If it is a question of carpentry, we do not trust a man to build even a hen-coop who has not had some little apprenticeship at the trade; but in this most difficult of all arts, the building of a State, the shaping of what is to be a moral habitation, the one, as Burke says, that " requires all the experience a person can gain in his whole life," how often are those chosen who have never spent one hour in studying the real nature of government and of morals, and whose sole qualification is their ability to manipulate a caucus, pander to a popular prejudice, or, it may be, buy outright the popular vote!

What are moral questions used for in politics? As soon as the first outburst of enthusiasm is over out of which the parties that take them up are born, how inevitably does the execution of their principles sink into a secondary place, and their main use become the keeping of their advocates in power! If Jove laughs at lovers' vows, how he must roar at politicians' promises! The performances of a circus on its advertising board fence and in its actual equestrian ring, or even the virtues of a citizen on his grave-stone and in his life, are hardly wider apart than those of a political party before election and afterward. The story is told in the adventures of the famous Baron Munchausen, that coming one night to what seemed a great island in the far-off sea, some of his sailors climbed up its steep sides and made on

its top a fire with which to cook their supper.
The supposed island, however, proved to be a
huge whale asleep on the water; and as soon
as the fire had burned a little into his blubber,
it waked him up and down he went, sailors, supper, fire, and all, to his home in the vasty deep.
And that is the experience reformers have had
again and again when they have climbed up on
the back of some apparently continental political party and kindled there the moral fire with
which to cook a supper of temperance, woman's
suffrage, or labor rights. As soon as it began
to burn down into the fat, how quickly has it
become a whale and left them and their cause
exactly where Munchausen's sailors were, floundering in the watery deep! As Hosea Biglow
declares:

"Constitouents are hendy to help a man in,
But arterwards they don't weigh the heft of a
pin."

Then the methods by which politics and legislation are carried on — the manipulations of
the caucus and primary meeting, the torchlight
processions, hurrahing and mud-flinging of the
campaign, and the log-rolling, bribery, and partisanship of the lobby-room — who will say they
are the ones out of which nice moral results are
likely to come? Is there really any evil in society to-day that politics can be set to run

down which is worse than politics itself, anything which needs reforming more imperatively than the would-be political reformer? A dudish hunter went out into the woods one morning with his equally dudish dog and started a wolf. An hour after, meeting a grim old farmer, he asked him if he had seen anything of the two. " Oh, yes," said the farmer, " I saw them going by here a little while ago fast as they could run." " And how near were they to each other? " anxiously inquired the youth. " Well," answered the farmer, " the dog when I saw them was about two lengths ahead, but the wolf was fast overhauling him, and I guess that by this time they are just about together." So with very much of the politics that we have started out to hunt down moral evil. The hunter may indeed be some two lengths ahead now, but the game is fast coming up with him, and the two very soon will be together — one inside of the other.

But even where politics is pure and honest, as, indeed, it sometimes is, even when the wisest and best of men get together to make laws, as, indeed, they sometimes do, there are limitations in the method itself which make it in dealing with moral issues only of partial value. The proposed law has to be cut and trimmed and pared down to meet their varying tastes. It never can be the embodiment of the highest and most advanced principles, never at the best ahead of what the average mind, the bare majority of a people, will sustain; otherwise it will be only a dead letter. And when it is enforced it secures to itself only an outward obedience, not the homage of the soul; cuts down the branch of evil, but leaves its root to unfold, it may be, in a far worse shape; suppresses the saloon, but drives the jug into the home; wipes out slavery, but puts in its place the race problem; shuts up the brothel, but sows the whole city with its inmates; provides, perhaps, in the very fact of obedience to its letter, a quietus to the conscience for breaking, all the more, its inward spirit. "Sammy," said a mother to her little boy who was playing in the yard, and whom she wished to keep from the dangers of the street, "don't you go out of that gate." "No, mother," he answered, "I won't go out of it." Ten minutes after, beholding him making mud pies right between the cart ruts, she angrily exclaimed; "Samuel, why didn't you obey me? Didn't I tell you not to go out of that gate?" "Yes, mother," he replied, "and I did obey you. I didn't go out of the gate; I climbed over the fence." How many are the grown-up Samuels who strictly obey the State mother when she tells them not to go out of the gate into evil, but who in doing so manage all the same to make for themselves plenty of mud pies out in the roads of vice and wrong by climbing conscience-easy over the unprohibited garden fence!

Worst of all, as a politically made law can express only the average morality as regards virtue, so also it can meet only the average need as regards justice. It can not discriminate, can not take into account an evil's intensifying and extenuating circumstances, can judge only by the outward act, has to saw off its punishment as we saw wood, by the foot measure; and the best legislation thus applied becomes sometimes an instrument of wrong that wrong itself would hardly dare originate. A little lame boy nine years old, with no home and no friends, who had stolen a few pennies, is seized by it and locked up in jail, at first alone, where, so timid and so little beyond babyhood was he, that the sheriff had to put a light in his cell to keep him from crying all night, afterward for four months with a vile, licentious negro. And at the same time the boodle aldermen, the defaulting cashier, and the downright thief, who have stolen moneys by the hundred thousand, are enabled — how many of them! — to walk, money and all, through law's unlocked doors. A woman with a nursing baby is sentenced to ten days' imprisonment for calling a man who had insulted her "vile names," so little hardened that on hearing the sentence she fainted away; while in every great political canvass a thousand newspapers on each side fling charges at each other and at the opposite candidates too outrageous to be expressed by the term " vile names," all not only unrebuked by law, but sustained by it as the necessary instruments sometimes of settling great moral questions. It was found a while ago in the city where I live that its charities were encouraging idleness among the overgrown boys in some of its families, and a law was made that no household should receive public aid which had children whose age was over twenty-one — a most righteous law apparently; but the very first case it cut off was that of a half-blind old lady of eighty who was doing her best to support an idiot daughter of forty — the most deserving case in the whole city. Visiting the veteran keeper of our county jail on one occasion, I expressed the opinion that in the twenty years of his official life he must have seen a very dark side of human nature. "No," said he, " the average of those who come here is quite as good as the average outside. Of course I get some downright rascals, but usually the big villains have too much shrewdness, or too much money, or too much legal help to get into my clutches. Most of those who come to me are men who have some one weak place in their nature which some one combination of circumstances has happened to assail, but who otherwise are exceptionally good men and men who in all other circumstances would have lived and died respected citizens."

Then, apart from the failure of the political method to reach the worst cases of immorality, how many are the lives of earth's noblest and best that it has sacrificed on its scaffolds and gallows, not unintentionally through mistakes of evidence, but knowingly because of their efforts to bring about a higher morality!

> "Alas! the blows for error meant
> Too oft on truth itself are spent."

What is it that has slaughtered liberty's advocates on a thousand battle-fields? The sword of law's defenders. What has been the worst obstacle that reform — our anti-slavery reform, for instance — has had to encounter? Notoriously the statute book. What stands next to church law as responsible throughout all time for the blood of the world's martyrs? Beyond question political law. A few years ago warrants were issued for the arrest of eight men charged with murdering the Chicago police. One of them could not be found and might easily have escaped even a trial; but conscious, apparently, of his own innocence and hoping by his influence to save his companions, he voluntarily walked into the court-house during

their trial and gave himself up to its officers.
It was a deed of trust in law and of gallantry
toward comrades that in the days of classic
Greece and Rome would have challenged the
world's admiration, and which might apparently
even in our day have weighed something in
showing that he was no ordinary criminal; but
law can have no eye for chivalry and no sense
of honor in dealing with its offenders. He was
proved guilty of throwing out, if not bombs,
yet dangerous sentiments, the guilt of reformers in all ages, and was hanged as remorselessly
as if he had been an actual murderer stabbing
for money and cornered, in spite of himself, by
a vigilant police.

Such cases are the result of what must always be a limitation of the political method in
dealing with moral questions, the fixedness of
its enactments. When nature has settled a
point of right, she immediately leaves it to
take care of itself thenceforth, and goes on to
help settle another; but when law has settled a
point of right, it immediately sits down square
upon it, and devotes all its energies ever after
to keeping it settled. It is like the old farmer's
horse — good when you want it to stand, but
very poor when you want it to go. In its eyes
the right is all accomplished good, and to be
defended; the wrong all unaccomplished good,
and to be resisted. The worst foe of new

morality is law-embodied old morality. Legislation is a man who makes barrels by putting the boy Principle inside of them to hold up their heads while he drives on the hoops — a good way if each barrel thus finished was the last ever needing to be built. But every time he is called upon to build a better one, it makes it necessary for the boy to smash the old one in order to get out — a process which naturally causes a good deal of disturbance, as very often the smashing has to be done with gunpowder. The path of the world's moral progress through the ages is marked by its smashed and abandoned laws. As Mr. Buckle puts it, "Every great reform which has been effected has consisted not in doing something new, but in undoing something old." And with such a record the satisfaction which is felt at getting the world's moral progress into law must necessarily be a good deal modified by the certainty that the very next question will be how to get it out of law.

In contrast with political action, look at man's other great method of aiding morals — that of education, of voluntary association, and of appeals to reason and conscience. "Where is your music?" said a bystander to a soldier of the Eighth Massachusetts Regiment as it was hurrying through the angry streets of Baltimore to the defense of the nation's capital at the outbreak of our Civil War. "Down in the breech of our rifles," was the grim reply. And that is how we want to carry out moral music as we go forth to the defense of right and justice on the battle-fields of human life — not so much in the drum and fife of a political caucus and a legislative hall as down in the depths of our souls.

"Within himself he found the law of right."

It is the naturally evolved successor to the method of law. There is no characteristic of our times more marked than the number, size, and sweep of the reformatory movements that with the decadence of politics and the loosening of the legal bond have sprung up into doing what was once considered to be almost exclusively the politician's and legislator's work. Religion, so long divorced from morality, has in our day recognized its claims and begun pouring into it the might of its divine inspiration. The Church itself is no longer, at least in free countries, a State institution, or governed, at least in its Protestant form, on State principles, but is simply a series of voluntary moral associations. And wherever any new issue comes up in the world at large, or any new and difficult work presents itself needing to be done, it is the instinct of its advocates to form among themselves a society to take it in charge — this even when the Government is to be asked ultimately to act as its agent. A salt dissolved in water

so that its atoms can act freely according to
to their own internal law does not more surely
arrange itself in a crystal than humanity individualized in the medium of liberty does into a
voluntary organization. It is a phenomenon
going on before our eyes to-day which transcends in beauty anything ever seen in the
chemist's laboratory, yet is looked upon by how
many as if it was only society going to pieces.
And in settling moral questions, who will say
that humanity thus crystallized is not a more
highly evolved agency than humanity in its
merely amorphous, political state?

It is the method of equality, of self-respect,
and of manliness. When a thing is done because of a law imposed by another, no matter
how worthy in itself the thing may be, and no
matter whether that other is a monarch or a
majority, it inevitably places its doer in a position of inferiority, makes him a thing moved
by an outside force rather than a man self-moved. But when it is done from inward principle, it makes each man his own monarch and
puts him on a par with every other man. It
appeals to and develops that which is noblest
and best in man — his power of choice and his
own sense of right.

> " A voice spake in his ear,
> And, lo! all other voices far and near
> Died at that whisper full of meanings clear."

It brings together in support of a cause only those who have a heart and soul interest in its success, those who love it and can lay on its altar the enthusiasm of love. It is indeed open to fanaticism, narrowness, crankiness; but it is lifted realms above the far worse vices, so common in politics, of selfishness, shallowness, and time-serving. All the noblest qualities of our human nature — altruism, self-sacrifice, the courage of conviction, and the living for an ideal, all the crosses and martyr stakes of our race, all its noblest poems and most heroic deeds — gather, if not inevitably, yet naturally around its standard. And, in spite of the popular odium attaching to the name reformer, if you want to stand on the mountain tops of humanity, want to see how near dust can come to Deity, want to breathe an atmosphere as far removed from politics as that of Shasta from a sink, go into the company of men who

"Ere its cause bring fame and profit and 'tis prosperous to be just"

have sided with a moral truth — men like Phillips, Garrison, Foster, Pillsbury, and their associates in the early days of the anti-slavery cause. So with the kind of morality that is attained by the moral method. It is the real article. What is done by it is done from principle, done because the thing is really believed in, and not from outward constraint. Take the man who is temperate from inward conviction, as compared with the one who is temperate because the law will not allow him anything on which to get drunk; can there be any question as to which is the higher kind of man? And a State all of whose moral questions have been settled in souls, can it be otherwise than a better one to live in than that which has settled them only on statute books?

It is a method, to be sure, whose outward instrumentalities are insignificant and unimposing; one that, in comparison with the enginery and majesty of law — the police officer, the court, the judge, the prison, the gallows — is a mere "voice crying in the wilderness." But what has been historically the most efficient moral agency this world has ever seen, the Christian religion, was at the start that very thing, a mere voice crying in the wilderness. It despised the aid of law — was, rather, so conscious of its own innate superiority that it did not take the trouble to despise it. Think of Jesus as lobbying in the Sanhedrim to get it to enact his Golden Rule, or of Paul as dropping the sword of the spirit to manipulate a caucus for his nomination to a position where he could introduce a bill against idolatry. Instead of being helped by law, it had from the start all the power of law, yea, the very principle of law, to contend against; and it did it triumphantly, did it even when its foe was the Roman Empire, that very embodiment of law — went on doing it against the whole vast empire of wrong, till, deserting its own weapons, it began arming itself with those of its antagonist. I saw a place on Cape Ann a while ago where a soft pine seedling had lodged itself in a cleft of rock, the most hopeless, apparently, of all localities in which to grow, a bit of soft woody tissue surrounded with solid walls of granite and with only impalpable light and air to be its nourishment. Yet the pine with the drill and dynamite of its inner life force had rent asunder the huge granite ledge, elbowed tons of it out of the way, and, as a tall tree, was waving its evergreen boughs in the April sunshine, unharmed even with a scar. And that is what moral force is in the ledges of wrong — a tissue softer than that of the pine seedling, yet rending into powder what defies the sharpest penalties of the statute book and finding food where the sword of law finds only flint.

With such a contrast between the two things, can there be any doubt as to which is to be sought after as at least the preferable one for advancing the world's moral interests? While believing thoroughly in woman's right to the ballot, is it not a mistake to measure her progress as a social factor by the degree to which

it has been attained? There are scores of
places to which she is being admitted — notably
to the college, the counting-room, the platform,
and the sacred desk — that are worth to her
infinitely more than anything, from polls to
presidential chair, that politics has to offer.
And however willing she may be to take it as
the symbol of her equality with man, is it worth
while for her to pay a very large price for what,
as an agency in helping morals along, is like a
seat in a country wagon to a girl who has got
her hand on the throttle-valve of a locomotive
engine? So with reformers possessed of the
ballot who never succeed in getting their ideas
materialized in any political measure — go down
to the grave, after years of struggle, with them
embodied, perhaps, only in their own tottering
forms; they are not on that account valueless
as moral factors. There are men in the world
— you have some in your own ranks — ripe
with age, yet blossoming continually with new
hopes and plans for humanity, orange trees in
the realm of soul, whose simple personality is
doing more for progress than any political activity could. A vote in the minority is lost; a
man in the minority always counts. And an
association like this, made up of such men,
young and old, and operating wholly through
ideas, is raising, if nothing more, yet a raw
material for ethics, without which at last all

the factors of it would come to a stand. So
with the churches that, refusing to meddle with
politics, give their whole energies to the making
of better souls. I know it is the custom of
progressionists to despise their work, and I am
very far from believing it is religion's whole
sphere. But they, too, have their place.
What this world wants more than anything
else for the solving of its moral problems is
moral men and women. Human nature is the
soil out of which all social fruits grow; and
whatever makes that richer will make everything above it righter.

Nevertheless, with all this immeasurable superiority intrinsically and philosophically of
the moral over the political method in dealing
with the questions at issue, practical sociology
is very far from saying that the political one
is yet wholly a thing of the past and never now
under any circumstances to be used for their
solution. Adaptation to the environment as
well as intrinsic excellence is what here, as well
as everywhere else, has to be taken into account.
First archism; then legalism; then anarchism;
or, if the words are better liked, first imperialism, then legalism, then individualism — prince,
politician, principle — that is the natural order
in which all government unfolds, that the one
each part of which has a corresponding phase

of social development it is best fitted for. And as in religion the law is the school-master to bring us to Christ, so in the State politics is naturally the path by which we go to principle. With social development the same everywhere, the progress from the one to the other would be everywhere the same. But it is notorious that while some parts of society are enlightened enough to act on principle, others, even in the most advanced communities, are yet in that savage and half-civilized condition for which the personal ruler and the strong arm of law are best adapted. And where this is the case it surely is the dictate of plain good sense to use the tool, whatever its intrinsic imperfection, which will best do the task. "I believe in blood as much as any one does," said the horse-trader; "but when I see a really good animal I go for him, no matter how mongrel his ancestry may be," a wisdom that will apply equally well to legal scrubs as compared with the bloodstock of principle. Electricity is a higher motive power for moving street cars than horse muscle, and a dynamo in each car a higher one than a wire connecting it with a central station. But, till the separate dynamo is perfected, we use the wire; and when the wire will not act, as is the case now and then, we bring out the old horses and hitch them on in the old way. And for the same reason, though moral

EVOLUTION AND POLITICS 185

principle is a higher force than law with which to move the car of progress, and a moral dynamo in each man's soul a better form of it than a central one at Albany or Washington, it nevertheless is a matter of practical wisdom, when the dynamo breaks down or can not be applied, to keep the old political horses as the force on which to fall back.

It is indeed true that law can never rise above the average morals of the State, never express its most advanced sentiment; but, on the other hand, it is an immense instrument for doing what in some respects is even more important — the bringing of its less advanced members up to the average and the keeping of them from dragging the whole into destruction. Here is a village where moral suasion has succeeded in shutting up all the drinking saloons but one. The very fact, however, that the others have been closed makes it all the more profitable to keep this open, all the more difficult, therefore, for it to be acted upon by moral suasion. Why now should such a premium on its baseness be allowed — why not the great majority of citizens who want it closed get together politically and shut it up with the power of law? Here is a state where a hundred factories have been persuaded not to employ children under twelve or fifteen years of age, but a dozen more selfish ones persist in their employment, and as a consequence are able to undersell the others, or else compel them to reduce the wages of their adult hands to a level with those of the children. Is not this a case where law can properly interfere to put them all on the same footing? Or, worse still, here is a man who, through ignorance or a flippant contempt for science, throws his offal into a brook or keeps open a filthy sewer till it threatens the whole village with a deadly epidemic. Ought there to be any scruple about lifting him up by political action to at least the average height of sanitary morals? A traveler attacked by a savage dog, as he was passing peaceably by a farm-house, seized his gun and poured its whole blazing charge down the creature's throat. "What did you kill my dog for?" exclaimed the angry owner, rushing out. "To prevent his killing me," was the answer. "Well, why didn't you hit him with the butt end of your gun?" was the next question. "Well, why didn't he come at me with the butt end of his body?" was the neat reply. There are some evils in society so savage and widemouthed that if a man waits to deal with them morally there will not be any man, the same as if the traveler had waited to tame the dog, there would not have been any traveler left. And in such cases, savage as the method seems, is there any other alternative than to give them the blazing legal end of society's moral gun?

Laws do indeed have a tendency to become the prisons of moral principle, needing often to be violently destroyed when any new onward step is to be taken. But that is true of all forms, all institutions, all growths, is true of the human body itself, is true even of the customs, habits, and societies by which morality as a principle acts, is true at last of the " grand old man " who for sixty years has stood at the forefront of England's reforms. It is the fundamental method of evolution, building up and then tearing down, imprisoning life in one generation, and then sweeping its forms all into graves in order to have it move on into better ones in the next.

> " Ever by losses the right must gain,
> Every good have its birth in pain."

And its operation in the field of politics, its having the laws which morality leaves in and blooms in during its spring become the dead leaves and dead petals which it has to shake off in its autumn so as to have its tree grow, only brings the political method the more clearly within the scope of evolution.

Laws at first produce only outward morality; but outward morality kept up long enough becomes habit, exactly the same as inward morality does, and habit inherited becomes nature, the inmost thing of all. It is the method that all parents use in the training of children, the forming of good habits through obedience to outward precepts. It is closely connected with "the influence of the environment," the working from the outward inward, which under evolution is certainly one of nature's recognized methods of progress. And with society freed by any means from immoral surroundings and its young trained up simply to good habits for a few generations, who can doubt that the moral gain, if not equal to that of inward personal struggle, would at any rate be immense?

There is no denying that laws are often badly administered and do harm; but, with all the tremendous value of inward principle, it must be confessed that its practical working is sometimes in this respect very far from being perfect. Who shall say that custom, fashion, public opinion, the channels entirely independent of law through which morality expresses itself, are not often as tyrannical and unjust as any legislation has ever been? Take the awful penalty that society inflicts on a fallen woman, laid down in no statute book; and in all the multiplied crimes of law against the sex, is there anything that for absolute damning wrong will compare with this? What is it behind judge and jury that in all ages has burned and shot and hanged the world's martyrs and reformers? There is nothing in the vilest legislation which is so much to be dreaded as the world's unlegalized spasms of virtue. It is hardly twenty years since the man who did more than all others to open the Pacific Railroad, actually putting his money, as the event has proved, "where it would do the most good," the manliest man Congress had that year, was hounded into his grave without judge or jury by the country's conscience. Trial by jury — law's method — is bad enough; but what is it in comparison with trial by newspaper, the public's method outside of law? And with all the dreadfulness of the reporter's pen as a panderer to vice, is it ever quite so dangerous as when it dips itself in the ink of righteousness and prepares to come out as the champion of virtue — any damage it ever does with its account of the murder's perpetration that can quite equal what it does with its account of the murderer's punishment?

While political laws, also, are often petty, inquisitive, and a severe restriction on personal liberty, are they more so than the rules and pledges of even the most pronounced voluntary associations? What State ever made regulations for its citizens that went down to a finer point than those which many temperance organizations and trades-unions make for themselves? The fact is, it is impossible to have anywhere the tremendous power which comes from associated action without the sacrifice to some extent of individual freedom. The most voluntary reform societies appealing to the world by moral suasion do have, and must have, rules among themselves of some kind in order to use to the greatest advantage even moral suasion; must have an iron-bound bucket with which to draw water even from the wells of liberty. The degree of their rigor and minuteness depends not on whether they are made by the State or by a voluntary association, but deeper down on the people themselves, Russian nihilism being just as despotic as Russian imperialism, and the town meeting in America quite as free as the town debating club. And so likewise the mean and objectionable things about politics — the caucusing, partisanship, bribery, log-rolling, bossism, and appeals to prejudice and passion — do not arise from the nature of the State, but from the undeveloped nature of man, are to be found in voluntary associations, even in churches and religious conventions, quite as devilishly developed as in ward rooms and legislative halls.

Crowning all else, it is to be said on the side of political action that it is not infrequently the direct means by which the moral method does its work. The politics of a free country is the great public school to which all its citizens go inevitably as pupils. It is impossible to get a law enacted which involves in any way their welfare without at least some discussion of its right and wrong principles. Every electioneering campaign is a debate of its members in which, mixed in with the meanness and the mud-throwing, the precious stones of right and virtue and moral obligation are flung from side to side. If the calendar of politicians is darkened with names that are the synonyms of cunning and self-seeking, it is starred also with such shining ones in the ranks of principle as those of a Sumner, a Gladstone, a Cavour. And even in the worst machinations of the caucus and the lobby there is often an unconscious, unintended moral wisdom that surpasses in its practical effect the sober designing of the churches and schools, a divinity that shapes the ends of politics to morals, rough hew them with bribery and trickery as their actors may, presidents elected from the ranks of pot-house politicians as one of themselves whom the dignity and responsibility of their position have converted into models of official conduct, microbes of political vice that have proved the best possible antidotes of some of the civil ones that were consuming the general body of society, and seeds of law sown in the dirt and filth of selfishness and corruption that have flowered in public virtue and fruited in moral progress.

Is there any improvement of politics, any

further development of the State, which can remove their defects and make them more efficient as moral agents? I do not see how State socialism — that is, the enlargement of their functions — is going to do it. It is a movement in the very opposite direction of that to which evolution naturally tends; a use of law greater instead of less, a working more from without instead of more from within. The evils of the political method which are now in a few fields it would transfer to all, bring everything under the control of the politician. And just in proportion as it relieved the individual of the moral strain under which he now so often falls, it would relieve him of the moral strength under which he now so largely stands.

Neither can I see any reason for going with Mr. Spencer to the other extreme — that of limiting the functions of the State to the punishment of crime and stigmatizing all laws for the direct promotion of a people's welfare as among " the sins of legislators." If it is right for the State to stop murder by shutting up murderers, why is it not right for it to do it by shutting up the saloons which make the murderers? If it can properly interfere with the man who maims another with a club, then why not with the one who maims another with a polluted stream or a dangerous wall? Or, if it can support a police officer and a jail for the sake of maintaining the peace of society, then why not a school-master and a schoolroom? The more evolved philosophy here, as everywhere else, would seem to be prevention rather than cure, dealing with the fountain rather than the stream. And on Mr. Spencer's own ground that the State is to secure to every man freedom to do all he wills, provided he does not infringe on the equal freedom of every other man, all laws needful for this, and especially all laws like those relating to education, which tend to make him less desirous of infringing on the equal freedom of others, would seem fairly to be within its province.

If the State is to be improved at all as an agency for dealing with moral questions, the principles of evolution point plainly to more freedom, more reliance on the individual, more the character of a voluntary association as the direction in which the improvement is to be sought. The worst thing about it now is its assumption that its laws have a special sanctity and authority by virtue of their being made by it, and that it has a natural right to impose them on all the people within its limits independent of their direct personal consent. The conception of it presented in such works as " Mulford's Nation," and in so many patriotic sermons and Fourth of July orations, designed to excite reverence for it as an institution innately good and necessarily to be obeyed, is quite as mischievous as that of the Socialist at the other extreme, who looks on it as a distinct personality which has special duties it owes to him — is indeed a kind of teaching that is largely responsible for socialism, the obligation to support on the one side implying the obligation to protect on the other. A remnant still exists of the old philosophy that it is the State that makes morality. For the divine right of kings we have substituted the divine right of congress. And as the pagan of other days took a piece of wood he had saved from the fire heap or the lumber yard and carved it with his knife into an idol which he fell down and worshiped as his god, so the citizen of to-day takes a piece from the timber of our common humanity and shapes him with his ballot into a legislator whose law he bows down to with a homage altogether different from what he would give it as the word of a man. It is an assumption that we need to get entirely rid of. The State is ourselves, what we are, and with only such authority as we choose to let it have. As Emerson says, " We ought to remember in dealing with it that its institutions are not aboriginal, that they are not superior to the citizen, that every one of them was once the act of a single man, and that they are all imitable, all alterable." There is no reason why a man should not join it and leave it as freely as he does a church or a temperance society; no reason why, if he refuses to receive its protection and partake of its benefits, he should be taxed for it, any more than when he declines to buy any other goods. It is toward this relation to it that all democracy, all civilization tends. And with the citizen thus its voluntary member there would be naturally the same appreciation of its value and responsibility for its conduct, and the same chance to act in it on principle, that there are now in all other voluntary associations.

With equal emphasis evolution points to more differentiation in the legislative department of the State as a requisite for its better dealing with moral questions. A large part of its mistakes and inefficiencies now arise from its trying to act on all its varied interests through only one set of men. With the complexities of our modern social life and the wide diversity of the matters to be attended to — coinage and crime, temperance and tariffs, Indians and imports, seals and silver — what can be more absurd than to expect one body of legislators to make laws intelligently on them all? Different hands for different work is what is as much needed in the State as in any other workshop. If an Indian question is to be acted upon, the only way in which to have it done properly is by the election of men for it who have made a special study of the Indian situation; if a temperance question, then of those who have given to temperance in all its bearings their life thought. So with all other matters requiring wide knowledge and nice discrimination. Thirty years ago our country had bitter experience of what it was to wage a military war by acts of a general Congress, setting politicians who could manage a caucus to managing a campaign, and leaders who could fire the country's heart to being leaders who should fire its cannon. We need to do now in our war against wrong what we had to do then in our war against rebels — put its conduct in the care of moral Grants and Shermans, have West Points at which to educate civilians as well as soldiers. It is this that is the real civil-service reform, the one that will bring law-makers within its scope, a hundredfold more important than that which includes only law administrators. Then when a law has been formulated it ought in most cases to be referred back to the whole people for its final passage — they who ought, in the old New England town-meeting way, to be their own ultimate legislative body. It is a reference which would give them a direct knowledge of the laws they are living under, a thing which in nine cases out of ten they are ignorant of now, would be a union of the nation's select and common wisdom, the voice of reason and the voice of the people, that might with some justice be called the voice of God. And moral laws public opinion had helped so directly to make, public opinion better than any policeman's club would help naturally to enforce.

Summing up the conclusions reached, society's moral questions include all those which relate to how its members in their dealings with each other shall best be enabled to promote the public good and to secure from it their own highest well-being. The right of any person to act on such questions is derived from the fact that he is not only an individual with his own conduct to attend to, but a part also of the social body, having interests that are affected by the conduct of others, and that his will and his work are the legitimate higher channels of that great indwelling power making for righteousness by which the whole universe is moved. Politics and the moral method both have their place under evolution as agencies to be used in their settlement, the difference between them being that the one is a stage farther along than the other, and that it works from within instead of from without. Each has its imperfections and limitations, each its special stage of social development to which it is best adapted; and while moral principle is to be looked forward to as the ideal condition, political law is to be used whenever for the time being it will best promote the great end to be attained, just as in the education of a child outward precept is imposed upon him by parent and friend till he is able to act always from his own inner sense of right, the acting from his own sense of right being always kept in view as the end to be reached. There is no inconsistency between the two, no reason why both of them should not join hands, when the opportunity offers, in helping do their common work. And the final tendency of evolution here, as in so many other things, is not to accentuate the differences of its factors, not to give the one supremacy by the other's annihilation, but to fill each with something of the other's life and to unite them all on a higher plane and, in a completer whole, evolve the State into more freedom for the individual, the individual into more voluntary associations that, like the State, shall act through self-imposed law, and society at large into a completer yielding to that Divine Power within it which of itself makes for righteousness. As the audience of a country church one summer afternoon were laboriously struggling through their congregational hymn, the wheezy old organ with its poor player trying to lead, and several scores of voices each with its own distinct degree of success trying to follow, it chanced that Emma Abbott, the famous opera singer, dropped into the service, and suddenly a voice rich, sweet, powerful, and thrilling with an accent of soul no word can describe, broke in with them from among the pews. It did not hush the others, but quickened, inspired, strengthened, led them — swept the hundreds of straggling voices and the wheezy old organ itself, glad now to follow, into complete harmony with each other, into a capacity, also, that surprised themselves; and there went up to heaven out of them all a burst of reverential song such as the old church in all its eighty years of service had never echoed with before. And that is what the inward moving power of evolution, the voice of God in the soul of man, is tending to do with our wheezy old State organ and its political players, and with all the hundreds of voluntary reform tongues that now, straggling apart, are trying to deal with moral questions; it is tending not to hush them up, or take their place, but to quicken them into new strength, unfold them into new beauty, and blend them all together in a song that shall be worthy of its glorious theme — a song of the eternal Right that in all this vast world of ours shall not be marred with one discordant note of wrong.

V

EVOLUTION AND PROGRESS

Radicalism is ordinarily supposed to concern itself entirely with the new, and to have little or nothing to do with the old. Its method of progress is thought to be the rooting up and sweeping away of the institutions and ideas of the past with each changing age, and the planting in their place of others revealed directly out of the heavenly world or originating wholly in the minds of this world's reformers. Destruction, it is said, must necessarily precede construction; the houses of the fathers be torn down, in order to make room for upbuilding those of the children; the handwriting of our predecessors be sponged off from the great social slate as the only way in which that of our own time can be made to stand forth distinct and clear. Advanced thinkers everywhere, but especially in religion, are apt to be impatient with men who cling in any degree to the doctrines, phrases, and forms of a bygone age,—

" Loving those roots which feed us from the past,
    And shored on every side
With landmarks of hereditary thought,"—

doubly so with those in their own ranks who hesitate about laying the ax at the root of each sacred tree, accusing them sometimes of trying to serve two incompatible masters, the god of tradition and the live spirit of reform. An historical faith is spoken of as a contradiction of terms, the very essence of all faith, it is said, consisting in the soul's immediate consciousness of eternal realities; and they would as soon attempt to live on last year's breathing as another age's taught religion. Even among those who, in some degree, respect and use the past, its truths are treated not as roots and seeds having their best place in its own soil, but as gems and coins to be brought forth and placed side by side with the treasures of the present. Conservatism is made only another name for preservation; progress conceived of as accretion and not growth, the adding of so many new things to so many old ones, and not as the life of the one fruiting itself forever in the forms of the other.

A generation ago this philosophy of the old and new was the only possible one for advanced thinkers to take. Their highest watchword then was necessarily revolution; their only source of fresh truth, the undiscovered and unknown; their devoutest attitude, a face turned to the future rather than to the past; and, as related to the conservatism of that day, they had inevitably to take the position of foes and to do largely the work of destructives.

But, since then, the great science of evolution has been discovered and taught; and not the least striking and wonderful of its many influences is the new significance and value it has given to what is old in the world's treasures, and the new attitude it has compelled all really radical thinkers to take with reference to the past. It is usually looked upon as a very destructive doctrine, making sad havoc with the pet ideas of conservatism and upsetting all established science, philosophy, and religion. And so it is. But it is a force which cuts both ways, supersedes the past theories of radicalism just as completely as it does those of conservatism, and succors the advocates of tradition, an established church, and an historical religion even more than it does the friends of intuition, freedom, and the living now. Under its teachings, the past and present are found to have a direct organic relation with each other, like that of root and branches, seed and fruit; the divine method of progress to be neither the destruction of the old to make room for the new, nor yet its preservation as the stock to which fresh gains are to be added, but its use as the base and means from which and through which to unfold forever a better new; the bygone ages found to be not dead things which have done their work and that are valuable now only for the light of experience shining out of them through the uncertain media of history, but the Josephs and Marys, older and younger, out of whose loins by the miracle of a greater incarnation are being born continually the Saviours of to-day. It is a science which has preëminently that ear-mark of all great truths, the reconciliation on higher grounds of apparently incongruous half-truths,— lifts all religious students, both radicals and conservatives, upon a broader plane where to observe and into a new light with which to see. And as the sunrise more than once in our Civil War revealed regiments which had been fiercely fighting each other in the dark as really on the one Union side and with the same patriotic cause at heart, so the dawn of this great luminous truth shows bodies of thinkers who have been striking madly at each other in the night of the past as on the same union side of the world's advance, and as toilers all for one eternal cause.

Look at the illustrations of this organic relation between the two things found in the realms of nature and of natural progress. It was the original theory of geology that the earth had gone through a succession of cataclysms or convulsions, by which its different orders of minerals, plants, and animals, after existing upon it for long ages, had been suddenly broken up and destroyed, leaving only their fossil remains in the buried strata; and that then, each time, the Creator had made a fresh start, introducing by a direct act of his will new and improved agencies and species, and that in this way, step by step, he had advanced to man and to the world as it has been for the last six thousand years,—a theory which embodies exactly the old idea of how all progress was made. But now it is known that one stratum of rock furnished the materials by the slow wearing down and mixing up of its elements to form another; that each species of animals and plants is the outgrowth by reproduction and variation of all those which went before it; and that the latest things produced out of the earth's treasury, while new considered as individuals, are, in their origin, substance, and deeper life, as old as nature, yea, perhaps, as God himself. The flower which blooms to-day has roots which go down through all the soils of the past; the child which is born to-morrow, qualities which antedate the race. Before Abraham was, we all are. The ancient fire-mist is still being worked over in our bones, the spirit which shaped it, perhaps, in our souls. The first spring which decked the earth blossoms in the last; the first worm which crawled on it has ascended, as Emerson says, through all the spires of form to man; and there was something reaching over from the primal savage, who is not yet really dead, that went to make a Plato, a Shakespeare, and a Jesus Christ. Never for a single moment has there been a wiping out of the slate and a beginning over again. The present condition of things all through, even in its newest fields, is an unbroken tradition of the past; a consequent to which every antecedent has contributed a part; a life which could not be except as it has for its pillars all the myriad skeletons ever made by death. In nature's progress, it is not destruction which precedes construction, unless by accident, but construction that always comes first; the new buds which are formed before the dropping of the old leaves; the life of the children which is made sure of before the death of the fathers; the Past forever which holds in its strong arms the infant Present. Nature, as a whole, is like a single tree. Its new seed is planted in the old dust. Its lifted blossom is possible only through its lowly root. The mellow fruit of its humanity hangs on the gnarled and uncouth limbs of its fossil brutes. Amid all the ravages of death, sweeping off individuals, nations, races, and species, its ancient stalk remains planted in the far-off spring of time, enwrapped with layers of fresh strength gathered from every blossom and every beast it has ever borne in the mighty past with which to bear new ones in the years to come. The most precious part of it is not the flowers and the fruit which it has on it this spring and this year, but the old, unsightly roots, trunk, and limbs of its bygone years so often despised, but in whose garnered juices are the possibilities of endless fruit and flowers. And every time a fresh growth appears upon it, whether it be of plants, animals, or men, it is still the one mighty householder bringing out of his treasures things new and old.

Equally conspicuous, when the eyes are once opened to it, is this relation of the old and new in the realms of politics, reform, society, and civilization. There are indeed convulsions and revolutions, winters of paralysis and springtime revivals, the disappearance of old forms and the manifestations of new ones without number, but no wiping out of the entire slate, no tearing up of the old roots, no house of the children which does not have in it very largely the lumber of the fathers. The war which preceded the formation of our Republican government, though we call it a revolution and glory in it as a new era in human affairs, was more properly an evolution, a new flower on a stalk already centuries old. The liberty which blossomed with petals of blood and flame at Bunker Hill and Yorktown had its roots in the battle grounds of Naseby and Marston Moor, Thermopylæ and Marathon, had been fought for again and again by the sires of the very men who on our own soil were marshaled against it. Our famous constitution incorporated principles which England had been nursing for centuries,— was not a new creation, but the outgrowth of a seed which the storm of war had shaken from its old tree and blown across the waters to this fresh virgin soil; and without the habits of self-government and of submission to the will of the majority wrought into our Anglo-Saxon blood under English skies and during our extended colonial childhood, how long would our outward Republicanism have lasted? Yea, traced back in its longer pedigree, it will be found that all government is of one blood; that the newest democracy has precious things in it which were nursed by the old tyrannies; and that without a throne there never would have been a ballot box, without a Cæsar never a Congress.

All scientific discoveries, even evolution itself, come by evolution; that is, are made not by looking into the realm of the dim unknown, but with sharper eyes into facts and principles already in the treasury of our race. The explorers of the new everywhere have to begin their investigations with conning over the mighty stores of the old. The civilized sciences, not less than the civilized races, have had their savage ancestry,— chemistry its alchemy, astronomy its astrology, the finding of the philosopher's truth the searching for the philosopher's stone,— without which they could not be. The accepted theory of to-day is shaped, not more by its originator, than by all the rejected theories of yesterday. When Galileo looked through the Tuscan optic glass and discovered the mountains of the moon, the phases of Venus, and the satellites of Jupiter, it was not he alone who saw them, but, with his eyes, all the other upturned orbs which, in Chaldea and Egypt and, back of them, in the uncalendared night of the past, had ever studied stars. Honest thought, though married itself to error in one generation, begets out of her a shining truth for the next. In the mathematics of progress, it is the negatives of failure, not less than the positives of success, which, multiplied together, makes its mighty plus. And the student of science, who should forget this law of dependence and argue that the best way to help it along would be to sponge the mental slate of himself, and of the world, free from all past attainments, would find the first other truth written there would be, "Thou art a fool."

Society all through is not of the present alone, but of the mighty past; it is a stalk like nature, whose roots go down into the heart of the first man that ever walked the earth; is a result to which the farthest back as well as the farthest up have contributed their part. Out of their lowly caves the despised troglodytes reach silent hands to shape the fair Parthenon, upbuild the majestic St. Peter's, and mold the luxurious mansions of our modern life. Amid the splendid charities and wonderful mechanical contrivances that are raising the asylums and hospitals of our own time, the philosophic ear, listening through the spirit's subtler telephone, will hear the click still of rude stone hammers wielded before Christ was even a Messianic dream, and by hands four fingers of which were red with blood. The wisdom of ancient Rome, not that of our living politicians alone, thank God, still makes the larger part of our laws. The domestic light which brightens up our homes has rays in it kindled on hearth-stones among

EVOLUTION AND PROGRESS 211

far-off Scandinavian tribes. Behind the little bands of policemen, who guard our streets in the silent watches of the night, there is a great army of other unseen ones, marching to their posts each eve from all the ages since law and order came to men. When the youth and maiden whisper their first love to each other in the soft summer night, its sweetness, purity, and refinement seem to them all new, — a gift direct out of heaven, such as no mortal ever felt before. Yet in it are the cumulative pulse and thrill of what unnumbered hearts now in their graves, whose throbbings and fires have beaten and burned the coarseness of mere animal passion into its fine and lasting gold. The very words of love and of all man's daily speech, though they seem to spring fresh and warm from his own heart and lips, have in them the accent of all the speakers who have ever laden them with their joy and sorrow, since the first cry of pain and shout of laughter stirred the waves of air. It is the past of society everywhere which makes its present; the developed Old which constitutes the shining New; the rich and toiling Yesterdays which, forevermore, are leaving their wealth to the young To-day, as their child and heir.

"The Present moves, attended
With all the brave and excellent and fair

> That made the old time splendid.
> Whatever of true life there was of yore
>   Along our veins is springing.
> For us, its martyrs die, its prophets soar,
>   Its poets still are singing."

And because our civilization is not yet perfect, because evils of many kinds are yet mingled with its good, who can think it would be a true philosophy to tear it down and begin anew? Its most ungainly parts, ideas and institutions which, to the superficial view, stand directly in the way of progress, and which, sometimes, a superficial reform would gladly get rid of, are often its most precious inheritance,— roots crooked and gnarled, it may be, but which concentrate in themselves all the juices of the past, and on which alone can grow the flower of the future. There is no ideal heaven, no factory of art or reason, no invention of man, out of which can come an improved social state so surely as out of this world's treasured past. Whether or not we believe with Pope that whatever is is right, we must believe that whatever is is the best that could have been made, up to this present hour. All the wisdom of God and all the work of all the ages have gone into its production; yea, are in it now. And the reformer's true friends and helpers are not only the living recruits, the fresh young hearts that gather

EVOLUTION AND PROGRESS 213

around his standard, but the myriads of the mighty dead mingled with them, and able now not less than of old to carry on their work; the most tremendous force at his command, not the new drops of spiritual influence which are now falling from heaven, precious as they are, but the great stream of what is old, the cumulative moral impetus of all the ages, beginning in the far-off mountain peaks of history, gathering momentum and volume from all the countless human hearts along its way, and, mingled with the life of our time, sweeping the social craft with irresistible might onward to its heavenly port.

It is a relation that with equal certainty holds good in religion and in all religious life and truth. It is indeed the case that all religions claim that in their growth, if nowhere else, this organic relation between the old and new has been broken; claim that their truths, if no others, have had a supernatural origin and a miraculous witness; claim that their new, if that of nothing besides, was not derived from any old, but interpolated into human experience from beyond nature and advanced on its way by the breath and nurture of another world. But the more thoroughly their rise and history are studied, the more evident it becomes that they are of divine birth only in the same way as all other blessings; that all which is in them at any one time can be accounted for as the logical unfolding of what was in them before; and that, however much they are nourished and quickened by the spirit of God, it is by his spirit in this world and not from beyond it, and by its acting on the past as the sunshine and the air do on the growing tree, and not by its own energy alone.

Look at Christianity as a good example of this relation. With all the emphasis which is laid on its miraculous element, its New Testament form, according to the testimony of its own writers, came out of Judaism,— not, indeed, as a mere continuance of the older faith, but as a child out of its mother, its teacher being himself of Jewish birth, its light a part of that true light which lighteth every man which cometh into the world, and its mission not the destruction, but the fulfilment of the law and the prophets. Judaism by the same process came out of the religions of Egypt and Persia and the far-off East,— Sinai with its thunders and all the long supernaturalism of Jewish history being but the poetic drapery of a natural evolution; and these religions in their turn out of others still farther back, which amid the attrition of the ages have now as little left of their original form as the soil beneath them has of its prim-

EVOLUTION AND PROGRESS 215

itive rock. In each case, however, there was not a wiping out of the old faith and the putting in its place of a new and strange revelation any more than in nature a destruction of the old species of animals and plants and the fresh creation of others, but a natural development of the one out of the other, all that was richest and best in the old passing over each time into the new. And, in each case, the old was the necessary forerunner to prepare the way for the new, and its work the absolute condition on which alone it was possible for the new to come. Without a Moses and the prophets there never could have been a Jesus and the apostles,— this the real sense in which they testify of him and predict his coming, as the animals by their very forms predict the coming man ages before his appearance,— without the Law, never the Gospel; without the worship at Gerizim and Jerusalem, never that in spirit and truth; and without the heathen religions and the old nature faiths, bloody, grim, and superstitious, never either Law or Gospel, Moses or Messiah.

But the process did not end with the coming of Christianity. Jesus himself calls his word only the seed. What a wealth of meaning in that one simple term! what a revelation of the true nature of his gospel! what a testimony beyond all miracle to his own transcendent fitness for leadership! Its utterance anticipated eighteen hundred years of the world's growth. It contains Darwin and Spencer, evolution and the nineteenth century. And it was not a chance word, not a happy hit, but the central truth of his religious philosophy; the idea under the guidance of which he did his work; the explanation of why he wrote no books, organized no church, promulgated no creed; the principle on whose correctness he staked the whole success of his life and ministry.

It is this fact of its seed nature, this tendency of its old to unfold forevermore into the new,— often lost sight of alike by its defenders and its doubters,— which solves the chief part of all the difficulties about it, drawn from its crudeness, imperfections, and wide diversities. Its form in the New Testament, so often asserted and assailed as its only real truth, is not Christianity itself, any more than the acorn is the oak, or the troglodyte humanity. Neither is Catholicism, or Orthodoxy, or Unitarianism, or Episcopacy, or any other system of truth its whole. They are all but the phases through which it is growing,— all but strata and species in the geology of truth, destined like those of nature to die out and be buried up. And yet, in the larger view, they are all parts of it, all essential to the future of itself and the world, all producers the old of the new. Without a Jesus there would have been no Luther, Wesley, Channing, and Parker; without Catholicism and Orthodoxy, no Protestantism and Unitarianism; without all the religions of the past, heathen and Christian, no Liberalism anywhere to-day. The freest church on earth in our time has roots which go down for its nurture amid the racks and pincers of the Inquisition. The sweet juices which are blossoming now in so many faiths all about us were drawn up a part of the way through the veins of Turretin, Augustine, and grim old Calvin, — yea, received from them a part of their elaboration; and, under the platform even of Free Religion itself, if a plummet were dropped far enough, an altar would be found with a human victim on it just as surely as under that of the crudest superstition; and, what is more, it would be found that an echo of his groans goes to make the sweetness of our songs.

But, if evolution, as thus applied to religion and especially to Christianity, conflicts with and undermines its supernatural and miraculous character, and so favors radicalism, it also confirms and upholds it tenfold more on its natural and historical side, and so gives the profoundest aid and comfort to its conservative interests. It shows beyond all possible question that it is not an invention, not a manufacture, not something which has been imposed on the world by the cunning of priests or the fancy of philosophers, but a normal and legitimate growth. A part of nature, it must share with all its other parts — with the flowers, the sunshine, and the solid earth itself — our faith in nature. Even in its newest, latest forms, it has all the uncounted ages as its foundation, witnesses, and proof. The superstitions and crudities out of which it has come, though recognized, as indeed they must be, as the old things in its treasury, are no more an argument against it than man's original savagery and barbarism are against civilization, — are in fact, according to evolution itself, the only road along which its truths could come. It enables it to stand before science not as an alien, supplicating for a place in which to live, but as one of the original tenants of its own soil, having all the rights of a first settler. And what evolution has thus brought forth, nourished, and made a part of itself, it surely will not do for any loyal disciple of evolution to cast out as unworthy of his belief.

Is there not, also, in this fact of its being so strongly rooted in the soil of the past the strongest possible pledge for its continuance in the future? There are some progressive

EVOLUTION AND PROGRESS 219

thinkers who prophesy that religion is about to die out; some timid believers who fear that without a new revelation from heaven it will; some who see in science its deadly foe, and in evolution the special phase of science which is to give it the final stroke. Vain hopes, vainer fears! The tree whose tap-root goes down through all generations into the heart of the first man who ever trod the earth is not to be blown down by any breeze which does not blow down human nature itself; the movement which has been gaining momentum through all the human ages, not to be stopped by any force less mighty than what stops life everywhere. Religion, beyond question, will change in the future, as it has in the past, will be as different six thousand years ahead from what it is now as it was six thousand years ago from its form to-day; but it will be the change of growth and not decay, the change from more to more and not from less to less. The real prophet of religion, the one in comparison with which the most glowing predictors of the Hebrew Scriptures are timid, short-sighted guessers, is this very science so fought and feared now by some of the churches. It is the old under its light which contains the new; its vast age — such is the paradox — which gives the assurance of its continued youth; its conservative element, so completely do the two things harmonize, which constitutes the root on which blossoms for all the future the radical's divinest hope. So long as man evolves, religion will. As the first relic of human building found on earth is an altar, so will be the last. And its final truth, transcending all men now can possibly conceive of, will be not a new revelation out of heaven, but a legitimate outgrowth of its own past, something to which all the truths, ay, and all the errors of all the ages, shall have contributed a part; something to which every faith and worship, not excepting the lowest, crudest, and most horrible in the far-off geologic ages, shall have led up as the necessary steps,— the whole, indeed,

> " The world's great altar stairs
> That slope through darkness up to God."

Finally, it is a relation which suggests the true method by which the work of religious progress needs consciously to be carried on in our own day. It is not by cutting loose, even on the part of the most radical thinkers, from Christianity, or from any of the great historic religions, and rubbing them out from the world's slate; not by giving up men's Bibles, traditions, and churches, and putting in their place some wholly new truth, new organization, and new cultus derived from science or reason or the spirit world, but by holding fast

EVOLUTION AND PROGRESS

to these as the soil and root from which under the eternal sunshine to have religion grow beyond them, being forever upheld by the one and nourished by the other. I know how contrary this philosophy is to the common idea; know how terribly the world's traditions and inherited customs seem sometimes to stand in the way of its progress; know from experience how powerfully old memories and old faiths drag down on the soul in its upward reaches; know how prone many of us are to look at the religious past as inevitably the fetter and chain of the religious present. But it is only a superficial view. The past of religion, the same as of all other things, is the great mother breast which holds the nourishment of humanity's present and future; tradition, the lifted platform only by standing on which can the builder lay new courses along the ever-rising temple of truth; the memories of religion reaching back into the buried centuries, the mines where alone the coal can be quarried for driving its engines up the steeps of progress and on into the fair and sunny fields of its larger hope. It is construction, the same here as in nature, which must precede destruction; the new buds that must be formed before the dropping of the old leaves; the larger faith that must anticipate the weakening doubt. An historical religion, instead of being a contradiction of terms, is really the only religion which is possible. What Lowell says of the individual is equally true of the race:—

> "The bird I hear sings not from yonder elm;
> But the flown ecstasy my childhood heard
> Is vocal in my mind, renewed by him,
> Haply made sweeter by the accumulate thrill
> That threads my undivided life, and steals
> A pathos from the years and graves between."

A person might as well cut the new leaves and flowers of a tree off from its old limbs and expect them, when exposed to the sunshine, to remain fresh and bear fruit, as sever the advanced religious life of the present from the doctrines and institutions of the historic past, with the hope that, exposed only to the light of our time, it will grow and ripen. Continuous tradition and continuous inspiration, the one the body of the great world tree; the other its surrounding light and air,— these are equally the factors of progress. Radicalism under the reign of evolution becomes not a lost word, but one with a deeper significance than before; means not a tearing up, but a holding on to the roots of things; conservatism, not an empty name, but a true and divine instinct, a clinging to the past, not to keep its form unchanged, but as the root to be unfolded into

EVOLUTION AND PROGRESS

an ever larger future. And the evolutionist in religion, to be consistent with his own faith, must be in this sense both a radical and conservative; must do what, with many thoughtless people, makes him seem only a trimmer and time-server, but which really is the extreme of independence and courage,— reach forth with his welcome evermore for new light and truth; yet, as the very means of doing so, must honor and use the past, draw his nurture from old Bibles, old exemplars, and old churches, and have roots of his being which, with some of their tendrils, reach down to the very dust of the world's primal beliefs; in short, must be, as Jesus proclaimed centuries ago, the householder which bringeth forth out of his treasures things new and old, and, as Lowell has echoed in our own time, the voyager who

"With the old sextant of the fathers' creed
Shapes his courses by new risen stars."

VI

EVOLUTION AND CHRISTIANITY

When Darwin's and Spencer's doctrine of Natural Selection and the Survival of the Fittest was first set forth — two names, as you know, for essentially the same thing — its novelty and philosophic aptness and the discussions it provoked as to its theological bearings, drew attention away for awhile from its deeper moral implications. But now that its truth has been in a measure established and leisure found for examining more carefully the prize so brilliantly won, the glow of delight excited by its scientific beauty has gradually given place to a feeling of deep depression over its awful destructiveness and its apparent evidence of an absolute disregard in nature of all ethical and humanitarian principles. It lets us into the world's workshop as no other discovery has ever done; but reveals its magnificent walls more stained with blood than was ever any wild beast's cave; gives us a hero to worship such as no other kingdom ever saw, but one with a Cyclopean greatness that even a Carlyle would hardly

EVOLUTION AND CHRISTIANITY 225

offer incense to; takes life on from its unorganized protoplasm to its Richmond of civilization, as no other principle ever has, but does it Grant-like through a wilderness where its uncounted armies are heaped upon battle-fields of uncounted slaughter. Even such an advocate of its truth as Mr. Huxley can see in it no ethical or philanthropic import. " The cosmical process," he says, " has no sort of relation to moral ends," is rather " the headquarters of the enemy of the ethical nature." And in its attitude especially to the poor and weak its contrast with Christian selection is so great as to give, with many persons, new strength to the argument that Christianity could not have come from nature and must, therefore, be a supernatural religion.

Before giving it up, however, as utterly hopeless for these higher things, it is well to remember that one of the most striking characteristics of evolution, as exhibited in other fields, is its habit of producing its richest fruits up above from what lower down are its most unpromising stems — unity from differentiations, the sky-seeking flower from the earth-seeking root, the rattlesnake's tail and Plato's skull from the same vertebrate skeleton, and Jephtha's sacrifice and that of Jesus from one religious sentiment. The real thing needed for getting out of the moral difficulties into which at first it so thickly plunges us is not less of it but more; the word of the Lord it speaks to the Moseses and peoples who in starting out of their old Egypt for a better land are confronted first of all with its Red Sea, "Go Forward." And obeying such a command, I want to take this doctrine of the survival of the fittest, so terrible in its beginnings, and try whether following it right through its blood-red seas will not lead us now, as of old, to a Canaan flowing with all the milk and honey of religion's and philanthropy's most loving care for the unfit poor and weak.

Starting with its operations in the physical world, it means there, beyond question, the preservation of only those animals and plants in each species and of only those species and genera in the organic world as a whole, which without any regard to their ethical character, excel in such qualities, whether of size or smallness, skill or stupidity, courage or cowardice, generosity or meanness, often the worst ones even physically, as best fit them for their environment; and the crushing out and crowding out, without any mercy or honor or justice, of all their unfit brethren. Nature provides herself with plenty of material to select from by having her creatures produce an immense number of offspring, more than are needed or able to grow up — is a mighty hunter who loads her gun not with a single ball, making everything depend on her accuracy in firing that — which was the old idea of Providence — but with a multitude of small shot, many more than she wants to hit the mark, so many that if they all did hit it, there would be no mark left, intending only two or three to take effect — which is the modern, scientific idea of Providence. Her shot are seeds, eggs, children, species, nations, possibly worlds. And it is the tests they are put to in reaching the mark of fitness which make her famous struggle for existence and constitute what is figuratively known as natural selection.

It is a struggle in which really the first round takes place before birth. Only the strongest and most attractive males are allowed to become parents. The whole vegetable world is an Oklahoma into which seeds carried on all manner of vehicles are vying with each other to get corner lots and promising sites on which to plant themselves. With eggs a favorite diet the world over, it is only those which get shielded and sheltered by the shrewdest devices that escape tongue and bill and boiler. Of the myriad germs which are called up to the gates of life in viviparous animals how few are chosen to pass through them into actual existence! The whole embryonic world is a battle of the pigmies against the giants, a battle in which the odds are so great it seems a wonder that any of the little folks survive even to the extent of getting born.

Victors in this preliminary contest, the outward elements,— heat, cold, moisture, dryness, earth, sky and the like, constituting the very home into which they are born, these fall upon them with their tests, giving a welcome and shelter only to those which can withstand their onslaughts, and giving to their weaker comrades sooner or later only a grave. The numbers perishing in this way even after they have reached maturity are enormous. Darwin estimated that the cold winter of 1854-5 destroyed in his own estate four-fifths of all its birds. With no extra wraps to put on and no warm fires to get before, every change of climate which affects man, affects the feeble among animals a vast deal more. Fifteen thousand hides were sent East a while ago on a single freight train, taken from the cattle out on a Western prairie that had died in one of its blizzards. Who shall count the frail mosquitoes and the aged flies that have their song hushed forever with the first autumn frost? Even the little tough, grip-making bacteria, resisting all the devices of man to prove their unfitness to survive, seem to have been compelled by the past winter's thermometric hard times to join the ranks of the unemployed. And going back to the geologic ages, we find that not only individuals, but whole species and genera both of animals and plants have been killed off in a like manner by their ever changing elemental environments. So far as Nature is God it is all fiction that she tempers the wind to the shorn lamb. She tempers it to the lamb which is not shorn, provides wonderfully for the well and strong of her children, provides well for the weakest and smallest so long as they are well and fit; but she has nothing which corresponds with human care for any of them, large or small, when they are hurt and sick,— never folds the little suffering bird in her loving arms, never makes any warm gruel for the chilled-through rhinoceros and tiger, has no soothing syrup for the restless cubs of the distracted wolf and bear, provides no surgeon for the broken-limbed deer and bone-choked fishhawk, and builds no asylums for consumptive lilies, mashed mosquitoes, and aged sharks.

It is pitiable sometimes to see how little her creatures expect such a thing from any one as disinterested, individual kindness. Visiting an unused room in my Ipswich home awhile ago, I noticed that a solitary bird driven from its flock apparently because of its feebleness, had been in the habit of creeping for shelter at night between the window pane and the closed half of the window blind. Seeing how the bitter wind was whistling through the open slats and remembering my own sensitiveness to drafts even inside the room, I was moved altruistically to fit a stray shingle over the open space so as in some measure to break off the wind. The little creature with the evening shadows came as usual to the sill, peered at the improvement on this side and that, with evident surprise, and then, concluding apparently that it was too good to be true otherwise than as a trap, flew away into the night shadows, preferring their certainty to any, even clerical, Greeks bearing gifts.

The care which nature does take of them is itself a sifting process, what are blessings to the strong being banes to the weak. Every farmer's boy who has tried to raise chickens, has noticed how the mother hen, as soon as they are hatched, begins leading them for food through the wet June grass and off, on long journeys such as only the strongest can stand, and that with all her diligence and self-sacrifice in providing for their wants as a whole, scratching the earth for their meat, covering them with her wings from the cold, and defending them from foes at the risk of her life, she herself kicks over the foolish ones which get in her way as ruthlessly as she does the clods their food is among. Nature is such a hen. The food of her creatures is always in some kind of June grass. She leads them off in migrations where even her wild geese grow weary, and her grasshoppers are their own burden. And the very suns and showers which scratch the earth so wonderfully for their sustenance, kick over into its dust the witless ones which get in their way.

Nor is any exception made in the case of her human children. Three-fourths of them die of her blows before they are five years old. She wades with her boys into green apples and snow water ponds, and with the girls into slate pencils and corsets and colored candy. "Don't strike him when he is down," is the rule enforced in even the most brutal prize rings; but in the struggle for existence it is when a man by reason of some weakness or misfortune gets down, that she rains upon him her fiercest blows. Nero used to select his victims for the wild beast conflicts of the amphitheater by taking all from a file of prisoners marching before him who came between two bald heads. Nature, fortunately for some of us, is not so particular about the bald heads, but, if she sees a person having anything the matter with his lungs, or liver, or stomach, or heart, he is handed over with equal indifference to her fiercer, elemental wild beasts. The old Burial Ground at Plymouth, into which one-half of the *Mayflower's* passengers were carried their first New England winter, is a witness to the rigor with which her sifting process is applied in finding out of man's migrations, the fit founders of a new nation. And the earth is everywhere full of graves warning her human broods who wish to survive, that it will not do for them, any more than for her brute ones, to get in the way of those mighty legs of hers, the earthquake, tornado, thunderbolt, with which she is scratching for them the earth's deeper soil.

Escaping the elements, however, does not end their struggle. Her scratching, vigorous as it is, supplies them with only a fraction of their needed food. The greater part of it they have to get out of each other's bodies; and that, too, by a system of "mutual murder" arising not through a fall from Eden, but instituted to begin with as a fundamental principle of the organic world, by which alone life can exist.

> "Then marked he
> How the lizard fed on ants, and snake on him,
> And kite on both; and how the fish hawk
> Robbed the fish tiger of that which it had seized,—
> The strike chasing the bulbul, which did chase
> The jeweled butterflies till everywhere
> Each slew a slayer and itself was slain."

EVOLUTION AND CHRISTIANITY

Several years ago, before I knew as a Darwinian that the fish is my elder brother, and that piscicide is no more justifiable as sport than homicide, I caught a cod, in the stomach of which, on dressing it, I found a pollock, in the pollock a young lobster, and in the lobster several fine protozoa, all fresh. It was a good representation of the whole organic world. Its highest beings holding in them as food everything down to the protozoa, are a genuine " codfish aristocracy." And in the struggle to see which shall be the eater and which the eaten, the well fitted not only get the prize sought for, but get with it as side dishes all their weak and witless competitors. Some of you may remember one of *Punch's* famous cartoons some thirty years ago, entitled " Misplaced Sympathy," in which a pious mother who has taken her heedless Sunday-school boy to a picture gallery to be impressed with a painting of Daniel and his companions in the lions' den, is horrified by his exclaiming, " O mother, mother, see that poor little lion down there in the corner; he won't get any! " I have always had a great respect for that boy. He was evidently a true lover of animals, thought vastly more of them than of any old Bible prophets, and became afterwards, I doubt not, a genuine member of some Anticruelty Society. But Nature is no such boy.

What she is concerned for is not lest the poor little lions in a corner should not get a share of her Daniels, but that the fierce big ones should get them all. She has not only too much company at her table, as the Hebrew host explained the difficulty in his case, but too few chairs and too little food, so she ekes out its scantiness by setting the guests to eat each other up. It is indeed

"A rage to live, which makes all living strife."

Then while their struggle is bad enough even in the best of seasons, it is aggravated by drouths and famines ever and anon into scenes of unspeakable horror, as for instance during the dry seasons of Central Africa when all the animals of the country for miles around, driven by their intolerable thirst, come to the few stagnant pools here and there into which what little water there is has sunk, the larger and fiercer ones taking possession of them entirely and lying in wait for the others, — huge hippopotami wallowing in their depths, long glittering snakes reaching out over their surface from the trees, ferocious beasts of prey watching with fiendish shrewdness their every avenue of approach, and on the outer rim rabbits, antelope, deer, scores of weak herbivorous creatures, looking with longing eyes and parched tongues for a chance to get one sip of their black, slimy, putrid, yet how precious drops, and having to choose at last between the ferocity of sharpened teeth and the fierceness of desert sands.

So with man: a large part of his struggle in all ages has been for the means of life, air, light, water, food, even ground; a large part of his social differentiations those between the big lions with a plenty of Daniels to eat and the poor little ones down in a corner with hardly a Daniel's bones to pick — on the one side Astors, Goulds, Rothschilds, Vanderbilts, millionaires tenfold over, on the other millions without a mill; on the one side corporations and coal mines, on the other families and freezing. And ever and anon there comes along some great financial drouth in which eyes as thirsty as those of the desert deer look on pools of wealth, some of them wallowed in by creatures as foul and circled around by teeth as sharp as those of the African waste. Men complain sometimes of the Church, the State, the whole social fabric as responsible for these awful inequalities,— think, perhaps, with Rousseau, that if society were only abolished and everything left to nature, everything would be equality and peace. Delusive thought! The trouble is that the original source of these inequalities and hardships is not Church or State or Society, but nature herself. Poverty, cold, hunger, are a part of her ways for sifting out the poor, cold, hungry. And to go back to her primitive reign would be only to go back from the ferocity of cities to the ferocity of desert sands.

Then, worse from the moral standpoint than even their struggle with each other for food, is the tendency of animals to war against those in their own ranks which are simply different from themselves, and to do so especially against such as are disabled and weak, the object being apparently only to assert their superiority. If there is a lame or sick chicken in the brood, or a stray one from another nest, everybody has noticed how the strong and at-home ones will peck at the unfortunates till they are either killed or driven away. "When I was a girl," said a lady, "and now and then got into little childish squabbles with brothers and sisters, I used to have quoted to me Dr. Watts's familiar hymn, 'Birds in their little nests agree,' to my shame and confusion. But after trying in later years to raise a brood of canaries and seeing how readily they made each other a funeral,— especially after leaving four of them in a cage one Sunday while I went to church, and finding on my return three hanging by their heads out of the wires, executed by their own brother, I began to think that bird nature was not after all so very

EVOLUTION AND CHRISTIANITY

much better than human nature." One of the most pathetic sights the animal world affords is its wounded members trying to get away from the well ones, even of their own species, to suffer and die alone — monkeys who carry off their disabled comrades from the battle-field, anthropoids, therefore, in something more than bodily form, being almost the only exception. It is notorious that no two roosters or bulls can be put together in the same locality without a fight simply to determine which of them is smartest; and no matter what the affections lavished upon them beforehand, there is not a hen or a cow which does not turn from the beaten one as promptly as ever a society belle did from a poverty-stricken beau.

Nor is it a kind of struggle which is left behind when nature comes to man. What are nine-tenths of the world's great historic wars but the fights of its larger barnyard roosters to see which is smartest? What the huge armaments all the governments of Europe are sporting to-day but the spurs to try sometime again the old question which of them shall crow the loudest? Big nations as regards little ones are all bullies, our own no exception, as witness its dealings with Mexico, Chili and the Indians. How ready all the different social classes are to set their feet on the necks of the ones that are in any way below them! What are the competitions of the business world but a crowding of the weak to the wall as mercilessly as any that ever ran with blood? If a man gets a new idea, or a woman a dress out of style, who does not know that they are pecked at and driven off by themselves exactly as a bird is with a new feather, or a beast with a strange form? And even in the church what are the martyrdoms, persecutions, anathemas and rivalries of sect against sect, things of which in all ages it has been so fearfully full, but the efforts of the strong to crush out what to them have been its unfit weak?

Such are the various ways by which natural selection is carried on.

Turning now to Christianity, Christianity not as an institution half realized, but as an ideal and aim, how transcendently different from all this is the new principle, new atmosphere, with which the inquirer is at once brought in contact! Its fundamental idea, as Mr. Huxley says, is beyond question exactly the opposite of that on which physical nature is carried on — is love, not hate, self-sacrifice rather than selfishness, and preëminently caring for the weak, poor, sick, unfit, instead of crushing them out. Its founder declares explicitly that he came to seek and save that which is lost; that to love thy neighbor as thyself, the wounded man everywhere being the neighbor, is one of the two greatest commandments; that whosoever shall give a cup of cold water only to one of these little ones shall in no wise lose his reward, and that he who is least among you shall be greatest. It was the poor, lame, halt, blind, that were invited especially to his gospel supper; the sick and sinful that his life was spent in healing, not crushing out. And in the same spirit his great Apostle declares that not many wise, not many mighty, not many noble were called to be his followers, but the foolish things to confound the wise, and the weak things to confound the mighty, and the base and despised things and the things which are not to bring to naught the things which are. Then with and by itself, in spite of all its alliances with pride and power, and all its subserviences to wealth and fashion, it is historically along this line and among this material that for 1800 years it has won its victories and done its work. It has built hospitals for the sick, opened churches for the sinful, scattered bread to the hungry, demanded freedom for the slave, championed the cause of the poor, and lifted up to a new level the weak and despised — has had a kind word even for animals themselves, recognized their rights, denounced cruelty in their treatment, established societies, newspapers, laws for their protection. And in the final building up of its kingdom its principle is to work into it every weakest, wickedest, meanest, poorest, unfittest soul, rejected of nature and despised of men, there is on the face of the earth.

How now, with this immensity of difference, this apparent utter antagonism between them, are these two things made under evolution the gracious parts of one majestic whole, and in the larger cosmic process the natural outgrowths, one through the other, of a common love-planted root?

The first step of the answer is to recognize the adaptation of each agency to its own especial part of the work. Looked at as simply the means for attaining what is physically best, and for laying at least the foundation of what is morally best, there is no difficulty in seeing, even with Christian eyes, that the principle of the survival of the fittest through a struggle for existence is one of immense practical wisdom. If a man is going to build a first-class house, he naturally puts his fittest timbers into its walls and his unfit ones into its waste. Every farmer aiming to improve his cattle and corn, has to pick out the most perfect of them to breed from and the others for his table and common work. And in all wars, wars for liberty and right as well as for tyranny and wrong, the general who wants to win victories enlists in his army not weak and sickly men, saints though they be, but the soundest and toughest ones the land affords, without asking for their standing in the church. So when nature wanted to build a first-class universe, improve her original protoplasmic cattle and corn, and win victories for her great final cause, how could she do otherwise than act on the same principle? Suppose that in her physical realm the opposite course had been adopted — that of preserving the sick and weak, what would have been the result? We have tried it to some extent with human beings, have for centuries been keeping alive the lame, halt, poor, blind, thousands of persons whom nature at a very early date would have put in graves; and the answer is — society overrun with tramps, the dangerous and criminal classes more numerous than ever before, and the unemployed poor mounting up into the hundred thousands. And if nature had been doing the same through her million centuries, how many more than now would have been, not her human, but her sub-human darkest Londons — her animal tramps, her Juke fishes, her sickly cornfields and her unemployed vegetable poor! Call it mercy to the weak and poor themselves to have them saved, what is it to their descendants, what lesser cruelty to have the myriad offspring of a crippled creature suffer and live than to have the one creature itself suffer and die? A well managed sawmill is run by its waste, run by using its slabs and sawdust, valueless themselves for lumber, as the engine fuel with which to turn out its straight and beautiful sticks. Nature's life-mill, in its system of having the weak eaten by the strong, is only acting on the same economic principle — utilizing its slab-animals in producing its straight and smooth organic timber. And what are their struggles with each other, and with the elements to get their food, but one of the factors in developing their strength, the exercise as needful for species and genera as it is for muscles and minds? Suppose that all of them had been so amply provided with sustenance that there would have been no need of their struggling for it, what would have been the result? The succulina has answered — a creature beginning life well organized, but which after fastening itself as a parasite on the hermit crab, where it gets safety and support without effort of its own, loses its higher organs and degenerates into a mere jelly-filled sack. Without this awful struggle for existence every animal would in time become a succulina. Starvation has been a part of the world's food. Our first stage in becoming angels is necessarily to fight like devils.

Cruelty to the individual has been kindness to the race; selfishness in the realm of physics has done the same uplifting work as unselfishness in the realm of morals. And horrible as the struggle seems from our Christian standpoint, out of it — out of only the bare and cindered rock and the organless and senseless protoplasm to start with, has come our Christian standpoint itself — come the beautiful, organized, intelligent world which is here to-day, the fragrant flower, the singing bird, the stately tree, the marvels of the brute creation and the race of man.

But physical perfection and an animal world are not the whole of nature's aim. She has had other things in view, a moral and spiritual being and a social, civilized, religious world. How were these to be attained? Self-seeking, eating each other up, trampling down the weak and poor, agencies so potent in her physical realm, were powerless for this higher work. Others were needed, those which involve love, justice, mercy, self-denial, self-sacrifice. And it is at this point and for this purpose that the principle of preserving the weak and poor, the physically unfit, comes in, the stone rejected by the animal builders, which is made the cornerstone in the temple of soul.

It is a principle which operates as a factor of this higher evolution in two ways. The first

is by bettering the poor, the sick, the weak
themselves, making them the fit, lifting them
up into health, strength, morals, self-support.
While nature was working chiefly on bodies,
and could use the unfit ones as food, it did not
pay to spend effort on what was imperfect; but
when she came to soul, it would seem as if
everything had been brought along so far and
had cost so much that it began to be precious
— paid better to be improved and kept on with
than to be broken up and used over. Then,
too, having the one do for the other brought in
gratitude, allayed antagonism, helped bind the
two classes together, and so evolved the higher
social world. It is a kind of work which the
hard times of this past winter have been the
occasion of on a grand scale. They have
brought the fit and the unfit into such kindly
relations with each other as not all the preaching
in the world could have brought about,
have compelled, too, a study of their problem
such as it never before has had — have done
it, also, just at a crisis when the two classes
were getting dangerously wide apart, a benefit
which more than pays for their money loss.
There is nothing else which can do it so well —
love, not law, which is needed to put down social
discontent, the loaf of bread thrown one
way which stops as no gallows can the dynamite
bomb thrown the other, capital's wives and

daughters basket-armed and love-sent who have been going every day this past winter into quarters of our large cities unharmed, where capital's police, bludgeon-armed and law-sent, could have gone only through blood. And though in the past such service has aimed chiefly at relief, it is being gradually found that it cannot stop there, but must go on, helping the dependent to become the independent, and the unfit to be in all respects the fit.

Better still, lifting up the unfit operates as nothing else can to lift up the fit themselves into being more fit. Bodies grow by self-seeking and by what they take in; souls by self-sacrifice and by what they give out. When a tiger meets a sick and wounded traveler, he is made the stronger and larger by eating him up. When a man meets a sick and wounded traveler, he is made the stronger and larger by saving him from being eaten up. All qualities which are put forth to help others — love, sympathy, kindness, justice — react and help the helpers; all the downward things which called them forth — weakness, want, sickness, sin — become the world's uplifters. Who has not seen families where the little crippled boy's feet have been the ones on which the strong, rough brothers have reached heights of gentleness and self-denial into which not all the physical vigor of the world, nor all the teachings of its Sunday-schools could have carried them alone? The live babies of the household may unlock for their parents the joys of earth; but it is the dead ones who open for them the heavenly gates. Look at the dark side of a great city, at its white faces, bleared eyes, brutal passions, bloody crimes, and you exclaim what a drag on the world's progress is their preservation. Look at the bright side of a large city, the white souls, pitying eyes, angelic graces, heroic deeds, which the struggle to save them has called forth, and you ask what other agency in all this world is aiding progress so much. Count the tramps who are walking the earth as the result of 1800 years of Christian care for their survival, and you question where is its wisdom. Count the saints who walk the skies as the result of 1800 years giving them that care, and you have a hundredfold the question's answer. It is the unfit who are the food of the fit in the new dispensation as truly as in the old, only now it is by their saving instead of by their being destroyed. The imperfections of nature are the raw material out of which are made the perfections of spirit. None of the shot with which Providence loads his gun really fail. Those which miss the animal hit the man — go astray of the mark at the distance of a generation, lodge in its very bull's eye fifty million years off. Reformers

EVOLUTION AND CHRISTIANITY 247

stand aghast sometimes at the immensity of our age's problems, those especially of poverty, vice and crime. They are the most precious commodity there is on this earth to-day, are worth more to it than all its mines and manufactures, are a grander field for its science than any sun or star, for they mean the mining and making of men, and are a shop where the things made, make also the makers. What if the material is so large and so constantly increasing as to preclude all hope of its being all made morally fit in this life? That only adds new need, new meaning for a future life, suggests that its hell instead of being the mere refuse heap of the universe, as so many have thought, may be the quarry out of which new stones are to be forever wrought for heaven's walls, its sinners more material out of whose saving its saints are to be continually more saved. And surely it is no unworthy thought, is in keeping with what is the divinest element of Christianity here, is what we have a hint of in the story of Jesus going down the first thing after his crucifixion to preach to the spirits in prison, is better than any endless psalm singing, that through all the eternal years souls are to lift themselves up by lifting up their weaker brother souls.

There is one vital question more — how this tremendous change in nature's use of the unfit has been brought about, what the forces and processes by which the principle of their preservation has been evolved from the exactly opposite one of their destruction. It was no gift of a supernatural world, no message brought to earth on angel wings. It began back of all religion, back even of man, back among the animals themselves, began in that source, as worthy always of scientific as of filial reverence, mother love. The first old hen,— speaking metonymically,— that scratched the earth for a brood of chickens, scratched it up along with the worms, kicked over with her clumsy legs some of the chickens, but kicked over with them the old self-centered universe, gave at any rate the blow which is to end with its toppling over. And it came directly out of the old system. The chickens being the offspring of her own body, care for them was at the start simply care for her own larger self, an outgrowth, therefore, of selfishness. But care is in its turn the natural nurse of love — what costs us something, that is, what is dear, becoming dear. The feebler, therefore, the offspring were, costing, as they would, more care, the dearer they became, the stronger the impulse to keep them alive; and this care which at first extended only to the brood as a whole, gradually differentiated to individuals, as everything under evolution does, till in humanity everywhere, savage and civilized, the weak, puny, physically unfit child, needing most the mother's anxiety and care, is the one to which naturally she gives the most,— the first cosmic step how easily, yet how wonderfully taken across the apparently impassable chasm between care for the fit and care for the unfit! The Christian housewife, when she cuts off part of the old hen's coarse, tough legs in preparing it for dinner, does not think of any connection between them and the subtle, sacred ties which bind her to her sick babe upstairs, or the Christian minister, as he eats the other part, a guest at her table, of their relation to one of the sacredest, grandest elements of his religious faith; yet not less certainly they have all been evolved in nature's factory out of one primal stock.

Another factor helping on the change is the underlying solidarity of all life in one grand organic whole, one vast and all-embracing self. The reason why animals prey on each other is not hate but hunger; why the strong prey on the weak, not tyranny but facility in satisfying the hunger; and why the weak and odd ones of the same family, even when not needed as food, are pecked at and driven off, is because difference from the common size and look has been so long associated with what is to be feared as predatory that the sight of it raises at once and blindly the instinct of self-defense. Just as likeness makes liking, for we like at first only what is like us, so unlikeness makes dislike. With savage and nomadic tribes, also, surrounded with foes and often pinched with want, care of the old and feeble is a source inevitably of tribal weakness; putting them to death, therefore, a condition of tribe survival, done with filial love and endured with patriotic submission. And thus it is that care for the original, larger, homogeneous self is overcome and held in abeyance by the necessity of providing for the smaller, differentiated, individual self. But the original oneness is not lost, any more than universal gravity was in the evolution of suns and planets; and as the world progresses and tribes become larger and more settled, it reasserts itself in a higher form. The differentiations of labor under the industrial stage of society give the weak kinds of work to do, and a tribal value that is impossible in war. Patriotism and pride come in, covering with their ægis every citizen, however humble, as a part of the common whole. And out of the original life-unity there emerges at last the mystic tie of sympathy reaching out with its nerves finer than those of flesh to everything which lives, even the feeblest creature, and making all others a sharer of its joy and pain, and so interested for their own sakes to secure its welfare — the subtle scientific truth which underlies the great command, "Thou shalt love thy neighbor as thyself," not as much as but *as* thyself.

Allied with this solidarity and growing out of it, the union of the weak with each other for mutual help and protection has contributed not a little to the general principle of their being cared for and preserved. Animals which individually were unfit, very soon learned that collectively they might have the highest degree of fitness; and driven off by themselves, their misery not only developed a love of company, but with it a strength of company which in securing food, building shelter, and fighting foes was the very thing needed for their survival. Misery, however, could not thus receive aid from its brother misery without giving aid back, could not have company at all without its being mutual; so care for the individually weak and poor became a necessity for the existence of the flock and herd; and when the weak and poor differentiated out of themselves the strong and well-off, what began as a necessity was inherited as a principle. The Golden Rule is a law of nature. Eons before it was taught by Jesus, it was acted upon by animals and plants. It is the underlying principle to-day of all trade-unions and labor organizations,— the association and united protection of the weak individual laborer against the encroachments of capital; benevolence organized as business; good wages and good treatment insisted upon by all for the weakest and poorest because it is the only way in which they all can secure for themselves good wages and good treatment. The church preaches it and too often that is all; labor practices it. And thus how wonderfully and beautifully the trampling down of the weak has pressed out of them the wine of care for their survival, and the iron hammer of ferocity driven home and clinched the golden nail of fraternity.

The unfitness has had, also, in its contagiousness, a powerful goad driving on the fit to its relief. It has been learned after many terrible lessons that no man can be sick or ignorant or vicious to himself alone; and that if we do not want him to make us all sick, ignorant and vicious, we must all go to work, and make him well, educated and virtuous. Why have all our large cities been so anxious this past winter to vaccinate the poor at the public expense? Because the disease of which it is thought to be the preventive, is so "catching." That word "catching" grows in very humble soil, but it has on its branches a vast amount of very precious fruit — one-half at least of all our asylums, poor laws, schools and churches. What we don't do because we love

EVOLUTION AND CHRISTIANITY 253

our neighbor as a part of ourself, we have to do because we fear him as a part of ourself. I knew of a woman down in Arkansas, the daughter of a cowboy, and inheriting her father's pluck and pistols, whose lazy, domineering husband tried to impose on her all the work. One day when the baby was sick and she needed some water for its washing, matters came to a crisis. Setting down the bucket on the doorway and drawing her revolver, she said, "If you don't start with it for that water before I count three, I'll shoot." He laughed in her face. "One." He laughed again. Bang! And he rolled over in the dust never more to get up. "Two, three," she counted, as leisurely wiping the weapon with her apron, she went back to nurse the baby. That is what Nature does with her husbands when they refuse to bring to her sick babies the water of life. It is One as a warning; then Bang; and not till after they have rolled over, the two and three. We call her severe when she deals with the babies herself in her animal realm; but it does not begin to equal her severity to those in her moral realm who won't deal with them at all. Plagues and black deaths have been some of her "bangs." The French Revolution was another. We shall have one in our own land, if we neglect things too long. And counting the husbands sneering at reform who as a consequence have bitten the dust, what wonder that the rest of us are gradually learning to seize its bucket with her first word Go, and no matter how unfit the babies are, faithfully fill it up to the brim!

Another potent factor in the evolution of this higher principle has been trade. The fearful competitions of the business world driving the weak and poor to the wall, so opposite apparently to any survival of them, are only one of its aspects. What is it the real interest of all great trading houses to bring about? Not the poverty of the world. With everybody else poor, who is to buy their goods? No; it is the real interest of all trade, whether of one person or of one people, that all other persons and all other peoples should have something to trade on; and it is this really which trade tends to give them. Whatever may be accomplished by rascality, there is honestly no such principle in this universe as the rich growing richer, and the poor poorer at the same time. It is like electricity. The rubbing which develops it at one pole has to develop it at the other also. It was business which abolished slavery at the North; the best business operation that even white men ever had done for them, its abolition at the South; business that in every direction has given the weak and poor a thousand luxuries that without it

EVOLUTION AND CHRISTIANITY 255

would have been only their vain wish. I congratulated a large manufacturer once on the interest he took in bettering the condition of his workmen. "Oh," he said, "that isn't goodness, it's only goods; there's no machinery it pays so well to improve as the human machinery." The first vessels sent by Christianity to heathen shores carried rum and missionaries. It was a mistake only in the kind of merchandise. The more gospel, the more goods. And even as a business transaction the best investment civilization could make of its money would be the lifting up the whole savage world into moral and religious fitness.

Finally, on these lower things as a basis, religion itself comes in — love, altruism, conscience, the sense of right, all the highest and best sentiments of our human nature, to complete the work. We care at last for the unfit because we like to. Weakness appeals to our gallantry. We shrink with instinctive horror from stamping out any creature simply because it is feeble and sick — "would not needlessly set foot upon a worm." "The Vision of Sir Launfal" becomes our favored poetry. The trumpet calls of reform thrill our blood as the bugle's blast did our sires. A mighty nation finds its inspiration for four years of war in the freeing of a slave. And when the world's greatest and best man, a Jesus, sacrifices his life to save its meanest and worst — a thing so utterly at variance with nature's old economy, eighteen hundred years unite in honoring it as humanity's crowning deed.

It is thus that I find a passage from nature's Egypt of destroying the unfit, right through its awful wilderness and Red Sea on to religion's promised land of their preservation and lifting up. The old way of writing a novel, as you know, was to get its characters and incidents all involved in a hopeless snarl, the lovers parted, the hero knocked senseless, the heroine in the villain's clutches, wickedness and wealth everywhere triumphant, modesty and merit everywhere trampled down; and then to unravel the snarl, have the hero saved, the villain shot, the maiden rescued, lots of other killing done, and somewhere about the fortieth chapter the mystery all cleared up, the lovers happily married, poetic justice done to everybody, and in the distance several fine children. Evolution is a novel more full of intricate snarls, dramatic surprises and thrilling incidents than any ever written by a Scott or a Sue, one also with killing enough to satisfy the most bloodthirsty schoolboy appetite, but which unravels at last all entanglements, overcomes all brutal villains, brings heroic virtue up out of all defeats, and does everybody and everything full poetic justice. It is to be noticed, also, that it is all accomplished by strictly natural laws, without any bringing in, or need of bringing in, any *Deus ex machina* to untie the cords in which the Deity within had become wound up. Instead of its being true, as Mr. Huxley says, that the cosmic process is the enemy of the ethical nature and with no sort of relation to moral ends, it is directly and inevitably out of the cosmic process and by the simple continuance of it that the ethical nature and the moral ends have been evolved. " The ruthless self-assertion," " the tramping down of all competitors," and the survival of only the physically fittest, so conspicuous and so revolting at the beginning of the work, were engaged after all in laying, as nothing else could, the foundations of the structure on which alone its ethical part could be raised; and if there is anything which argues the height of the pinnacle in the coming ethical sky as a part of the original design, it is the depth and breadth of its base in the physical earth. It is a process, to be sure, which is yet very far from being completed. Nature never makes her changes all at once, never lets go the old till her creatures have got a good grip on the new. We are now in the transition stage between the two — indeed have been so ever since civilization began — are partly under the old law of the survival of the fittest, and in part under the new law of saving the unfittest; and it is this fact which explains not a few of the difficult problems of our time — our tramps, our Juke families, our cut-throat business competitions, our military conflicts, our evils of democracy and our aristocratic churches — explains the conflict between the cosmic and Christian with which Mr. Huxley and others are so deeply impressed — is what makes philanthropy and reform, a reaching for the ideal and yet never cutting loose wholly from the old real, one of the most difficult of all arts. But it is a stage of the work which is full of hope. The shuttle in nature's mighty loom, the same as in that of man, is shot back and forth two opposite ways, but it carries only one thread and weaves only one piece. Egoism at the animal end does the same work as altruism at the spiritual end, serves the race by serving self; altruism at the spiritual end the same work as egoism in the animal, serves self by serving the race. And as out of the two there has come already a being who has not only the inner desire to lift out of their death-stream his unfit brothers, but, what is equally important, the bodily strength and the solid shore of flesh to stand upon which make it possible, so out of them both there shall come at last a world in which the unfit, never, perhaps, so long as life

EVOLUTION AND CHRISTIANITY

is progress, ceasing to come, shall everywhere be developed into the fit, a realization of Tennyson's splendid trust —

> "That not a worm is cloven in vain;
>   That not a moth with vain desire
>   Is shriveled in a fruitless fire,
> Or but subserves another's gain;
>
> That nothing walks with aimless feet;
>   That not one life shall be destroyed,
>   Or cast as rubbish to the void,
> When God hath made the pile complete."

VII

IMMORTAL YOUTH

Man has always wanted youth and dreaded age. The one is associated with beauty, health, activity, joy, and love, the other with weariness, wrinkles, decay, and death. The hardest thing about life, to most people, is its growing old; is to see the bloom fading out of the cheek, the sparkle out of the eye, the vigor out of the limb, and, worst of all, the poetry out of the soul; is the coming of that time when

> "Those cheerful suns are set forever
>   Which light to youth's gay dreams impart,
> And dried that deep ideal river
>   Which fed the fountain of the heart."

As the October of the year, even when lighted with all the splendors of ripened fruit and reddened leaf, has a sadness about it that is never felt in the stormiest days of spring, so the October of life, even when surrounded with all the accumulations of maturity's success, has a shadow hanging over it such as never comes to youth's dreariest March. Lord Palmerston, when congratulated at the age of eighty on his position as prime minister of England, laden with honors and lapped in wealth, answered, "Yes, they are indeed things to be grateful for; but I would gladly give them all up to go back and be a boy again as I once was,— poor and unknown outwardly, but in the prime of life, and with all the measureless wealth and possibilities yet within me of boyhood's heart." To be always young, to have the bloom of life's springtime remain forever on the cheek and the sparkle of its morning in the eyes, to feel that days of pleasure can be quarried with no end to their golden mine, and years of love be sailed with no limit to their ocean swell,— this, to many, is the ideal of life.

" Fair laughs the morn, and soft the zephyr blows,
  As, proudly riding o'er the azure realm,
In gallant trim the gilded vessel goes,
  Youth on the prow, and Pleasure at the helm."

And there is nothing in the ambitions and dreams of the world's past more pathetic than its chemists' long search for that Elixir of Life which was to bring back to its old men their boyhood's freshness and vigor, and its voyagers, long wanderings for that Fountain of Youth whose waters were to wash away all the aches and stains of age, and restore it again to its vanished prime,— nothing, perhaps, has contributed more to the success of Christianity than its hope that what had been failed of so long ago beyond the seas of earth would at last be found beyond the river of death.

Yet, with all the attractions of youth, there is no one who wishes to go back to all that it was; and, with all the drawbacks of age, no one who wishes to give up everything it has brought him to. Oliver Wendell Holmes, in one of his charming poems, so full of human nature, represents a listening angel as coming to an old man who had been sighing after his lost youth, with the offer to restore him to it again, but asking him to consider first whether there were not some things in his present possessions that he would like to take back with him into the past. To whom the old man replies:

" ' Ah! truest soul of womankind,
    Without thee what were life?
  One bliss I cannot leave behind:
    I'll take my precious wife.'

" The angel seized a sapphire pen,
    And wrote in rainbow hue,
  ' The man would be a boy again,
    And be a husband, too.'

" ' Ah, yes! and memory would recall
    My fond paternal joys.
  I could not bear to leave them all,—
    I'll take my girl—and—boys.'

IMMORTAL YOUTH

> "The smiling angel dropped his pen:
> 'Ah, this will never do!
> The man would be a boy again,
> And be a father, too!'"

And this is what, I suppose, we all of us do really wish for,— the blessings of youth along with those of maturity and age, the beauty, health, vigor of body, and freshness of feeling which belong to life's prime, accompanied with the balance of character, the breadth of experience, and the treasures of love and knowledge that have been gathered up in its later years,— want life to be an orange-tree, bearing on its branches at once the fragrant flower and the luscious fruit; this, I suppose, that is the common idea of mortality,— a state in which we shall have all the bloom and vigor of youth without its ignorance and inexperience, and all the wisdom and worth of age without its wrinkles and weariness; a state in which through all the eternal years we are to ripen to celestial fruit, yet never lose the celestial flower; see children and children's children coming to join us from the ranks of humanity as long as earth shall endure, yet remain ourselves, equally with them, in all the purple bloom of unfading youth.

But, fascinating to the fancy as it may seem at first, is such an immortal youth either possible or, in the larger view, really desirable,— such a combination of youth and age, progress and permanence, otherwise than incongruous in itself and incompatible with the very laws and nature of all growth? We know how it is in this present world. Growth is not outward accretion, but inward development; not continuous enlargement, but progressive heterogeneity; not youth with the addition of maturity and age, but youth unfolded out of itself into new capacities and attainments. The apple is not a combination of the flower and the fruit, not something which can be itself and at the same time the bud and blossom, but an evolution of the flower into the fruit,— something which is possible only by the dropping of its fair petals and the giving up of its floral life. So with the blossoming and ripening of the human soul. The man is not merely an enlarged boy, not merely the qualities of youth increased with those of maturity and age, but the form and faculties of the boy unfolded out of themselves into those of the man. And while each period of life, taken by itself, has its own special charm, the effort to combine the two artificially — as when the ancient belle puts on the dark tresses and pink cheeks of a young girl, and the antiquated beau the dudish dress and frisky airs of a young man — only destroys the beauty of the one, and adds to the other an ugliness it never has by itself alone. What reason is there to think that it will be otherwise in the eternal world,— that growth there will not be of the same nature and follow the same laws as growth here? And, if it were possible for the qualities of the two extremes of life to be blended in the future state,— if the soul were to rise out of the grave at eighty with the spiritual rouge on it of twenty, and the saint with his burden of eighty thousand years go skipping about the streets of the New Jerusalem as friskily as he did, a sinner, at the age of eighteen about the streets of New York,— would not the contrast be even more ludicrous in the sight of the angels than it is with us now in the case of their earthly rejuvenation?

Must we, then, give up utterly this hope of immortal youth, look forward to a rising out of death with all the imperfections as well as with all the excellencies that the soul had on going into it, think of immortality as a continuous forever of that growing old which gets to be such a burden in these few brief years of time,— an increase endlessly, it may be, in wisdom and knowledge and virtue, but an increase endlessly also in conservatism and inactivity, in spiritual stiffness and fancy-baldness, in heart-wrinkles and soul-rheumatics! If such is indeed to be the case, then we may well anticipate our immortal destiny with the tremblings of despair rather than with the throbbings of hope. When Gulliver, that famous traveler, who had visited Lilliput with its inhabitants only six inches high, and Brobdingnag with its people sixty feet tall, arrived at the kingdom of Luggnagg, he was told among its other wonders of a certain class of Luggnaggians called Struldbrugs, who had the peculiarity of never dying, but whose old age developed, along with its shrewdness and knowledge, such unpleasant qualities of avarice, opinionatedness, and selfishness, expressed, too, in their faces, that, to keep them from frightening and entirely overwhelming the other Luggnaggians, they had to be shut up in pens. Gulliver, having expressed a desire to see a few of these earthly immortals, was conducted to a place where several very ancient ones were closely confined. He looked at them as long as he could stand their ugliness, then, having rested his eyes, looked again, and at last tried to borrow two or three specimens of them to take home to England, as the best possible means by which to cure the English people of the fear of dying. The story is one of Dean Swift's exquisite bits of satire against certain aristocratic families of England who had their antiquity to glory in, and nothing else; but, if the inhabitants of the spirit world are indeed

IMMORTAL YOUTH

to go on through all eternity, growing old in the same way and with the same traits that some people do here on earth for their fifty, sixty, seventy years of time, the story will apply equally well to their case; and the result would be at last a set of spiritual Struldbrugs one specimen of which would be enough to make us mortals content to remain forever in the finer beauty of the grave and in the sweeter brotherhood of the worm and the clod.

These things, however, thank Heaven! are not the only possibilities which are before us in the way of immortality. There is a form of it conceivable which does combine, to a certain extent, the two things craved for,— what is best in youth with what is best in age,— and which is in exact accordance with the laws and nature of all earthly growth. It consists not in the preservation forever of our present youthful faculties, feelings, tastes themselves, but only of a subtle essence out of them, stored up in the soul itself, and in the unfolding repeatedly, as the first ones grow older, of other new ones having their times of vigor and freshness, and so on as long as soul shall last,— the youth being thus the changeable factor by which the growing is done, and retaining, or rather passing on, forever its freshness; and the age the permanent factor, embodying all the finer results of the growth and leaving behind all its deadness; and the means and conditions, the larger spring, by which the unfolding is induced and stimulated, are new scenes, new truths, new friends, new kinds of work, everything acting on the soul which is in advance of what it has had acting on it before.

It is a kind of immortal youth that we have an illustration of here and now in the phenomena of the natural world. Every year nature is growing older and older in its life, every year richer and richer in its own inherent nature; yet every year it is showing more bloom, more vigor, more of those qualities which are preëminently the characteristics of youth, than ever it did before. It will be almost an eternity, this present spring, since the rising of its first seed out of the ground. But, instead of exhibiting any signs of decrepitude and old age, it will burst forth in a few days, as we know, even in spite of these east winds, with a richness and variety of verdure beyond anything that was even hinted at in its far-off beginning. And this law is so vivid and constant that our very ideas of old and young, so far as nature is concerned, have become completely reversed. We think of its early geological days, the time actually of its youth, as its antiquity, and of the animals and plants it produced then — fossils now — as its ancient ones, and of its last

IMMORTAL YOUTH

and really its oldest season, its millionth perhaps, as its youngest time, and of the animals and plants that are being produced now in what, counting by years, is actually its old age, as the offspring of its youth. And it sings truly through its Emerson: —

> "No ray is dimmed, no atom worn;
> My oldest force is good as new;
> And the fresh rose on yonder thorn
> Gives back the bending heavens in dew."

How is this immortal youth of nature brought about? Notedly, not by preserving the forms of life it produced at first undecayed, but by letting them continually die out, leaving only the subtle results of their growth behind them, and having new and improved ones take their places,—" life living upon death,"— rising gradually from the beauty of color in the shell of a mollusk to the beauty of poetry and of religion in the soul of a man. And, so far as we can see, there is no end to the process. The older nature grows, the younger nature is; and ten thousand, perhaps ten million, years from now its springs will have a bloom on their cheek, its animals and plants a vigor in their limbs, its young men and maidens a romance in their hearts, beyond anything that can be conceived of to-day.

"Still on the seeds of all that's made
　The rose of beauty burns;
Through times that wear and forms that fade
　Immortal youth returns."

Human nature is another illustration of the same great law. The babe that is born of it to-day is really the offspring of its myriadfold octogenarian age; inherits in its blood something out of all the multiplied growth of the past; is in its deeper life as old as the race itself. Yet who, looking into the cradle at its fair face, can detect there any marks of this immeasurable antiquity? Who can say it is not as fresh, as innocent, as lovely, as richly endowed with all the finest qualities of youth, as any Cain or Abel ever was of its far-off prime,— infinitely more so than any babe of its beginning, simply preserved till now undying and ungrowing, could possibly be? And, plainly, human nature keeps itself thus forever fresh and young by putting forth forever these fresh young lives.

Human society,— is not that also immortally fresh and young in the same way? Timid souls do indeed talk as if it had about come to its last days; see in its shattered creeds only a dying out of its religious life, and in the thousand anarchistic, socialistic, and labor throes with which it is convulsed, the evidence only of its general breaking-up. Fools, so to misread the very signs of its continued youth! Dying trees do not bourgeon forth with new buds and blossoms, or dying men with new undertakings and plans. Society never before was so fresh and young as it is to-day, never before had such vast activities, such wide and warm affections, such unbounded hopes and dreams and ideals of a better coming state — all youth marks — as it has now at its topmost age. If some of its old foundations have crumbled, it is only to have their materials used in raising new and better superstructures.

> " Ever the rock of ages melts
>   Into the mineral air
> To be the quarry whence to build
>   Thought and its mansions fair."

Why, its races have but just come to the love-making period of their lives. It was only week before last that the battleships of nine of its greatest nations — things which hitherto have belched at each other's sides only destruction and death — vied with each other in seeing whose tongues of fire could speak loudest the salutes of peace, and in proclaiming out of their iron throats, with a powdered emphasis that hate never had of old, their messages of united good will. And this very last week this grand old earth of ours has blossomed forth with a World's Fair petalled and stamened with all the arts and industries and sciences and charities and reforms, ay, and religions, of its myriad people,— a mayflower indeed of its latest spring blooming in the prairies of the West, which transcends how infinitely far anything that was ever dreamed of under its rising sun, even in its Eden of the East! And here, too, the continuity of youth has been brought about and kept up in precisely the same way as in the other cases, by its putting forth continually new shoots from its old stalks, and moving into new scenes with its old races. See how Christianity, eighteen hundred years ago, sent the blood of its fresh life pulsing through the veins of what seemed then a worn-out and effete world, filling alike hovel and throne with its shining hopes, and impelling gray old Time himself to begin counting his years from a new date. All Europe blossomed forth a new world intellectually, morally, religiously, and in its impulse to liberty, under the discovery four hundred years ago of this new world, of land across the seas,— Ponce de Leon being a wiser man than he has ever had the credit of being in coming to these shores in search of his Fountain of Youth. An Elixir of Life richer than alchemy of old ever hoped for has been given to our own day in Darwin's thought and in Spencer's long toil. And the thousand reformatory, religious, and socialistic

IMMORTAL YOUTH

movements with which our age is fairly crammed, as they are the signs of its existing youth, so they are the means by which that youth is to be continued and developed in the future, making it indeed true that

"Through the shadows of the globe we sweep into
 the younger day."

It is a kind of immortal youth, moreover, which is not only illustrated in these great worlds of nature and humanity as a possibility for the individual soul, but one that we can see the actual beginnings of now and here in its growth. Man's faculties do not unfold all together, but, as we know, in a natural order and succession,— first the bodily appetites and senses, then the affections, the imagination, the memory, then the moral nature and the business faculties, then reason and judgment, and at last the spirit's insight and love. And each of these, as it comes along, and as it mounts up into new fields and into new phases, has its own special period of youth, shared in to some extent by the whole soul. I know how it is in my own case; and I doubt not all of you here have had something of the same experience. I never feel the awakening within me of new powers and interests, never rise into a new set of emotions and ideas, never enter on a new field of work,— and, the more advanced and unpopular for the time it is, the more it brings of this splendid reward,— without finding in them something of the same thrill, romance, springtime glow, that I felt in childhood at the opening of the bodily senses, and in youth at the blossoming of mind and heart. Who has not known women that have found in toil for some noble cause a toilet more efficient than any that art ever furnished for keeping even the body radiant with the spirit's youth,— women whose beauty, more truly than with any voluptuous Cleopatra, " age cannot wither, nor custom stale "? It is the true explanation of the enthusiastic delight the young convert feels at the awakening of his religious life. As Jesus tells us, literally he is " born again,"— has new faculties unfolded within him, a new world opened to his view. . And it is all normal, therefore, that he should have something of the same fresh delight that he had in the first years of his bodily youth. It is what every great discoverer experiences when he lays hold of a new truth; is what sent Archimedes of old rushing naked out of the bath, where he had solved his problem of specific gravity and King Hiero's crown, shouting with all a boy's enthusiasm, " Eureka! Eureka! " " I have found it! " Conservatism, timidity, narrowness of aim, loitering at the rear in the march of thought, — these are what hasten on age: progressiveness, courage, breadth of view, keeping abreast of the times,— these what stave it off. "Always young for liberty," Channing's noble motto, is what all of us can be. The old miracle of Joshua, stumbling-block so long to the literalists of Scripture, is repeated again and again in our modern age. The sun of life's sky does stand still over Gibeon, and the moon of its youth over Ajalon, to all men who are fighting the battles of the Lord. And it is when the blood has been heated in the tropics of reform that is shown even here on earth

" How far the Gulf Stream of our youth may flow
Into the Arctic region of our lives."

Why, now,— to complete the thought,— should not this same law hold good and this same process go on in the spirit world and in the immortal life? Yea, why should not a new environment do there what a new environment always tends to do here,— intensify the process, break up all the deadness of age, awaken within us a crowd of new feelings and faculties, and in the new work which it gives them evermore to do give the doers a sense of sharing evermore in their freshness and youth? Of course, this does not imply that we are not to retain all of our earthly faculties and feelings which can be of any use there, the same as we do here the older ones in the midst of the new.

And, emphatically, it does not imply that with the unfolding of the new affections the old objects of affection are necessarily to be given up. The old tools, the old creeds, the old institutions,— these, indeed, we are to leave behind us, the same as we do the toys and the games of our childhood, for they, in their very nature, are fixed, and cannot grow. But the old friends that we have loved,— the supposition is that they, too, as living beings, are equally with us to grow young, unfold new traits of character, new breadths of being, new graces on which for the new affections to fasten themselves.

" Burned on her cheek with ever-deepening fire
The spirit's youth that never passes by."

And thus love to those above, whom we have learned to love below,— father, mother, husband, wife, child, friend,— may have through all the eternal years something of the freshness, romance, thrill, something of the eternal youth, that love, to start with, always does have here in time.

Who will say that such a conception of immortal youth does not make it infinitely richer and more desirable, as well as vastly more reasonable, than any mere return to the qualities, however purified, of our earthly prime? Who, with it in view, will mourn so very much that he is drifting away from the rose and gold of life's earlier morning, that the dreams and hopes of its opening years are fading, and that its pink on the cheek and its wild thrill of the senses can never come to him again? Who, rather, will not press forward with new ardor in that onward path, opening to-day as never before, that will fill his noonday sky with a richer rose and gold, make him a sharer in humanity's larger hopes and dreams, and give him the freshness of a great enthusiasm and the thrill of a forever-growing soul? To keep our minds open to the grand new truths of our time, to join the ranks, when thin and few, of some new and therefore hated reform, to stand at the forefront in the fierce battles that a larger liberty is fighting now for our race, to take some part, however humble it may be, in dealing with those awful problems that are seething in the social cauldron of to-day,— here is the Elixir of Life in nature's own laboratory that crucible and chemist never found; here the Fountain of Youth, flowing at our very doors, that voyager of old sought in vain beyond the seas. And, having thus learned the secret of keeping young in these years of time, what can eternity be, with its larger sphere, but a new opening in which to use it for making the immortal years mean more and more an immortal youth, and for showing, even so far as the freshness of life is concerned,

> " That men may rise on stepping-stones
> Of their dead selves to higher things "?

SERMONS

I

CHILDHOOD

A CHRISTMAS SERMON

The child Jesus.—Luke ii. 27.

Christmas is coming. Even if there were no calendar to tell us of the time, even if we were away on another planet watching the earth, the outward aspect of things, the preparations for it which have been going on for weeks in all Christian lands, would warn us of its approach, would indicate, at any rate, that some widespread, periodic change, like the double lines on the planet Mars, was taking place on our puzzling star. Right amid the chills of winter our churches and parlors suddenly adorn themselves with vernal hues. Right amid the shortest, darkest days of the year a mighty wave of joy rises up and sweeps over vast sections of the earth. Great crowds of people surge through city streets, bearing all manner of strange bundles. Parents are seen in corners planning mysterious things for their children; children in groups, plotting wonderful surprises for their parents. The current of human nature seems reversed. Persons, who all the rest of the year are eagerly getting from others all they can, are now seized with a mania for giving to others all that is possible; and, morally, this old earth of ours, on the 25th of December, must present a picture which transcends in beauty all that it reaches physically, even on the 21st of June.

What is the occasion of this marvelous change, what the central figure in this charming commotion?

It is the birth of a little Jewish boy in a manger nineteen hundred years ago, is the idealized face of a little, speechless child.

The cause is one which seems at first glance utterly inadequate for such an excitement, the figure one which, in contrast with the honors paid it, is almost ludicrous in its smallness. Why, it may be asked, should so much stress be laid, even by Christians, on the birth of Jesus, involving, as it does, the memory of him as a mere babe? If he was indeed a supernatural being,— angel or God, as so many excellent people profess to believe,— would it not have been vastly more in harmony with his celestial nature and more likely to have impressed the world and to have won him followers, if he could have been celebrated as descending out of heaven in the fullness and strength of his maturity rather than in the weakness and insig-

CHILDHOOD

nificance of a puling infancy? And those of us who find it impossible to accept literally the wonderful legends of his nativity, those of us who believe he was born into the world precisely as every other child is, why, especially, should we fasten our attention so largely on his cradle? Why not take him at some one grand moment of his manhood — that in which he spoke the law of love or bade defiance to scribe and Pharisee, or placed himself at the side of the despised woman of Samaria — as the figure to honor with our memories and make the center of our joys?

These are questions which suggest naturally for our Christmas thoughts the significance to himself and to the world of the infancy of Jesus, and, as represented in him, the significance in the divine economy of all birth and babyhood.

I. His entering life as a little babe is the strongest possible testimony to his natural and simple humanity. Good old Dr. Watts could indeed sing of him.—

> "This infant is the mighty God,
> Come to be suckled and adored."

And there have been countless other men who have professed to believe that he was really such. But they have been able to do so only by looking at him in a creed rather than in a cradle. No one can picture to himself the actual infancy of Jesus,— his rounded face and limbs, his being nursed at Mary's bosom and carried in Mary's arms, his dawning smile of intelligence and love, his tottering steps as he learned to walk, and his thousand little blunders as he was taught to speak and read and know right from wrong; and then, with any claim either to reverence or sanity, believe that he was, at the same time, the Infinite and Eternal Head of the universe, worshiped in the courts of heaven and pervading all worlds with his majesty and might. Even Raphael, with all his genius, could not paint him as otherwise than a perfectly human child, having in his eyes the same light, only a little more of it, which lighteth every man that cometh into the world. And all Christendom each Christmas morn, whatever its professions at other times may be, is at heart entirely humanitarian in its faith.

Regarded, however, as simply a natural event and as a type of what it is in the case of all other children, the birth of Jesus is a marvel worthy of all the commemoration it has ever received. The mystery everywhere of humanity's opening life, the utterance of a soul into its sphere, the flowering even in its humblest form of that great tree of being whose roots go down through all soils and all ages,— there is no mystery of a miracle, no birth of a planet, no inauguration of an empire, which can compare with it either as a marvel or in its immeasurable significance. All the forces of all the past have been at work for its evolution: all the animals of all the rocks have been its prophetic announcers. Its ancestors, not with Jesus alone, but in the case of every child, reach back to the first Adams and Eves who stood on earth,— yea, and include among them, as truly as its parents of flesh and blood, the Holy Ghost, the overshadowing of that Power, more than matter, without which no life can ever be. Its tiny form is the bridge between the mighty past and the mighty future over which, by the laws of heredity, there go in a condensed shape all the attainments of our human nature through its eons which have gone, and all the possibilities of our human nature through its eons which are to come. Wise men journey not from the East alone, but from all lands, to lay their gifts at his feet,— gifts of science, poetry, philosophy, religion, " the gold and frankincense and myrrh " of the soul. And, if there is any truth in the doctrine of a personal immortality, the life which is then begun is destined to endure when all the glory of empires shall have faded into oblivion, and all the splendors of science, even that crowning science which solves the problem of the universe, shall be only a far-off memory. And such an event, exemplified for all humanity in the birth of the Nazareth babe,— may it not well have all that is sweetest in song and tenderest in love and most reverent in religion gathered up to do it homage?

II. Again, the infancy and childhood of Jesus, little as they could accomplish directly for his work, were not a lost period out of his life, not an experience which, in accounting for his after career, can be left out of sight, but are one of its most important parts, one without which some of its maturer features would be wholly inexplicable. He never could have loved and won to his arms children as he did, never could have spoken those gracious words about them which are such a precious part of his gospel, had he not once been himself a child; never could have sympathized with the weak, childish, and tempted of all ages, as he did, had he never, in his own person, grown up through weakness, immaturity, and temptation into favor with God and man; never could have built the kingdom of heaven on earth with the wisdom he did had he not, first of all, learned how, from boyhood up, to build himself. It was the child in him, as in all of us, that was father of the man,— the year next his cradle, as well as the year next his cross, which had its part to do in making him the Saviour of the world; his training as an infant in a home which

CHILDHOOD

did for him what never perhaps could have been done by the training of him as an adult in a heaven.

So in every human life. There is no possibility of laying too much stress on what is done for it by its opening years. Infant baptism is sometimes ridiculed as a senseless rite; and, considered as the means of a literal salvation, or in any way as having of itself " made this child regenerate," it doubtless is deserving of its increasing disuse. But, looked at symbolically, it is the expression of a great educational truth. Single drops of the water of life at its starting-point are more potent in its shaping than whole rivers of it in after years. It is what is put as seed into the baby that comes out richest as fruit in the man, the influence which surrounds the first year of its cradle that will be felt by it down to the remotest year of its eternity. And, with us all, to grow up as a child in a home is a diviner blessing than, were it possible, to be dropped down out of heaven as an angel or a man.

III. Once more, the infancy of Jesus as told in Bible story has been, as a matter of history, no small part of the agency which has secured for his religion and for himself their grand positions in the world and in the heart. All mothers, the world over, turn instinctively to a baby with their love: all persons, even the

rudest, yield something to its sway. A gospel
which came to humanity in dimpled cheeks and
laughing eyes and chubby hands had a winsomeness from the start beyond anything which eloquence or logic or miracle could offer,— a religion whose beginning was a home, a cradle,
and a child, a vantage-ground such as one with
only a church, a sermon, and a priest never
could have known. And the infant in Mary's
arms, pictured first in Scripture words, then incanvassed and idealized by Raphael and the
great painters of all the Christian ages, and
found to-day under the multiplications of modern art in almost every home, has spoken a
language and touched a chord which all classes
of persons — prince and peasant, savage and
civilized, wise and witless — could alike understand and feel. Out in Western Texas, where
I was a while before our Civil War, there stood
an old Spanish mission church, named San
José, nearly ruined by having been made the
scene of repeated battles, but still having over
its altar a very fine picture of the Crucifixion.
One day a party of roughs from San Antonio,
fearing neither God nor man, broke into the
building, and, with their pistols, began making
a target of its picture. The old priest in
charge of the place implored them, with tears
in his eyes and with every persuasion piety and
horror could prompt, to desist from the sacri-

lege. In vain. They only threatened to fire also at his own white head. At last, with happy inspiration, he seized a picture of the Sistine Madonna near by, having in it the wonderful child face of the infant Jesus, and, holding it up before that of the Crucifixion, bade them, if they must shoot, to fire at that. The brutal leader, with a ringing oath, at once leveled his revolver at the child face. But those calm, sweet, unfathomable eyes, the marvel of all art, looked straight and trusting into his; and he did what, fronting man, he never yet had done, — dropped its muzzle with a bit of tremor. His companions jeered at him for his cowardice, and again he raised the weapon, but with the same result. A third time he tried and failed. Then, with a strange look in his own eyes, but a voice there was no jeering at now, he faced his fellow-ruffians, shouting: " Away with you all! The man who shoots at that child, I'll put a bullet through him!"

So in the great cathedral of history, amid the insults and derisions leveled so often against Christianity's altar. It is not the Christ on the cross, but the Christ in the Jewish mother's arms, which again and again has saved it from desecration. And in the Church itself, sometimes as rude and ruffian with its priests and theologians as any outsiders have been, it is not its saints and sages, not its majestic walls and stately columns, which have endeared it to the popular heart and made it a home, but the fact, as with so many other homes, that in it was a baby.

It is a service for religon which is shared in by all children. Not in poetry alone, but in sober fact, is it true that

> "Heaven lies about us in our infancy,"
> "And not in utter nakedness,
> But trailing clouds of glory, do we come."

Faith, hope, and love are their natural endowments; and the innocence, the truth, the heaven, which look out of their eyes are what no brutalities of doubt can easily muster the courage to destroy.

IV. Nor is this all. The infant Jesus has not only helped save religion to the world, but has also been a most potent factor in saving religion to itself and in aiding it to be for the world a real saving power. You remember the story of the rough miner at the theater in the early days of California before homes and families had gone there, how, in the midst of the performance on the stage, when an infant among the audience burst into wailing and the poor mother tried in vain to hush it up, he shouted, "Stop the play, and let us hear the baby cry"; and how the whole assembly of rough, strong men sat there, listening to its little voice, thinking of their own homes and loved ones far away, and finding in the memories it brought up a joy never felt in drama and a wealth never found in mines, till their silence hushed it to sleep on the loving mother's breast. So in the Church, amid the great tragedies of theology which for eighteen hundred years have been enacted on its stage, the wrangling of priests, the blood of martyrs, and the clash of sects, the rough ages with every Christmas eve have stopped the theologians' play and, with softened hearts and bettered souls, have heard the Christian baby cry.

Here, also, Jesus is only a type of how it has been with children everywhere. Among the many striking truths brought out by evolution one is that the plank by which ethics crossed over from egoism to altruism — that is, from the love of self to the love of others — was laid for it by these little ones, they as the offspring of the parental self being the "others" in caring for whom selfishness itself had to become altruistic; and another truth is the one first pointed out by Mr. Fiske, the longer period of infancy in the human species which compelled its parents to remain united and in one place, and so originated the family and the home and made civilization a possibility.

It is a principle — this use of infancy as the agent of progress — which is acted on all through the organic world. What the shepherds of Switzerland do with their flocks when, as the season advances, they would get them up into higher and better pastures, accessible only by narrow, precipice-edged paths along which it is impossible to drive the grown sheep, take the lambs up in their arms and go with them ahead, the whole herd then following freely their bleating, is what Nature in all ages has done with her flocks in getting them up the steeps of time into better mental and moral pastures, taken the young there first, given them ever finer instincts and nobler desires, knowing that, where they call, the race at last will climb. Looking back through the centuries, the evolution zoölogically of each new class, order, and species has been not from the perfected old ones, but from the offspring of their feeblest contemporaries. The vertebrates did not come from the most highly developed of the preceding articulates, but from the amphioxus, a creature inferior to all the others of its class in everything but a bit of spinal cord. The mammals descended not from megalosaur and labyrinthodont, hugest of reptiles, but from microlestes and dromotherium, animals hardly larger than their scientific names. The ancestor of man was not mastodon and machairodos, the mighty among mammals, but an anthropoid so helpless otherwise that in the struggle for existence its only way of survival was to climb a tree. And in social evolution it has not been a stock from the great nations of antiquity, Egypt, Persia, Greece, and Rome, which in after years has done the most for civilization, but that from the ones which of old were only tribal infants; not the adult descendants of the world's great generals, scholars, and statesmen, who have pioneered it in its upward way, but how often the children of men who intellectually were only the little ones of their own time,— all a fulfilling of the Scripture words, "Thou hast hid these things from the wise and prudent and revealed them unto babes."

V. Finally, the respect paid the child Jesus has reacted powerfully on Christianity itself in making it an agency for securing to all other children new happiness, attention, and esteem. Its development for awhile, to be sure, was in exactly the opposite direction. There is nothing in all paganism more horrible than that doctrine of infant damnation which was taught for so many centuries as an article of Christian faith. And, indeed, the whole mediæval doctrine of original sin and total depravity involved their degradation, made them, as one of the old divines expressed it, only "serpents' eggs."

But it was a theology as hostile to real

Christianity as it was to the natural human
heart, and is what the prominence given age after
age to the childhood of Jesus was bound
sooner or later to kill out. It was impossible to
honor infancy in him, and not at last to honor
it everywhere; impossible for art to paint year
after year the Nazareth babe for cathedral and
church, using often living babes as models, and
not see sooner or later that one divine image
was in them all; impossible to read again and
again the Master's own words, "Of such is the
kingdom of heaven," and continue always thinking
that the constituents of that kingdom were
only "serpents' eggs."

It is an influence in their behalf which has
fruited how richly in our day! There is not a
theologian in Christendom now, however ruthlessly
he may send all other unconverted souls
to perdition, who dares do otherwise than make
an exception of all the children. And the place
they occupy to-day in literature and education,
the laws which are enacted for their protection,
the industries which are set at work for their
entertainment, the presents which are lavished
upon them at this season of the year, and the
new gladness which is infused into their lives,
—is it too much to say that all these have some
of their rootlets running back to those kindly
Scripture words which were written of old about
the childhood of Jesus?

Surely, then, it is not without solid reasons that we have one day in the Christian calendar, synchronous properly with Nature's new-born year on which to honor the birth and babyhood of him who was the beginning of humanity's diviner year, and to honor through him all babyhood and all birth. Whether viewed scientifically or spiritually, there is nothing else in all the realms of knowledge — no book, no scroll, no fossil rock below or shining star above — which is more packed with subtle meanings, more written over, body, mind, and soul, with Nature's own hieroglyphics, more worthy of society's careful keeping, than every new-born child. It is out of their unfolding lives that comes history, along with their little heads in the cradle that sleeps the State, the solution of the problem of their purpose that will solve the problem of the universe: —

> "Here at the portal thou dost stand,
> And with thy little hand
> Thou openest the mysterious gate
> Into the future's undreamed land."

It is the legend of Saint Christopher, the mighty Syrian giant, whose duty it was to carry travelers across a swollen mountain stream, that one dark and stormy night a tiny child came down to its brink and begged to be set over on the other side. Lightly the giant undertook what seemed the easy task. But, staggering and trembling with him amid the raging floods as he never had with adult weight, he exclaimed, when at last, faithful to his trust, he laid him safely on the further shore, "In Heaven's name, who art thou?" To which the reply came soft and sweet and full of recompense, "The Christ-child, and, bearing me across the stream, thou hast borne the whole world's weight." The legend is true of all infancy. Bearing it safe across the raging streams of sin and wrong bears with it all that humanity is. It is its children forever, no matter what its wealth may be in saints and sages, who are the world's hope; a new miracle which is wrought with each new one's birth, even though it be in poverty's manger; a new song of good will out of heaven which is sung over each new one's cradle, even though it is met on earth with only a hiss of shame. And faith's millennial year will begin and the sun of righteousness start forth afresh on its mighty circle when the Christmas morn shall dawn on which religion with the same reverence with which it now says of Jesus: "*Ecce Deus! Ecce Homo!*" shall say not of Jesus alone, but of every child, *Ecce Infans*,—Behold the Babe!

II

STAND-BYS

I was having an exchange of pulpits a while ago with a brother minister in a little country town of New England. It was a dark, stormy morning late in November. The members of the society, few at any time, were scattered through a farming community, some of them at considerable distance from the church; and as Fred, the minister's son, walked with me up to the building at the appointed service hour, the lad, with inherited ministerial anxiety, expressed a doubt as to whether we should have a multitude of people assembled with us that day to keep holy time together. Not a person was to be seen at the door, not even the faithful janitor, not even one of the group of well-dressed and observant young men usually at its side. The long line of horse sheds was entirely empty. No small boy sent ahead to keep him out of mischief, and to save his clothes from destruction on the stairway banisters at home, was visible stoning the geese, or trying to walk the path of rectitude on the top of a rail fence. And, as I looked abroad over the wet desolation, the unencouraging question arose as to whether the preacher himself would not have to be the chief part of his congregation.

Just then in the distance, down through an avenue of trees tossing their branches as if in warning and astonishment, the glimpse was caught of three female figures, cloaked and umbrellaed, struggling with the sleet and wind in the direction of the church.

"Ah, there they come," exclaimed Fred, "the three stand-bys! I thought I should see them! Father calls them his three stand-bys, because it makes no difference how hot or cold or stormy it is, they are always sure to be present; and father knows that, even if nobody else is on hand, he will at any rate assuredly have them to hear his sermon."

I watched the figures thus designated with no small degree of interest, as in a zigzag course, with many a tack and close hauling of the dress, they made their way slowly up into the meeting-house portal, and thence with us around the register into its otherwise vacant room. One of them was past middle life, the gray locks the wind had displaced falling softly over her forehead; the other two, sisters, not so old, but still no longer in the strength and freshness of youth. All three were wholesome, good-looking women, evidently of the large-hearted rather than strong-minded type, and with something in their faces, a sort of divine glow, finer than the light of intellect, which at once arrested attention. It was easy to see that the fidelity and steadfastness from which they had got their title were not of the outward act alone, but born and nurtured in the soul; easy to understand how three such faces as theirs could light up any place, even in the darkest day of winter. And, as I thought of the other little groups like them to be found in all churches and all departments of life,— we had a few more that day,— and of the service they are rendering every good cause, a sermon was preached to me a great deal better than anything I could have said to them.

The simple presence of such persons in a church is itself to every minister a powerful encouragement and help. He is of course glad to see his occasional hearers,— the guest from some other denomination who drops in to learn his side of infinite truth; the poor mother, the stand-by of home, who has a breakfast and a husband and three or four children to attend to in the morning, so she can get out only now and then; the young men of his ecclesiastical garden, rare flowers, whose eyes and religious natures open usually only in the latter part of the day, but who, once or twice a year, under the stimulus of a new suit of clothes, blossom out in the forenoon; the religious casual, well described by Horace as the small and infrequent worshiper, owning, perhaps, a pew, but occupying it so seldom that, when used, it has to be found for him by the janitor; the bevy of bright girls, always active at socials and church suppers, who remember sometimes that Sundays and sermons are also a part of religion; and the crowd of strangers who appear Sunday nights when it has been advertised that he is going to preach on "The Kingdom of Satan" or "The Doings of the Devil" or "The Sowing of Wild Oats," or some similarly sacred theme. But, after all, it is the stand-bys, the men, often old ones, and the women, often farthest from the church, who are absolutely certain to be in their places punctually at every service, whatever the season or the weather or the subject of the sermon,— these that he learns to look upon with special delight and to find the sources of his greatest earthly inspiration. What is winter, what are rainy days, what are snows half a fathom deep, when he has before him the prospect of their bright faces looking up to his and their warm hearts ready to drink in his truth? I know of a minister who never goes to church with such a light step and elastic spirit as on stormy Sundays, sure, as he then is, of meeting there the picked audience, the sifted wheat of souls, who are present because they really want religious help and want at the same time to help religion. Fred's father is a type of all preachers. There is none of them who, with three stand-bys to encourage him, cannot face bravely what is sometimes regarded as the devil's most powerful artillery, the gaping mouths of threescore empty pews. Their winter cloaks and brightening eyes allure him on amid bare walls, murky shadows, closed hymn-books, broken fans, and the awful echoes of his own voice from truth to truth and from charge to charge, as the white plume of Henry of Navarre led on his followers amid the shouts and groans and carnage of the battle-fields of France. And, when the sermon is over and he comes down from the pulpit, and they stop to shake hands with him, as real stand-bys always do, and ask him if it is not hard preaching to so few, he answers, without even a minister's white lie, that it is the jolliest thing in all the world to preach to such a few; and he goes home to his slippers and cold meat, feeling that he has fought a good fight, and that his seed — for that is what a minister's shot ought always to be — has fallen into good ground, even though it be into a patch of it no larger than three pews.

Equally valuable is the attendance of such persons at prayer-meetings, Sunday-schools, sewing circles, Alliances, and at all parish gatherings. Numbers are nice, newcomers needful, and doubtless it is well to have a religious excitement, now and then that will bring into them all the floating material of the community. But every minister, every worker, knows that such flood tides of interest will not, cannot, last. The enthusiasm dies, the crowded rooms thin out, and there comes a lull when only a few of the old plodding, never-tired workers are left. They are the stand-bys. They bridge over the intervals from excitement to excitement, are the only members, sometimes, who give societies a continuous life. They are not noisy, not conspicuous, not always the leaders and go-ahead people; and in the full sweep of prosperity, like the rocks on the seashore when the tide is in, are often lost sight of and forgotten. But, when the tide ebbs, when there is no minister to the society, and no popularity, when trouble and trial and disaster come, then, like the rocks, they rise again distinct and visible, and the society endures, endures, perhaps, as a lighthouse amid the stormy waves, because it has their strong souls on which to rest. Rev. W. H. H. Murray several years ago had a lecture on "Deacons," in which he easily raised a laugh at the two or three officers of this name, always on hand at prayer meetings, who used to stand up year after year to make the same long prayer, and give the same juiceless exhortation. But, after all, it is just such old men, always there and always doing their best, even though it is the same antiquated best, who for more than two hundred years in New England have kept these meetings in existence and afforded religion the limbs, whistling and bare as they were in the cold winter, on which to hang its leaves and flowers and fruit when the springtime of revivals came round again. A hard, ungrateful heart must that clergyman have, who does not love and bless these old, faithful, always-present souls, whether deacons or not, whose only gift is — as truly a divine one as any dash of leadership or brilliancy of prayer — simply to stand by him in times of loneliness, unpopularity, and spiritual deadness.

It is not in religious matters alone, however, that there are stormy Sundays and empty seats, nor in sewing circles and prayer meetings only that there are glacial epochs, ebb-tides of interest, and the need of slender bridges over which life's forces have to march, but they occur in every field where human beings are called upon to act.

During the golden years of youth we like new friendships, new faces, new homes, new gods. The more lovers, the more popularity, the more changes of scene, the more happiness, it is thought. Every fresh opening is hailed with enthusiasm, every fresh acquaintance with delight. Every good-looking girl outside of his own home is to the young man an angel, every sprucely dressed man to the girl a possible hero. And age, experience, fidelity, tried and familiar things, have no show then by the side of novelty, dash, and brilliancy.

But no one can go far on his way without finding that the real gold of friendship is not in the crowd, not in popularity, not in the sparkle of new eyes and the clasp of new hands, however pleasant, but rather in the two or three old stand-bys whose worth trouble has put to the test. The warm, true, faithful hearts, the men and women who have stood by us in the midst of darkness and disappointment, mistakes of judgment, failures in business, losses of popularity,—ay, and in the midst of our sins,— the stormy day friends who come to us in our solitude, all the more certainly because, as they fear, nobody else will come,— no person has ever known friendship, all the joy and strength it can give, till he has had two or three of such friends. It is worth meeting misfortune and disaster, worth losing the friendships of the crowd and the world, just to catch the gleam of their bright faces looming up through the darkness and to feel the clasp of their warm hands reaching out through the coldness. They light up the world's great temple with a splendor such as never came from the eyes of beauty; cheer us on amid empty purses, dismal times of trade, and the silence of all other songs with an inspiration never breathed by the tongues of gathered thousands. I heard of such a one once, an old maid, always doing kind deeds, who, in addition to the twelve spools of black thread already in her work-basket, went down the village street a cold, rainy day, to buy still another of a merchant having a hard time, whose store no one else for twelve hours had entered,— how weakly insignificant as a matter of business, "but the turning point," said he afterwards, "of my fortune and the saving of my soul." Happy is that man or woman arriving in life's journey, some stormy morning, on a hill-top which all others, perhaps, have deserted, who can look down the avenue lined, it may be, with leafless winter trees, and see struggling up to him against the sleet and rain two or three of such old stand-bys.

It is friends of this stamp that God gives naturally to every human being in those of the family and the home. The fathers and mothers, the brothers and sisters, they who have watched over us in our cradles, played with us in our childhood, grown up with us side by side to manhood and womanhood, their life-stream one with ours; they who, amid all faults and failures, have loved us simply because we were ourselves, drawing nearer to us with every stormy day of life, and whose affection sometimes not even prison doors can shut out,— a heritage of devotion more or less perfect, to which every child of earth is born,— it is these who are true stand-bys, these that are worthy types of the fidelity and steadfastness of the Everlasting Love.

And when extreme old age has come upon them and they can give to others no longer their care and devotion; when children and children's children have to do for them, upholding their feeble steps, dressing their aged forms, consoling their aches and pains, and smoothing their way down to the last long slumber, not less are they deserving of the name. It is well-known that the tall trees of the orchard and forest are able to brave the winter's storm and lift their heads aloft in the summer skies, not by reason of their fresh life alone, which exists only in the narrow circle between the trunk and the bark, and is renewed every season, but because they keep at their core, sheltered and protected by the new life, the old fiber stored there, some of it thirty, fifty, and a hundred years ago. And who has not known of families held together amid all the storms of human life and growing every year more beautiful and saintly because they had at their center an old father or mother or grandparent folded in and cherished by the currents of their fresh young hearts? Thank God, it is not only by the love, sympathy, and care received that we live, but often, far more, by those which we give. Children never grow up so nobly and well, homes are never so genial and lovely, as when there are aged and, it may be, invalid forms among them, mourning, perhaps, that their life-work is over, because they can no longer care for others, but doing, perhaps, the best part of it in being cared for themselves. And unwise, as well as ungrateful, is that boy or girl, that man or woman, gone out into the rush and glitter of the world and rejoicing there in other friendships and other loves, who does not remember and cherish the old father and mother left at home, and keep the paths still open and worn which lead back to their doors and to their hearts.

Of a similar character is the blessedness which is possible for the ripeness and old age of wedded life. The theories and practices which make the marriage relation only a partnership to be dissolved at pleasure, whatever else may be said in their favor, strike a deadly blow at an element in it which has the possibility, as time goes on, of becoming supreme over all others. Marriage in some of its practical

manifestations is undeniably the occasion of
an immense amount of misery, crime, injustice,
and down-dragging, is one of the most
perplexing institutions with which society and
religion have to deal; but in its ideal shape, of
all the evidences of God's goodness to be found
on this earth, all the indications that he cares
for human beings with the love of a Father, as
well as with the wisdom of a Creator, there is
none quite equal to his providing for them a
relation between the sexes in which the members
of each are moved by the strongest of all
ties to stand by those of the other in all the
varied scenes of human life. If it is an ideal
not always realized in full, it is one that is approached
a great deal oftener than those who
satirize it are willing to allow. Many a
couple living together thirty, forty, fifty
years, have found that the most blessed part
of their union was not the romance and splendor
of its early days, not the richer development
which it gave all through to their characters,
not even the children who were
gathered around its shrine, but the intimacy
and reliability of its companionship, the fact
that it gave them each in the other a near and
faithful stand-by,— a blessing coming to
them the fullest when the fervor of youth had
gone, and their children had left the home
nest, and amid the chills of age they stood on

the threshold of the great eternal house. "I had a happy marriage," said a lady, "but its happiest memory is what I did for my husband in his long final sickness, as I think it was also his happiest experience that I was with him to do it." And, apart from all questions of morality, who, if he is wise and wants the best the two sexes can give, would make marriage the transitory affair that would take out of its vows this stand-by element?

Stand-bys are usually thought of as conservatives upholding the past, and having no part to perform in revolutions, reforms, and the progress of society into new fields of truth and duty; and indeed all such movements are sure to find men in plenty who in the lower meaning of the words stand by when they are going on,— stand by with indifference and let others do their work, or stand by as Saul did at the martyrdom of Stephen, consenting to see them stoned and holding the raiment of those who do the stoning.

Yet even in progress and reform the opportunity and need are not lacking — yea, are imperative and abundant — for those, also, who will stand by them in the better sense of being their active and steadfast friends. For progress and reform are like trees of the garden. To put forth new leaves and bear new fruit they must have a trunk of unchanging principles, those of justice, liberty, right, and humanity, on which for the new leaves and fruit to grow; and they who stand by these principles when men, and perhaps nations, are tempted to forsake them in the pursuit of some seeming good, why is not their work as valuable for progress and reform as that of the men who grow on them the world's improved conditions?

Nor are the new movements themselves entirely without need of their special kind of help. It is not the dashing leaders, the brilliant orators, and the advanced thinkers alone, important as their service is, who constitute the whole force by which the success of a cause is won; but the sturdy men and women who, when the first enthusiasm for it has cooled off, and persecution, or, what is worse, indifference, has come in, go up all the same into its sanctuary and give it and give its leaders the cheer of their two or three bright faces and faithful hearts, they who not only stand up for it, but stand by it,— their work, surely, which is to be counted in.

We smile sometimes in reading Virgil's Æneid at the way in which his "fidus Achates," "fortis Gyas," "fortis Cleanthus," characters having but one attribute, appear again and again in its scenes as actors with the "pius Æneas"; but the story in this respect is in perfect accord with actual life, every hero being supported in his progress by a few just such faithful comrades. "What good can I do here?" many a man and woman has mournfully asked in going to a temperance meeting or Anti-slavery convention, or other reformatory gathering, where they had no ability to speak, no possibility of making further conversions, and no new thing to hear. The good of standing by them is the answer, one of the greatest goods of all. The plan of Wellington at the Battle of Waterloo, as is well known, was simply to form his regiments in hollow squares, and then exhaust the enemy by repelling the attacks made against them. Again and again his squares were assailed with all the dash and brilliancy of a Frenchman's charge. In vain: their efforts were like the rush of the sea against the sharp angles of its granite shore, the legions which made them being broken and rolled back in the foam and spray of human blood. "Hard pounding this," said the Iron Duke, as he threw himself into one of these fortresses of living hearts, "but it all turns on who can stand pounding the longest." And Waterloo's bloody field was gained, one of the sixteen decisive battles in the world's history, because Englishmen that day stood pounding the longest, or, in other words, were such good stand-bys. So in the world's great moral battles the men who can form themselves into hollow squares, squares whose lines are trued by the everlasting right, and in the darkness and discouragement of the battle's pelting rain have learned the tactics of standing firmly by their cause, and of standing longest the pelting of their foes,— they are the ones who will remain at last masters of the field.

All honor, then, in the church, in the home, in the world, and in the battle-fields of truth and right, to those whose genius and mission are to be simply stand-bys. They may not win always the laurels of earth, their position may be less strikingly brilliant than that of the world's inspirers and leaders, and sometimes they may be despised and laughed at by their restless brothers,— sometimes may despise themselves, but not the less they are the Lord's anointed, not the less the doers for him of a precious work. And, when the end comes and the laurels for the eternal years are given out, the Lord of the whole earth, whose causes they have stood by here, will in turn stand by them there; and out of thin churches and wearisome prayer-meetings and long years of faithful service in the home, and out from the world's great battle-fields, they shall be called up to the front ranks of honor, and be stand-bys forever around the eternal throne.

III

LIBERAL CHRISTIANITY AND LIBERAL ORTHODOXY

One of the most frequent questions Liberal Christianity has to meet when it goes forth now to establish new churches, and to push forward its work, is that of its need any longer as a distinct religious organization. Fifty years ago its ideas stood out in violent contrast with those of other denominations, and, whether it was believed in or not, there could be no doubt that the ground on which it stood in the world of thought was exclusively its own. But in our time the lines which separate it from other churches have in many places almost entirely faded away. The whole religious world during the past generation has become liberalized as it never was before. Eloquent, scholarly, and broad-minded Orthodox preachers are to be found in almost every community, setting forth more or less of what was once known as pre-eminently Unitarian and Universalist truth; beautiful, well-equipped and hospitable Orthodox churches in almost every village opening their doors to welcome equally all comers to fill their pews, enjoy their worship, and help pay their bills. And amid such a state of things it is asked, Why should Liberal churches, one of whose aims is to get rid, so far as possible, of sectarian lines, seek to perpetuate their denominational existence? Why not go into these new Orthodox churches, and join hearts and hands with their members in doing what seems to be their common work? Said the clergyman of such a church a while ago, in a city where there are several of like character, to the minister of a new Unitarian society, who had complained to him of the practical disfellowship he had received, "It is because we think you Unitarians had no call to set up another society here on the ground of Liberalism, and our people feel a little 'put upon' by your tone in making such a claim over them." And there are many Unitarians themselves who look at the matter in the same way. They have pleasant relations all the week with their Orthodox neighbors; their sensibilities are rarely jarred by anything in the preaching and worship they hear in Orthodox churches; and they very naturally say, "Why, then, be at all the trouble, expense, and apparent inconsistency of setting up and maintaining a separate and perhaps insignificant Liberal society?"

It is a question which deserves a fair answer. If these other churches are doing the full work of Liberal Religion, if there is no large, distinct, and positive want in human hearts and in general society which Unitarian and Universalist societies can satisfy better than all others, no way in which earnest-hearted men and women can work for the kingdom of God more consistently and more successfully in organizations of their own than in those of a broad Orthodoxy, then unhesitatingly these other churches have a right to feel "put upon" by our presence and our claims, and have a right to ask that our time, toil, and money shall be put in with theirs for religious service, rather than be used for perpetuating a useless sect. So in this paper I address myself to considering candidly the need of Liberal Christianity in the midst of Liberal Orthodoxy.

I. It is needed because with the Liberal faith it aims to give, for its holding, the Liberal form. There is indeed no denying the sweetness, breadth, catholicity, and genuineness of a large element of what is called Liberal Orthodoxy, an element which is found alike in Baptist, Congregational, Episcopal, and Methodist churches. It has the new wine of Liberalism, has it sometimes in its richest, finest flavor,— has it, I am free to say, in a far better condition than many of our stagnant Unitarian societies have. Its preaching for the most part is up with the times, is in harmony with science, and is as little bound by the mere letter of Scripture as God's sunlight is with a parrot's iron cage. Its ministers — I say it from long acquaintance with some of them — are as genial, large-hearted, and companionable men as are to be found anywhere on the face of the earth; and though now and then, under some special disturbing influence, they may lapse for a moment, not into the old doctrines but into the old phrases and methods, yet, as soon as the pressure is removed, like a steel spring they are back again to their true selves and to this nineteenth century. Unitarianism denies with all possible emphasis that it claims to be the exclusive representative anywhere of Liberal thought. So far as the thought is concerned it is glad to believe that there is hardly a single point at which it is not paralleled, if not in degree, yet in spirit, by Liberal Orthodoxy.

But how is it in passing from the thought to the theology, from the sermon to the creed, from the living faith to the lettered form? Why, there is hardly one of these churches which does not have for its confession — a confession which its minister and often its private members in uniting with it are obliged to assent to — the same old theology, with all its rigidity and horror, which in past ages has borne so terribly on the human soul. Having occasion, not long ago, to examine the creeds of the different churches in a city somewhat noted for its Liberal Orthodoxy, I found them made up of the very doctrines — some in one and some in another, softened it may be in their setting, but as hard, narrow, and repulsive as ever in their substance — that the pioneers of Liberalism were fighting against fifty years ago: such, for instance, as original sin, total depravity, the infallibility of all Scripture, the tri-personality of the Godhead, salvation by sovereign grace alone, the resurrection of the body, everlasting damnation, and the like,— down even to those about the corrupt nature, and God's wrath against it, of little children. Religion's new wine is put by them in theology's old bottles, the liberty with which Christ made men free entangled again in the slave's yoke of bondage, the live man of belief bound, as in the ancient mode of punishment, to the corpse of a dead faith. And it is here, rather than in the belief itself, that we come to the real difference between Liberal Orthodoxy and Liberal Christianity,— here that we begin to find the need of the one even in the midst of the other.

Such doctrines, to be sure, are not emphasized by it now as they were of old by those who believed literally in their awful significance; indeed are often kept almost entirely in the background, like a superannuated or imbecile relative in a polite family, while only the youthful, well-dressed Liberalism is brought to the front; but now and then the two things, by some malign accident, will come together,— right in company, too, and often into a most painful contrast with each other. A friend tells me that a while ago he dropped into a Liberal Orthodox church where the pastor was preaching a sermon on the nature of the resurrection. It gave up the whole of the old idea of a bodily rising, and was as broad, philosophical, and spiritual as the most advanced thinker could wish, a credit alike to the preacher's heart and head. My friend listened to it with the utmost delight, and said to himself, What now is the need of Unitarianism, when Orthodoxy is preaching such sermons as this? Just then he happened to glance from the preacher's lips to the church's creed written out on the wall in the background, and there his eye fell at once on the words, "*I believe in the resurrection of the body.*" If the corpse of some old acquaintance long buried had actually come forth and stood in all its ghastliness by the side of the living preacher, the difference between them could hardly have been more startling than it was between the dead and the living faith; and the gentleman came away more impressed than ever with the importance

LIBERAL ORTHODOXY 319

of a church where there is no danger of such resurrections.

Still worse is the contrast when a deliberate profession of these old creeds is made the condition of church membership, as it still is in many cases, to men and women who in their hearts are holding the new faith. I knew a young girl who while living in a Unitarian family had imbibed Liberal sentiments, but whose mother was Orthodox in her faith, and who naturally wished in her religious connection to be united with her parent in the same church. She told her minister, a noted Liberal Orthodox preacher, what her situation was, and he assured her that, so long as she had a personal faith in Christ himself, her special doctrinal belief on other points would make no difference about her admission to Christ's fold. Judge of her feelings, however, when, standing up in the broad aisle with a score of others to be received, there was read for her to assent to, besides the church covenant, a list of nearly forty theological articles. Being a modest girl, unwilling to make a scene, she allowed her assent to be implied; but it was with a terrible wrench to her moral nature; and writing to her grandmother about it afterwards she told her that of the whole forty articles there was only one she positively believed, and that with regard to the larger part of them she could not even understand the meaning of the words. Now, in all earnestness and solemnity, what kind of way is this with which to begin that Christian life which beyond everything else demands of its followers perfect sincerity? Of course, if people really believe these harsh creeds, there is no objection to their saying so. All doctrines are but the vessels in which to hold God's truth, the tools with which to do God's work; and, if some persons find the old ones are better adapted for their wants than the new, there is no genuine Liberalism which will not say that the old ones ought to be used, and which will not respect their users. But to impose a deliberate profession of them on young minds that know nothing about their meaning, and whose real faith is wholly the other way, as the imperative condition of their coming to Christ, and that, too, in the most solemn moment of human life, what is it but an outrage on the very name of faith which not only every lover of liberty, but every friend of honesty and truthfulness, ought to denounce? And yet how many thousands of people there are every year who are made to enter the church with just such a lie on their lips; how many church members who, if they worship at all, are compelled to stand up Sunday after Sunday and repeat a creed about the resurrection of the body, the birth of Jesus Christ from a vir-

LIBERAL ORTHODOXY 321

gin, and his descent into hell, the evidence of which they have never spent one single hour in examining; how many business men, who on becoming Christians are obliged to support doctrines, ay, and to utter sentiments in prayers, to be charged with which in the counting-room or on the street they would resent as a foul slander.

Of course I know very well the methods by which men try to reconcile their consciences to such professions; know they are told that the resurrection of the body means of the spiritual body, total depravity totally imperfect, a trinity of persons a trinity of manifestations, and the like, know how mental reservations and such modifications as " for substance of doctrine " are put in for the sake of sensitive moral natures. But what is this but the covering up a lie's body with a truth's garment, a form in which it is infinitely more corrupting than when it stands out in its own nakedness? What but the teaching in religion of that very principle which leads in society at large to the stamping of a piece of paper with the word dollar, and then using it as the means with which to pay a debt which was contracted in solid coin; to the treating of grease and tallow with a few chemicals so as to make them look well, and then selling the compound for our tables as genuine butter, and to the signing of obligations or the swearing of oaths, and then the repudiation of their force under the plea of a different meaning to the terms? If every one is to be allowed to put his own private interpretation on language, as Liberal Orthodoxy is teaching men to do in their creeds, what form of bargain can ever be made binding? Words are sacred things. The sanctity of all obligations depends in a large measure on their sacredness. Every member of society who would keep out of it a sea of falsehood is as much interested in having them untouched as every Hollander is that no one shall meddle with his dikes. The man who can bring himself to tamper with the meaning of words in the solemn profession of his faith before God has acquired a habit which must inevitably prove to him a terrible temptation in his relations with men. And is it not just here that we find the explanation of why so many church members are false and frail in their business affairs and in their domestic relations; the explanation, too, of why so many persons in the world at large, seeing how easy it is for professed Christians to hold one thing in their creeds and another in their hearts, have lost faith in all religion, and concluded that its professions are all of the same character, full and fair to the eyes, quibbled away and meaning nothing to the understanding? The new wine

LIBERAL ORTHODOXY 323

has been put in the old bottles, and Christ's words about it have been fulfilled,— the bottles bursting, and the wine, the precious wine of religion, itself, spilled.

Then, too, though there are many Christians on whose souls these solemn professions sit very lightly, many who seem to think that church vows, like lovers' vows, Jove laughs at, there are others who cannot reconcile their consciences to such a Protean use of language; and then, alas! their lives too often become a long, long conflict between the leadings of the spirit and the bondage of the letter.

Who now will say that in such a state of things there is not need, real soul need, of a church into which men and women can come with no other condition imposed upon them than that simply of a hunger and thirst after righteousness and truth, and an honest and free soul in their pursuit; a church which, having dropped the old theology, drops with it the old theological creeds; a church in which men are not only free to think for themselves, but free to choose the expression of their thought; a church which believes that truthfulness is a more important element of religion than even truth, and an honest doubt a more sacred thing in the sight of God than any hollow faith? If you should go down South and find that the negroes there made free by the

President's proclamation, and entitled by our laws to all the immunities of American citizens, were still keeping possession of their old manacles and chains, and still feeling obliged with every feast-day and every coming among them of a new member to put them on as a symbol of what they ought always to wear, would you not say that the work of emancipation was not yet complete,— say that there was need of some one to go there and proclaim that American citizenship meant not only freedom from slavery itself, but freedom from all its badges and signs? And this is the kind of work Liberal Christianity is trying to do for the citizens of Christ's kingdom, this one of the points in which it goes beyond its friend Liberal Orthodoxy, and in which it finds its need,— relieving men not only of the old bondage, but of the old bonds; giving them not only the new wine of Liberalism, but, as the vessels in which to hold it, the new words of liberty; making discipleship its only condition of membership, and saying to each one of its followers, " Form your own creed, utter it in your own speech, and above all other truth be yourself a true man."

II. The second great reason why Liberal Christianity is needed, even in the midst of Liberal Orthodoxy, is that it furnishes the only possible ground on which all churches can come

LIBERAL ORTHODOXY

into practical fellowship with each other, and the only possible tie by which they can be held together as one organic body. The ground of fellowship they have striven for hitherto, as is well known, has been that of outward, formal unity, unity of doctrine, ritual, and polity, the tie that of symbol and creed. And what has been the result? Division, persecution, hatred, weakness, almost every quality that is the opposite of a genuine Christian union.

Look at the religious world to-day, at the innumerable sects into which it is divided, permeating every little town and village, at the antagonism and strife of its different parts against each other rather than against sin, and at the enormous expense involved in simply the keeping up of its multiplied organizations; and how far removed is it from that one body, set forth by the New Testament as its type of union, in which those members thought to be less honorable receive more abundant honor, and in which they all have the same care of each other!

And this state of things must continue, from the nature of the case, so long as mere outward likeness of any kind, whether of doctrine, ritual, or polity, is insisted on as their ground of union. God has so constituted our minds in their very nature that they never can be true to themselves and true to him and see things, especially the great things of religion, all in the same light. The moment men begin to think and act they begin inevitably to differ; and the more vigorous and free the thoughts and actions are, the wider apart their results are certain to be. Liberal Orthodoxy, to be sure, may do much to smooth over and soften these differences and to bring those affected by them into relations of kindness and humanity with each other; but the very fact that it is Orthodoxy at all — that is, that it makes a right faith the connecting link of its members — renders it a negative work and prevents it from uniting those, the larger part of all Christendom, whose faiths, from the nature of their minds, are radically different. So with Liberalism alone of every kind. It never can unite. Its whole mission is to dissolve, to allow every man independent of every other to form his own creed, and to reduce the religious world, as it is fast doing under Protestantism, to a mere mass of individuals, as incoherent and unorganized as a bed of sand.

What is wanted, evidently, is some other principle to go with this, something that while giving to each man the right of private judgment and of making his own creed, Orthodox, Roman Catholic, Unitarian, or Jewish, recognizing and honoring the peculiarities of each, will at the same time supply the link deeper and diviner than any doctrine, ritual, or polity, which can bind these parts, bind their very differences, all together in one grand organic whole. And that principle beyond question is given to the world in Christianity. The gospel, in its subtlest essence, is not a doctrine, not a set of rules and forms, not a church organization, but a unifying, life-giving spirit, ready to permeate all doctrines, all rites, all churches, just as the human spirit does the human body. It is love, not creed, which is stated in the most explicit terms to be its connecting bond; the human body, consisting of many diverse members, which is given as the type of its outward form; having the spirit of Christ represented as what makes us his; the doctrine of the Holy Spirit its great transcendent idea, and the unity of the spirit the object it keeps in view,— the one faith sometimes spoken of being a subjective, spiritual quality, not an objective creed.

And it is the putting together of these two principles, Liberalism on the one hand making many members, and the spirit of Christ on the other uniting all these members, down even to the least, in one organic whole, which constitutes Liberal Christianity. It gives up, as you see, the whole Orthodox idea of making a right faith, the whole Presbyterian and Roman Catholic idea of making a right polity, and the

whole Baptist and Episcopal idea of making
a right ritual, its ground of fellowship and
bond of union, and turns for them within; finds
them in their common spirit and animating
principle; finds them in that Christian love
which under all beliefs, rituals, and polities is
one and the same; finds them in that broad
Christian living to which all sects were meant
to contribute a vital part. It is the only platform
on which all Christendom by the laws of
our human nature can come into fellowship;
and just because Liberal Orthodoxy and
Liberalism in all its secular forms is doing its
work so well,— the work of making men free,
— who does not see that Liberal Christianity is
needed all the more as furnishing the tie with
which to hold them together, many members in
one body, the great natural and scriptural type
of a perfect union.

III. But free thought and spiritual unity
are very far from being the only objects of
Christianity. They are merely the beginning,
merely the tools. Beyond and above them is
its work of saving, uplifting, and sanctifying
the world, and of unifying the human race; and
it is here that I find the third great need of its
Liberal form. The one supreme object of the
church hitherto has been to save individual
souls, and to save them more especially out of
a hell and into a heaven thought to exist on the

other side of the grave. Prepare to die; prepare to meet thy God; turn or burn,— these have been its rallying cries; and the great wide world itself, in which these souls have lived, with all its myriad interests, has been represented as under the Divine curse, destined in a few short years to be destroyed with fire, and utterly unworthy of a moment's religious thought otherwise than to be abused and scorned. This old idea itself of a lost earth trembling on the verge of a fiery fate has in a measure passed away, but the type of Christianity which grew out of it, the saving preeminently of the individual soul, and the doing of everything with reference to a future state,— this still remains as the characteristic of many Orthodox churches, even of those which in other respects are emphatically Liberal. Religion is made by it a thing apart from life; the intimate connection of body, mind, and soul, sacred and secular, market and meeting-house, the growth of corn and the spread of virtue, recognized now in all true philosophy, is largely ignored; and its churches are used for worship alone, pointing with their steeples away from earth, and looking down with stony walls and darkened windows six days of the week on all the interests and struggles of this great, weary, toiling world.

Look at the relation of this type of Orthodoxy to reforms, such reforms, for instance, as anti-slavery, temperance, the uplifting of women, kindness to animals, the advancement of science, and the suppression of vice — apart from some noble exceptions, what help in their infancy and unpopularity, when help is especially needed, have they ever had from its hand? A gentleman of the city where I live, himself a professed Orthodox believer, was talking with me a while ago about what could be done towards shutting up a den of shame in its midst notoriously leading young men by scores into vice, and I suggested that it would be well first of all to enlist the aid of the churches. "The last thing of all to appeal to," said he; "we can get the help of their individual members, noble men and women, by the hundred; but the churches themselves — you might as well try to drink milk with the great dipper in Ursa Major, or pay for the sweeping of the streets with the gold in sunset skies, as try to get the churches' influence for any earthly work; they are too much taken up with saving souls from hell to do anything about saving cities from vice." He may have stated their inefficiency in somewhat exaggerated language for general application, but, alas! are not his words too true of many of them with reference not to one vice alone, but to almost everything which concerns our common earthly morals?

Far be it from me in saying this to criticise these sister churches for thus devoting themselves to worship, piety, and soul-saving. I believe fully in such work, believe it is a side of religion there is a divine need of somebody's attending to; and I thank God he has placed men on earth who have the taste and talent for its doing. But with this world and the human race here as the field and stock out of which souls age after age are growing; with hells of vice, sin, and wrong right under the very shadow of our churches as deep and damnable as anything Dante ever dreamed of; with thousands of human beings every year going down before our very eyes into their pits of moral death; and with all parts of our nature and all the interests of society, earthly and heavenly, bound together with indissoluble ties so that the one cannot be saved without saving the other,— is there not, I ask, the need of a Christianity to go with that of the churches which is broad and liberal enough to take in all this work; a Christianity which aims to save for time as well as for eternity, save humanity itself as well as individual men, save homes, cities, nations, and society out of vice as well as souls out of sin; a Christianity not ashamed to plant itself at the forefront of unpopular reform, and which when it sees any human interest fallen among thieves, wounded and half-dead, and priest and Levite go by on the other side, is Good Samaritan enough to cross over with its oil and wine to where the victim is; a Christianity, in short, which writes over its door side by side with the first great command of love to God, the second, as in very truth like unto it, Thou shalt love thy neighbor as thyself?

Fred Douglass tells the story in his autobiography that in his early life when a slave at the South he used to pray with all the earnestness of his soul that God would give him freedom. Month after month and year after year he prayed in this way, but still the freedom did not come. At last one day, while thus pleading with all his soul before God, he heard a voice out of heaven whispering to him, "Pray with your legs, Fred, pray with your legs;" and obeying this divine behest, in thirty days the prayer was answered, and Fred Douglass was a free man. So now, while our brethren are wrestling with their souls in prayer before God that he will free them and the world from the slavery of sin, is there not need at least of some churches that will hear again the divine words, "Pray with your legs, pray with your arms, pray with your whole bodies, as well as with your hearts"?

One night during the war I was in an ocean steamer off Cape Hatteras in the midst of a terrible gale, the wind blowing us directly towards the foam-covered lee shore. The captain stood on the ship's bridge full of anxiety; two pilots were at the helm, every mate and sailor at his place. The huge vessel creaked and groaned, plunged and reared in the waves, and heaved from side to side like a living creature writhing in some awful agony. The sky looked wild as hell; the wind shrieked like demons through rigging and shroud; and every now and then there came on board, like a monster of the deep, a huge torrent of water. It was impossible to remain on deck, and after trying it a few moments I went below, stopping on my way to look in at the engine-room. Down there stood the two engineers calmly at their work, oiling the machinery, watching the time it made, and giving now and then an order to the stokers heaving in coal to the furnaces still further down. Every bit of brass and steel was shining with light; the clock ticked gently in its place, and steadily as a sleeping child's pulse the piston plied back and forth and the huge walking-beam trod up and down. Just then the captain appeared at the window: "Engineer," said he, "how are your engines? I have done all I can on deck. Every rag of sail is blown away, and we are barely holding our own against this miserable sea. Cape Hatteras lights are down under our lee; and if anything in your engines gives out, we are surely lost. This ship and its eleven hundred men all depend on you." "All right," replied the enengineer, "I will do my part"; and then he and his companion looked at the steam-gauge, tried the stop-cocks, gave another order to the stokers, wiped away the bits of lint from the shafting, and turned on at the joints a few more drops of oil. And it was because those engineers and stokers down there in the hold, where they could not see light of land or sky, did their work faithfully and well, that the grand old ship with its thousand men, a whole regiment of soldiers, came safely through the gale and added their strength to the Union forces of North Carolina.

So with this great world-ship of ours caught off the foaming capes of sin, blown upon with all the gales of passion, and writhing and tossing with sorrow, vice, and wrong; if it is ever to come through to the great celestial haven with its freight of a myriad souls all saved, as I believe it will, it must be not only by the religion on deck which guides the helm, watches the far-off heavenly lights, and trims the sails of prayer to catch the spirit's breath, but by the religion which is humble enough to include with this the work lower down of regulating the fires of bodily appetite, wiping away the stain of corruption from its shafting in the market, oiling the joints of labor and capital, and seeing to it that the great walking-beams of commerce, manufactures, and trade tread back and forth true to Heaven's eternal law. And when a little company of such religionists come into any community to help this work, who shall say they are not needed there,— who that their brethren higher up, managing the steeples and watching the heavens, have any reason to feel " put upon " by their presence, or to refuse them their fellowship?

Such are some of the grounds on which Liberal Christianity believes that in the world everywhere, and not less so at the very side of the most liberal Orthodox churches, there is still a call for its own peculiar work. It does not antagonize or undervalue these other churches. It recognizes that their faces are set towards the same light as its own, that their hearts are throbbing with a kindred life, and their hands sharers with it in one larger task. But in every army there must be the pioneers, the vanguard, and sometimes the forlorn hope; and its aim is to act as these in the army of the Lord. The principles which others carry out in part, its idea is to carry out in full; the work which they are doing, burdened with ancient traditions, it would take up in the freedom of the spirit; the new wine they are offering to the world in old bottles it would set before it in forms which are fresh and strong with all the philosophy and science of our own time. The difference between them is well expressed in their very names, Liberal Orthodoxy and Liberal Christianity, the one emphasizing a right belief, the other a larger word standing not only for belief, but for love, righteousness, truth-seeking, practical work, and the unity of the spirit. It is the true place for multitudes who are now in the ranks of Liberal Orthodoxy, the place to which the ultimatum of their own principles will surely bring them, and which for their sakes, therefore, ought always to be kept open. The men and women of our own faith can feel that in putting their time, toil, and money into the support of its churches and the advancement of its interests, they are putting them not into a dead or dying cause, not into a sectarianism whose outward growth must be at the expense of its own inward life, but into a movement which is alive with all that is broadest and best in the religion of to-day, and on whose platform all other believers can consistently stand equally with themselves. It is the natural standard for all young people, all brave, earnest, progressive minds who in their march to heaven want to keep step with the onward march of this world, to rally around; is the nat-

LIBERAL ORTHODOXY 337

ural position for all lovers of their kind, who want not only to work for truth and reform, but to do it under the inspiration of religious sentiment and amid the associations and memories of a religious home, to take. And so long as there are these classes in society and this work to be done on earth, no matter what progress Liberal Orthodoxy may make, there will be for their sakes a need and place for Liberal Christianity.

IV

A DEDICATION SERMON

OMAHA, 1871

Who commanded you to build this house and make up these walls? And they returned answer saying, We are the servants of the God of heaven and earth, and build the house that was builded these many years ago.—Ezra v, 9-11.

Thus saith Jesus to those Jews who believed on him: If ye continue in my word then are ye my disciples indeed.—John viii, 31.

CHRISTIAN FRIENDS: It gives me pleasure amid all the other evidences of enterprise and thrift that I see rising up so wonderfully in this new community to congratulate you on the completion of another place of worship, and with my brother in the household of our liberal faith, whose energy and patience and genius for hard work have carried your movement on thus far to success, to bid you welcome this first time within its walls.

You know what is the special object to which the services of the present occasion are to be devoted. The architect has wisely planned the house for the conveniences of public worship.

A DEDICATION SERMON

The builders have wrought his idea honestly and faithfully, it is to be trusted, into the stone and brick and wood of its outward shape. The hand of taste has touched its windows and walls with pleasant and cheerful colors, and scattered here and there its modest and appropriate adornments. You yourselves have put into it the hope, and, perhaps, the sacrifice that are already something of the interest, and faith, needed to cement its parts together as a spiritual home. We feel, however, that all these elements, important as they are, have not yet made it a church. There is need of its consecration, need of a finish to the seats, a beauty in the walls, a light in the windows, a warmth in the air, a grace in the shape and ornament such as no power of art can give, such as can spring only from the touch of the Eternal Spirit, need that the unseen owner come and make it his; and it is for this purpose, the formal surrender of it to God, and to the great ends and object of religious worship that we have met here today.

But the question arises, what is our worship? What the faith in which we are to dedicate it? What the thing it is to stand for in this community? Is it truly and distinctively a Christian temple? Are we to meet in it emphatically as a band of Christian worshipers? Is it indeed the God of heaven and earth who has commanded us, as he did his servants of old to build its walls, build it as a part of the unseen temple that was builded these many years ago?

You all know the estimate as to these points in which our denomination is held by a large part of the religious world. We are not recognized by the great body of Protestant churches as truly and distinctively Christians; are separated from them not only in doctrine, but in fellowship and communion; are made to occupy a position widely different from that in which they stand to each other, and to the world at large — oftentimes one of entire isolation. The Congregationalists, the Baptists, the Methodists, the Presbyterians, and even here and there a brave-hearted Episcopalian will venture occasionally to fellowship with each other, to exchange pulpits, and to unite in common religious movements; but, however much they may differ in other respects, they are all alike agreed in leaving the professors of Unitarianism outside of their communion. We are called deniers of the Lord Jesus, spoken of and treated preëminently as heretics. The only pulpits in all Christendom with which ours can exchange, with only the rarest exceptions, are those of our twin brethren and twin sufferers, the Universalists. The Young Men's Christian Associations, which in many of our large cities are doing such a noble work, exclude us expressly from all active participation in their affairs. Union prayer-meetings ignore our existence as having any possible access to the God of heaven. No Unitarian church member is asked as such to come to the communion table of those who are called evangelical. And, if a person united with their branch of the church wishes to leave it for ours, it matters not how perfect his character, or how conscientiously he may have changed his views, instead of being furnished with a letter of recommendation, he is excommunicated and turned out into the world precisely the same as though he were a sinner guilty of some terrible crime.

Far be it from me to refer to these things in the spirit of bitterness and reproach, or to forget the nobler traits of these same churches, and the many pleasant things that from time to time they have said and done to ours. It was in one of them that I was born and bred, in its Sunday-school that I learned my first lessons of divine truth; in its communion that are now some of the dearest friends I have on earth; and I would as soon think of hating the spots and blemishes of my childhood's home as of bearing ill-will against any part of the body with which I have had such associations, and which as a whole, stands for such glorious truths. A large part of the exclusion we receive is doubtless the inheritance of another age, a custom it has become hard to break through, even though the feeling on which it was grounded has passed away. The members of these same churches take us by the hand in every secular relation with all the warmth and cordiality of brother men. The great liberalizing influences of our land and age, the warmth of that religious tropical clime towards which the world evermore is moving, is having its influence greater or less on all sects. And, no doubt, if the question were put to the American people themselves to-day, to be decided simply on its own merits, the large majority of them would welcome us heart and soul to their communion.

The fact, however, remains that for some reason, either ignorance, or prejudice, or tradition, we are yet outside the pale of Christian sympathy. It is not a thing to cry over, not without its dignity and glory; is what the advance guard of Christendom, through all ages from Christ down, has had to experience. And yet it is not a pleasant position — not one we desire of itself to hold. We say frankly we should be glad to have the fellowship of all churches; glad to stand heart to heart, if not side to side, with all the vast army of the Lord, provided, always, we could do it without being false to freedom and self-respect, and false to our own special work. And on this occasion, when we are dedicating a Unitarian church, 1

A DEDICATION SERMON

hope it will not be out of place for me to try to set forth, not in the spirit of opposition to others, but of simple justice to ourselves, the claims, yea, the right, of Unitarians to the name and fellowship of Christians.

We claim it, first of all, on the simple ground of being the friends and followers of Christ. A small part of our number may hesitate about using some of the terms which have been applied to him in a way which has given them a false significance; and we may not any of us speak about him with the exalted awe and reverence of those who believe he is very God; but in the plain matter of love and discipleship and dependence upon and effort to follow him, we do not yield to any body of men that bear his name. He is our Saviour, Exemplar, Master, the head and fountain of our religious faith, the vine of which we are the branches, the door by which we go in and out of the Eternal fold. Our hearts reach out to him through the long vista of the ages. We read with ever increasing wonder the story of his life. The melody of his celestial voice, the light of his unshadowed eye thrill down to the very depth of our souls. We hear his call, as he stood by the sea of Galilee; catch the glistening of his robes, as he stood on the Mount of Transfiguration; listen to those words of wondrous meaning, as he sat by the well of Samaria; go with him heavy-hearted and bearing the world's burden, as he went up the hill of Calvary; stand with all Christendom, thrilled with a new, unspeakable hope, by the side of his open grave. And we follow him, not only over the page of Scripture, not only amid the hills of Judea, but down through all the centuries, down to where he is standing this very day, in the vanguard of every great and true reform.

What though we may not have the same opinion of his nature as the larger part of those who claim to be his friends, may not be able to distinguish within him exactly how much was human and how much divine? This does not vitiate in the least degree the reality or the strength of the tie by which we are his and he is ours. What is it that binds us to any beings that we love? Is it a knowledge of their metaphysical nature? Is it because we have measured the length and breadth of their minds and the number of their faculties and the greatness of their origin? No; the very idea of such a thing is absurd. It is the knowledge of their character, their deeds, their life; it is the greatness, not of their wisdom, their power, their origin, but of their hearts. And it is they who have the least power of metaphysical discernment; they who have never fathomed one faculty of the human soul, that are often the ones who love the most. It is so in our attachment to Christ. It is the living, breathing, loving man; not his theological anatomy, to which our souls go out. There is no lengthening his life into eternity; no expanding his features on the scale of infinity; no conception of his voice as coming from the abyss of Deity, which can make them seem to our hearts more divine and fair and melodious than they now are on the page of Scripture. He who does not love him as simply Jesus Christ will never be made to love him by writing under his name the Eternal God. How was it with his first disciples? When Matthew heard his call at the publican's bench; when Mary Magdalene poured over his head the box of ointment; when the apostle John leaned upon his bosom at the last supper; when they all suffered him to wash their very feet, do you suppose they then knew him as the Lord of heaven and earth, the Almighty and Everlasting Father? There is no one believes it. Yet were they not his true disciples, his followers and friends then? And, if we take him now just exactly as he appeared to them — just exactly as he was when he said, " Come unto me all ye that labor and are heavy laden and I will give you rest," — are we not equally worthy to bear his name?

But even on the ground that we must, indeed, have a true belief about what he was, before we can call ourselves Christians, our claim is not by any means weak. We adopt, as Unitarians, the exact language of the Bible in regard to his person. "Thou art the Son of the living God; Jesus Christ was the Son of God; my Father is greater than I; why callest thou me good? there is none good save one, that is God; of mine own self I can do nothing; of that day and that hour knoweth no man, no, not the angels in heaven, neither the Son, but the Father; there is one God and one mediator between God and man, the man Jesus Christ, who is the first-born of every creature, and the image of the invisible God." These are all the exact words of Scripture. Whatever else we may say and believe, there is at least no getting rid of these. They express exactly and literally our Unitarian belief. And are they not enough? Are they not more worthy, a thousand times, of our lips, as Christians, than the man-made phrases of the creeds in which he is called the second person of the Trinity, and very God?

But, as if to free us from all doubt on this point, the Bible itself declares they are enough. The Epistle of John states explicitly, "whosoever confesseth that Jesus is the Son of God, God dwelleth in him and he in God." How is it possible to have anything more definite?

The pen of inspiration writes that in order to have the indwelling of God's spirit, which certainly is the highest gift of Christianity, it is necessary to confess — not that Jesus is God, but that he is the son of God — our very Unitarian doctrine about him. And, with such authority before us, we ask — ask especially of those who believe in the letter of Scripture — is there any church under heaven which, at least, on the mere score of opinion about him, has the right to deny us, in any degree, the privileges and communion of his discipleship?

Still further, we rest our claim on the fact that we accept, not only his own doctrine concerning himself, but concerning all the great points of religion; in short, that we believe in Christianity. There is not a single thing which he has ever taught that, as a denomination, we do not fully and implicitly receive. All that is most distinctive and characteristic of our faith; all that we hold the most dear and precious in our hearts and lives — the unity and Fatherhood of God; love to God, and love to man, as the sum and substance of all duty; free forgiveness of our sins, on the simple condition of their repentance and confession; the everlasting worth of all human souls; the divineness of this present earth, and the glorious hope of immortality in the world to come, each and all we own as coming from him; and what is more, we adopt them, not as they are set forth in the creeds and confessions of earth; not as they come to us second-hand, from the councils and synods of fallible men, but in the beauty and sacredness of the Scripture words, and just as they fell all glowing from his own heaven-anointed lips. What more could be asked? If a man accepts all the doctrines of Calvin, do we hesitate to call him a Calvinist? If he says, I take all my theology from Swedenborg, is there any scruple about calling him a Swedenborgian? Why, then, should the Unitarians, who take all the doctrines of Christ in his own exact words, be denied the full name of Christians? Yea, does not the fact that we receive them without any intervention of theological skill give us, if anything, a superior claim to this title? Is it possible that any wisdom of men can put his truth in better form than that in which he has put it himself? Is not the fact that so many churches will not accept from their candidates the simple statement that they believe the New Testament, but insist on having them say they believe, also, in a man-made creed, whose words are entirely different from those of the Bible — an indication that, somehow, they feel that Christ is not enough? And the church which throws aside all human creeds, which says to every man who comes to it, declaring with his lips and life, I believe the gospel of Jesus Christ as taught by himself, it is all we want,— is there not, at least, a presumption that such a church is a little nearer his truth and his person, than the one which has to supplement his words with those of man's device? What does he himself tell us? "If ye continue in my word,"— most significant phrase; if ye continue, not in the words of Calvin, or Edwards, or Hopkins, or the Westminster Confession, or the Thirty-nine Articles, but " if ye continue in my word,"— in the truth as I have spoken it — " ye are my disciples, indeed." And, if he can look down now on earth and take cognizance of what is going on in his Church, what must be his surprise, what his sorrow,— a wound deep as any that was made on the cross,— to see that the one church of Christendom, which throws aside all other formularies from its confession, and bases itself simply on his own free gospel, should be the one that is especially refused his name?

There is one other test, furnished by the Bible — the most inward and severe of all — to which not only every denomination, but every soul must be brought at last, which it will not do ever to forget. Have we the spirit of Christ? Do we obey; do we live his truth? Are we bringing forth his fruits? Are we like him in character, in temper, in our treatment of others, in our daily walk and conversation? It is this which is the real criterion — the word of God sharper than a two-edged sword, piercing even to the dividing asunder of the soul and spirit, the joints and marrow. It is his own test. He himself says, "Ye shall know them by their fruits." "Not every one that saith unto me, Lord, Lord, shall enter into the kingdom of heaven, but he that doeth the will of my Father which is in heaven." " Herein is my Father glorified that ye bear much fruit, so shall ye be my disciples." "Ye are my friends, if ye do whatsoever I command." How plain and direct and crucial are these words. It matters not how great is a man's attachment to Christ, or how lofty he exalts his person, even though it be to the stature of Deity, or how implicitly he receives his truth, even though it be as the voice of God, if he is not Christ-like, if he does not do his will and bear his fruit, he is not in the innermost sense of all a Christian. And if he has this spirit, if he does live his life and his truth, then no matter whether he calls him God or man, master or brother; no matter whether he has never heard his name, he is in the divinest sense of all a Christian.

It is worth while to notice, moreover, that it is no imputed righteousness, no trusting in the merits of Christ to make up for the lack of our own, which can aid us in deserving the name, but what we ourselves have and are. The words read, "*Ye* shall know them by their fruits," "that *ye* bear much fruit," "*he* that keepeth his commandments," as if on purpose to show there can be no substitution. The religion of Christ in its very nature is intensely personal, something which goes to the very quick, something which takes hold as nothing else ever does of the spirit's life. To have it at all it must be not as a robe, a thing which can be put on and off, but as a part of the inmost self.

Far be it from us to claim that we bear all the fruits of the Gospel, that we are Christians in the full length and breadth of this glorious word. We know our short-comings too well, know that humility is one of the chiefest of those fruits; and the nearer we get to the perfect standard of Christ, paradoxical as it may seem, the farther do we find ourselves away. But it is the thing at which we aim, the very fault of which we are accused when it is said, as it so often is, that we hope to be saved by mere good morality. Yes, we do hope to be saved by good morality, the good morality of which Christ spake when he said, " He that doeth the will of my Father shall enter into the kingdom," the good morality which runs like a stream of silver through all the Sermon on the

Mount, the good morality of which he himself is evermore the great exemplar. And, though we come very short of his divine measure, very short even of our own ideal, yet when compared with those who are regarded and treated as Christians in other churches, do we so utterly fail as to be excluded altogether from the name? Look in the community around you. Do not Unitarians bear in any degree the fruits of the Gospel? Are they never honest and upright in their dealings? Do they never visit the fatherless and the widow, and keep themselves unspotted from the world? Is there no love to God and love to man among them? Are their purses and their hearts closed always to the cry of distress? And do they refuse absolutely to act on the great principles of the Gospel? If you were going to select a man to be the guardian of your children, or to take care of money for you, or to subscribe liberally for some public charity, or to put in any position where kindness of heart and unswerving honesty, and a high devotion to principle were needed, would you go only to those prayer meetings and communion tables from which all Unitarians are excluded in order to find him?

But, if the Unitarian faith does produce men endowed with these virtues, if they bear at least as much as other disciples the fruits of

A DEDICATION SERMON

the spirit, why should they not have equally with them the name and fellowship of Christians? Is it not a little queer, is it not apt to give the world's people occasion for sharp remarks, that the worst men should be so often treated as the best Christians, that the pillars of God's temple should be the rotten ones in a house of business, that the names placed on a church register, and supposed to be written on the Book of Life, should not be worth a straw when placed on a note of hand? Would it not be a thousand times more for the interests of religion and the honor of Christ and God, if, instead of making the distinction which now exists, the best Christian was made always and everywhere to signify the best man?

Our claim is based, however, not only on these tests furnished by the Bible, but, still further, on the great Protestant principle of the right of private judgment. It is well known that the Roman Catholic Church regards all denominations outside of her own body as heretical and unchristian. How do the rest of us maintain our position as against her? It can only be done on the broad ground that every church and every individual has the right to judge for itself and himself what is true and what is the best form of worship and ecclesiastical organization, responsible for their conclusions only to him, the great head of all things, to whom we are responsible for all our work. It is this which is the very Magna Charta of our Protestant liberties. It is adopted, in theory at least, by all of what are called the evangelical sects. And it is in the exercise of this right, and this alone, that they each and all have arrived at their present position, and in spite of their differences are able to claim and hold the name of Christian. And yet, what more have we Unitarians done than to plant ourselves and act, act to the fullest extent, on this same eternal right? We have gone to the Bible, gone to nature, gone everywhere that we could find one stroke of God's handwriting, one syllable that could illustrate the meaning of Christ, and out of it all made a judgment of what is the true faith and the true worship. Is there any doubt that we have tried hard and faithfully to get at the real facts? Have we not had among us ripe scholars, men not only with strong minds and deep, critical insight, but of fervent piety and spotless lives, and that spirituality and pureness of heart to which alone are promised the sight of God? Is there any special inducement why we should fall into error more than other men? Is not the absolute truth as precious to our hearts and lives, and as absolutely essential to our eternal welfare as to theirs? Why, then, have we not the same right to be re-

A DEDICATION SERMON

garded and treated as Christians as all other Protestant sects? How is it that any one has a right to use the principle rather than any other? Is it to be expected that we, any more than they, will give up what we believe is true, for the sake of agreeing with somebody else? And for any Protestant sect, or any number of them, to judge us and say we are not Christians, because we have not arrived at their conclusions, and, worse than all, to persecute us with the petty ways of excommunion and bad names, is it not denying the very principle on which we all stand, opening a mouth that would swallow up them as well as us? Is it not using the skin and voice, if not the teeth and claws, of the old dead lion they have tried so hard to kill?

Finally, we claim our place in the Church because the Unitarian denomination is equally essential with all the others to make up the completeness of Christ's body. The fact that our views, our work, our church organization is widely different from those of other sects, is so far from putting us beyond the pale of Christian fellowship, as to be one of the very best reasons why we should come within it. We do not pretend to have in ourselves all the elements of Christianity; do not pretend that our worship as it now is, can satisfy all the wants of the human heart. Denominations are all around us endowed with virtues and powers which are far in excess of ours. The Methodists have more of warmth and zeal; the Roman Catholics a better church organization; the Orthodox, doctrines which better reach peculiar minds, and the Episcopalians a richer and completer ritual. There are only a few things in which we can claim a preëminence, such, perhaps, as a severer and simpler faith, a clearer setting forth of our Saviour's humanity, the application of religion to the affairs of every day life, a new emphasis on the worth of this present world, and the best weapons with which to meet the assaults of atheism and scientific doubt. But what of this? Because we are all hands and no nerves, or, as is sometimes charged, all head and no heart, are we of no use at all? Are we not, therefore, a part of the body? Yea, because we are not heart and not nerves, because we are simply hands and head, are we not all the more needed to act in fellowship with the other parts? The fact is, there is no one denomination which can embrace the whole of Christ, no one worship which can possibly satisfy all hearts, any more than there is any one organ that can become the whole living body. The figure of Paul, in the twelfth chapter of Corinthians, is true to its very letter, one of the broadest and richest truths in all his teachings. We are many members all of

A DEDICATION SERMON

one body. The Methodist heart, the Episcopalian flesh, the Orthodox bones, the Roman Catholic stomach, cannot say one or all to the Unitarian hands, I have no need of you. God has given us each one his own special work. Even our little radical ganglions, which seem to be cut off from all the great centers, have their place which nothing else could fill. It is our very differences, not our likeness, which make our union of such absolute importance. The very fact that one can see and do and believe what the others never can, that is the strongest reason of our working together. So long as we have the one spirit thrilling from nerve to nerve, so long as we are faithful each to the use of his own talents and place, we are all a part of Christ, all " should have the same care one of another."

Here, then, we rest our claims to the name and the fellowship of Christians. How is it possible for any denomination to have those which are stronger in themselves, or which are founded more entirely in reason and in Scripture? They are what we ourselves are ready to grant, in all their fullness, to others. We hold out our hands to the right and the left. We look abroad over the whole range of Christendom, and wherever we see an earnest and true soul, wherever a human being touched in any degree with that glorious light which

1800 years ago broke over the mountain tops of Judea, there we own a fellow Christian, there see a life which is one with ours through our eternal head. It is the only broad and true platform, the only one which all humanity can ever stand upon, yea, the only one which is large enough to hold the whole of Christ. The great souls of all sects even now are planting themselves upon it. We have to-day, in spite of our visible exclusion, an unseen fellowship wide as the broad world, nerves of sympathy and feeling thrust through the stout walls of creed, and going over and around the deep gulf of rite and form, which thrill with the touch of kindred hearts in every church and every land. And the glorious hour shall come at last when all barriers shall be broken down and covered up; when each denomination, yea, and each soul, bearing still its own name and true to its own work and its own faith shall yet stand up together one loving band of Christian brothers, one mighty army of the living God.

My friends, it is in all the length and breadth of this glorious fellowship, is it not, that you now dedicate this house of worship? You come into it as a band of Christian worshipers. You claim your place and work here as a part of the great body of Christ. It is to be, first of all, before the name of any sect or party, a Christian temple. And you mean, so far as

your words and hearts can make it so, that it
shall stand in this community for all in our
faith which is loving and liberal, wide-reaching
and divine. Welcome within its doors the people of all parties and sects, of all forms and
faiths. Welcome, in exchange, within its desk,
the preachers of every church and creed, Ro-
manist or radical, orthodox or liberal, male or
female — all that will speak in the Saviour's
spirit and pray to the Christian's God. Welcome around its communion table and to its
warm right hand of fellowship all that will
come, even the poorest sinner and the vilest out-
cast, in the remembrance of our common Lord,
and with the hunger and thirst of his immortal
truth. Better that its walls should echo sometimes with error than with narrowness and
bigotry; better its aisles be trod with a want
of faith than a want of charity. He is no true
Unitarian who has a heart too small for the
whole of Christendom, even its darkest borders
and its roughest peaks. And any honest and
true man that God has been willing to anoint
and send forth into his own great temple of the
universe, it surely cannot be very offensive to
him that we, as the children of God, should
welcome, heart and soul, into ours.

But while the church is dedicated in the
largest Christian fellowship, we would not, by
any means, set it apart the less pronouncedly

for the worship and proclamation of our own Unitarian faith. We dedicate it to the One True God, Our Father in Heaven, the being whose highest name is Love, the object of all worship, and the source and center of all life. May he make it to be in very truth part of his own abode, a vestibule of that mighty temple whose arches spring beyond the beams of heaven's remotest star. May the light of his glory shine in at its windows, the voice of his truth echo along its walls, the beauty of holiness be the chief among its decorations. And when from week to week the sweet voice of the Sabbath bell shall swing forth its silver speech on the morning and the evening air, calling in his children from far and wide across its threshold, may it be to meet him here, the Everlasting Spirit, in awe and love and adoration.

Again, we dedicate it to Jesus Christ, to him who is revealed as our Lord and leader, our Saviour and Mediator, the head of the church, a son, but the Son of God. It is he who is the corner-stone upon which its unseen timbers are laid. It is his religion freed from all the traditions of men and in his own broad and liberal spirit that we would have proclaimed within its walls, proclaimed, it may be, with different tongues, but ever out of his love. And it is through his presence, subtler than all truth, that life which went out of his bleeding

A DEDICATION SERMON

heart on the cross to be the vital power of the broad world, that it is to be made a living church.

Once more, we dedicate it to humanity, that humanity in which Christ lived and for which he died; that humanity which, even in its lowest form, our faith teaches, is made now, as it was of old, in the image of God. Open its doors not only to all names and sects, but to all classes and all ranks of men and women; open its desk, too, open it wide and free, not only to all religious teachers, but to all human interests, all that are connected in any way with our broad religious life. It is the church, not less than the Sabbath, that is made for man. Temperance, education, civil equality, political morals, the rights of labor and race and sex, everything which bears on the spiritual well-being of any of God's children, is to go up to God in its prayers and be argued and enforced in its preaching. And if there is ever again a gospel reform despised and rejected of men, any that like the anti-slavery cause thirty years ago, is shut out of town hall, and school-house and lecture room, it is that chief of all that is to be welcomed and given its utterance within these walls.

And now, friends, it remains for you, day by day and year by year, to set the seal of your hearts and lives to these formal words of dedication. May you come always within its doors in the spirit of the largest Christianity, the spirit of love to God and faith in Christ and good-will to man. May the experience of a true religion within its walls, of sins forgiven, of faith strengthened, of sorrow consoled, of work inspired, of hopes brightened, invest it little by little with the memories and genius of a sacred place. May the buds of promise in your children bloom forth in its air to that fragrance and beauty which only the light and warmth of a true religion can give. May the ties which unite you as brothers and sisters, husbands and wives, be woven around in its prayers with the golden thread of celestial love. May you ripen with its truth into better men and women, into truer citizens, into kinder neighbors and friends, into greater fitness and strength for all the labors and trials of daily life. And when you go out of its doors for the last time, and look back upon it from the eternal world, may you be able, each one, to say, It has been to me indeed none other than the house of God and the gate of heaven.

V

A MINISTER'S IDEAL

A FAREWELL SERMON, HARTFORD, 1888

Not disobedient unto the heavenly vision.—Acts xxvi, 19.

DEAR FRIENDS: Meeting with you this morning for the last time in our relation as pastor and people, my thoughts go back irresistibly to the aspirations, enthusiasms and plans in the glow of which ten and a half years ago my work among you was entered upon. Not with any merely routine and perfunctory ministry in view, as you know, did I accept your invitation to take charge of the revived movement here, then in its fluid, unorganized condition, but under the inspiration of what to me was " a heavenly vision," as to the kind of work it was possible for its leader to do. It was a vision to which I had long wished an opportunity somewhere to be obedient. And the spring air was not more full of glint, hope and the mystic impulse towards summer's larger life, than my heart was that May morning when I stood before you for the first time as preacher, and saw in your eyes, as the sunshine does in the grass and flowers, the light reflected back which had come to mine. It is what to me is still a " vision splendid; " what with all its disappointments has never had the moment come when

> "At length the man perceives it die away,
> And fade into the light of common day;"

is what many another minister is sharing. And standing now in the late October of our pastoral year together, amid the few golden-rods and scattered star-flowers which seem the chief outcome of its toil, I want for this closing service, not despairingly or reproachfully, but with cheerfulness and good-will towards all, to set before you again, as the best review of my pastorate, the vision of a minister's and church's work, dawning upon me at the start, to which, through all these ten perplexing years, I have tried to be " not disobedient," and to express anew my faith in it even as a failure.

Its first distinctive feature relates to the kind of church that was to be built up, not its outward edifice alone, but with this its inner foundation, material and organization. The churches of the past have all had reference to past needs, and been shaped in accordance with a vision set forth in Scripture, rather than descending now fresh out of heaven. But, grand as they have been in themselves, and grand as their service has been for their time — a fact about them amid all their shortcomings that no Liberal will deny,—who even of their most devoted adherents can say that either outwardly or inwardly they are exactly adapted to the fresh work of our day, or who reasonably expect them so to be, any more than the weapons, the tools, and the governments of the past are for our present widely changed world? Taught by experience how hard it is to remold for new uses things which the traditions of ages have made sacred, and coming here to a fresh field and to material, as I supposed, that was plastic and unhampered, it seemed a splendid opportunity, without sacrificing the essential church idea, so precious an inheritance from the past, to break away from its old bonds, and to shape its rising form into harmony with great living needs — adapt it, as the scientific phrase is, to its environment.

With this principle as a guide, the aim has been from the start to base it not on a creed, a set of opinions about religion but on religion itself, love to God and love to man; to condition its membership even in this respect not on profession, a declaration of having attained religion, but on discipleship — a desire for its attainment; to make it up not of the rich, the educated and the respectable alone, or of the poor, the ignorant and despised merely, two things equally bad, but of all classes and conditions of people in their one relation of brotherhood as the children of God; to put no price on its privileges, so many dollars of money on so many square feet of opportunity, but to offer them, like the Gospel itself, to all who came, without money and without price; and to make its building not merely a house of worship to be opened once or twice on Sunday, but a divine workshop, to be opened every day of the week for every object that would make its members better, a class-room for study, and a larger home, where the stranger in the city, and the young man and woman, now with only a saloon or a cold lodging-room to live in, could find books and games and social warmth, and assistance in all the relations of life.

As regards Unitarianism, the aim has been to build it up in it not as a saving dogma, but as a helping idea, and as meaning not only the unity of God, but with this, the unity of man, — all nations, all religions and all interests. The brotherhood of different churches has been a part of its ideal; the divinity of other religions outside of Christianity an element of its Christianity; the sacredness of all honest employments and of all honest thinking, one of its own most sacred thoughts. And while setting forth with all emphasis and clearness its own convictions, it has believed in remembering the beliefs of the unbelievers, and has taken as its motto, equally imperative in both its parts, " Free speech in the pulpit, free judgment in the pews."

Especially has it had in view the broader Unitarianism of its being a church, not for the rich or poor, the high or low, the laboring man or the employer alone, but a common ground on which all the different classes of society, believing in religion at all, could meet together as equals, and in its mighty heart-tie find an offset to the influences which are at work everywhere else to drive them apart. We all know how it is in the world at large. With the use of machinery and the formation of great corporations, employer and employed no longer come into those direct human relations with each other which once did so much to unite them — in many cases never look into each other's faces, or know each other's names. With the filling up of our large cities, the rich have gradually clustered into one set of streets and the poor into another, destroying all their old neighborly interest in each other's welfare. Labor and capital with their repeated struggles have come to look on each other as only inevitable antagonists. Fashionable society is drawing its dividing lines more and more rigidly every year between its favorite few and its unrecognized many. Even religion itself has its costly churches for the rich and its humble mission chapels for the poor, its saints of one faith in one denominational fold, and its saints of another in a different one. And in all our great communities there are thousands of people even now as divided from each other as the dwellers on different continents, and as hostile to each other as foes on battle-fields. It is these class divisions and antagonisms, these sectionalisms, not between North and South, East and West, but between street and street, house and house, that are the danger and problem of our land today; these, if allowed to go on, which are sure in the future to blossom into flowers of blood and to ripen into fruits of revolution, as horrible as any that the world ever yet has seen.

How are these divisions to be met? how the feelings between them to be overcome? The mere preaching of love as a duty, first to one and then to the other, will not do it; markets and workshops have no power to bring it about; and railroads and telegraphs and ships of commerce, so mighty to unite nations in a closer union, operate only to drive classes farther apart. What they need is to come oftener together on mutual ground, to know each other in some other and higher relations than those of business, and to feel the impulse gleaming from eye to eye and throbbing from heart to heart

A MINISTER'S IDEAL

of some common, overmastering interest. There is only one thing which has even a tendency in this direction, not a credal, but a heart religion; only one place where there is even a possibility of its being realized, not an exclusive, but a wide open church. And who will say that such a bringing of them together is not a worthy experiment for religion to try? who that in every community there ought not to be at least one place where the representatives of all its classes and all its ranks can meet each other from time to time, remembering only that they are all alike high born in being the children of one Eternal Father, and all alike rich in having one common human nature? who say that the man who tries even in one case to realize such a vision of the church, no matter how opposite its results may at first be, is working on false lines of human need, or outside of the religion of him, who, though incidentally a divider, had for his foremost aim the making of his disciples all brethren?

Building up a religious society, however, to be helpful to its own members, no matter how broadly so, can of necessity be only one part of any true minister's ideal. Religion is altruistic all through, as imperatively so with relation to churches as in dealing with individuals. Its law is everywhere, "Whosoever will find his life shall lose it, and whosoever will lose his life

for my sake shall find it;" and the more it
holds to breadth and liberality as golden doctrines the more imperative its law becomes to
send them forth outside of itself in golden
deeds. It is a principle which all churches in
all ages, to their honor be it said, have in some
form recognized, all of them counting the whole
world as indeed their field. But their aim, for
the most part, has been not to save the world as
such — with their doctrine of its being under
the Divine curse a hopeless task — but to save
as many as possible of its individual souls out
of its darkness into the spirit world; and all
their schemes of redemption, so wonderfully de-
vised and so fervently preached, have had reference only to individual sins and been such as
only individuals could apply. Gradually, however, in our time there has come to the church,
some parts of it, a larger conception of what
it is to save the world — the saving of the thing
itself, its institutions, its governments, its
homes, its businesses, its whole social structure,
the saving of it now and here as the kingdom
of God on earth. It does not despise or ignore the saving of individual souls; but as the
farmer who would have good fruit does not attempt to cure directly his knurly and worm-
eaten apples, but goes to work on the tree
which bore them, grafting, pruning, digging
around and protecting that, till he makes it

bear naturally only good fruit, so the larger church idea goes to work on this great world tree, developing and nourishing all its parts so as to make it bear of itself, to begin with, only saved souls. Its religion is sociological rather than theological. It preaches not so much repentance as reform, not so much doctrine as duty, not so much rites as rights. A Baptist brother went to Robert Ingersoll and asked if he believed in immersion. " Yes," was the reply, " if taken with plenty of soap "— profane but after all expressing exactly the new religion's plan of salvation, the mingling of the heavenly cleansing with a large degree of earthly purification. It would save bodies as well as souls; save them out of sickness as well as sin; save them to good wages as well as to good works. Its prayer is, Thy kingdom come; its doctrine of the incarnation, Christ in the naked, hungry, sick and imprisoned. And of the food and drink given even to the lowest leper, it says:

"This crust is his body broken for thee,
This water his blood that died on the tree;
And his Holy Supper is kept indeed
In whatever we share with another's need."

It is such a conception of the church's work, as indeed a heavenly vision, that I have set before you and tried myself to be obedient to.

Believing intensely in reform as the gospel word of to-day, I have not sought to make any one of its phases a hobby, not believed in having the church take the place of the Temperance Society, the Woman's Suffrage Association, or the Labor Movement, but have tried rather to bring it into fellowship with them and with all organizations for the suppression of evil, counting them all as the secular branches of the one true church, and to supplement their own forces with all the inspiration of religion's motive power. There is nothing in all the world to-day which, it seems to me, is so divine, so direct a continuance of the Scripture's Holy Ghost, as the reformatory spirit. It does indeed take a great many queer forms, drives some men to be cranks, and some crazy, and some into movements which violate every principle of sound philosophy and of practical common sense,— I acknowledge that as freely as anyone can. It is like the inventive genius of our country, filling its Patent Office at Washington side by side with models which have proved of enormous practical value, with others of perpetual motion devices, self-acting steamboat propellers, and the like, that dynamite itself would not make go; is like the rain, which comes down from heaven, much of it falling on the parched field and making the drooping plant revive, but a vast amount also, into muddy gutters, on barren rocks, down the necks of belated travelers, and on the waste of ocean. But as both invention and the rain, taken as wholes, are of priceless worth, the one giving us such grand instruments of human progress as the locomotive engine, the telegraph and the printing press, the other all the wealth of the harvest field, so the reformatory spirit of our age, amid all its cranky devices, flying machines in the realm of morals, Keeley motors for running nations, and showers of philanthropy poured into social gutters, is nevertheless to-day our human world's most precious hope. Its motive power is altruism, doing for others, in its truest form. Wealth, honor, power, selfish good of any kind, is the very last thing its subjects can hope to get from its pursuit; poverty, persecution and ridicule,—

"A weary work of tongue and pen,
A long, harsh strife with strong-willed men,"

their almost sure reward. Whittier's words of one are true of all:

"Forego thy dreams of lettered ease,
   Put thou the scholar's promise by;
The rights of man are more than these!
   He heard and answered, 'Here am I!'"

And to attempt to have the Christian Church share in such a spirit, the very soul of all religion, to admit its advocates on to its platform, and to have a word of kindness in their trouble for even the wildest of its workers, is it unworthily a part of being obedient to the heavenly vision of its work?

But especially have I believed in that reform which underlies and includes all others, the reform of society itself. With all its glory, all the contributions to it of the ages past, who will say that the social structure is yet perfect; who claim it has reached its final form; who deny that in it are some enormous imperfections? And, if it is indeed to be improved, if we can expect saved souls to grow on it only in proportion as it is itself saved, who does not see that the very first thing to be done with it is to study its laws, find out how it is put together, and apply its remedies not empirically by administering haphazard pills of goodness, but scientifically, as the wise physician does to the human body. It is in this sense that I am a Socialist, a believer in making society better, and proud of the name. There is nothing in all this universe which is more worthy of study; no shining star that is fuller of splendor; nothing in the realm of nature that more fully illustrates the process of evolution; hardly the soul itself that is more alive with God. Let any one read the first two chapters in part second of Spencer's great work on Sociology, and he will find that romance itself will hardly compare with it in fascination. It is the anatomy and physiology of humanity's vast body, the resultant thus far of all history, the foundations already laid, out of which the kingdom of God on earth is to come. To study its costly past is the surest safeguard against the madness of attempting to break it up for reconstruction; to study its mighty possibilities the surest safeguard against the equal madness of attempting to keep it where it is. And the church, the minister, the men who are going to live in it, going to take part in its affairs, going to help bring out of it saved souls,— if there is anything they need to be, is it not Socialists?

Yet while sympathizing with this larger work of helping society as a whole, I have tried not to forget that the Christian ideal includes, also, the humbler one of helping the weak, poor, sick and wronged of its individual members, the men and women who are suffering to-day with its imperfections, and who cannot wait to share in its far-off completion. All churches, thank God, are giving them something of this help, have branched out into something a great deal wider for their good than merely their technical soul-saving, but, alas, how often is it confined even now to what are respectable and established philanthropies; and how many are the wounded travelers, some with the worst wounds of all, that its priests and Levites are still passing by on the other side, or as Samaritans never healing with a drop of that oil and wine they need most of all, a little heart-help. A man charged with a desperate crime was being taken by the police through one of our large cities. The crowd was terribly excited against him, and followed his steps with loud threats of vengeance. He answered them back with like ferocity,— seemed the last person for anything but hanging to draw the wickedness out of. Just then a little newsboy ran up to him with a copy of his morning paper, exclaiming cheerfully, " Here, boss, take this; I'm sorry I can't do something more for a fellow everybody is against, but I am glad to do this." The man burst into tears. " They are the first words of kindness," said he, " I have had spoken to me in forty years; and oh, if I could only have heard a few such before, I never should have come to this." Forty churches in that city, and a little despised newsboy the first person in forty years to speak to one of its unfortunates a word of kindness! And how many such wretches there are in the world, not only with the crowd against them, but under the ban of philanthropy itself, for whom a little humanity would do what no harshness ever can. I have no maudlin sympathy with vice and crime, as such — have a great deal of doubt as to the value of any mercy human or divine that would remit a deserved punishment, and of any benevolence, official or private, which takes merely the form of a gift to the needy. But I do believe with all my heart in the value of sympathy with them as men and women; do believe with all my conscience in the benevolence of righting their wrongs, giving them a fair chance in the world, and helping them to help themselves. When I entered the ministry, it was with a solemn vow that however much I might fail in the religion of piety towards God, about my capacity for which I always felt dubious, I never would lose a chance of being true to the religion of humanity, and of humanity especially in its more humble and neglected forms; and it has been in obedience to such a purpose that I have put in, from time to time, an earnest plea — as some have thought, too earnest — for such wounded travelers along the road of life as the enslaved negro, the persecuted Mormon, the despised Salvationist, the panic-hung anarchist, and the toiling men and women at our own doors, some of them wounded themselves in their frantic efforts to heal the wounds of their fellow-men. Nearly a year has now passed since I preached a sermon with reference to one such group, so under the ban of all society that even philanthropy itself went by them with averted face. I did it, not as a believer in anarchy, but as a believer in Christianity; did it as the little newsboy gave his paper, not out of any liking for crime, but as an act of kindness to human beings everybody else was against; did it because I felt that in a panic to vindicate the name of law a wound was being made on the soul of law such as not all the dynamite in the world could inflict. You know the cyclone of criticism it brought upon us, pastor and people both, the one for giving and the other for upholding such outrageous obedience to the Sermon on the Mount. It has brought me, also, a multitude of letters from all over the land, some written in tears of gratitude from men whom society's threats had hitherto only provoked to worse threatenings back; some testifying from long acquaintance with the executed men to their real innocence and to their high personal worth; and some from persons of high literary and social standing endorsing heartily the position of the sermon with regard to the utter injustice of their treatment,— all throwing a flood of direct light on what was spoken of at first only in the dimness of faith. And to-day, looking at the whole matter in this clearer light, I want to say, not out of persistency in a course once taken whether right or wrong, but from a calm review of all the principles involved and of all which being true to them has cost, that in those words of kindness so unwise from any earthly standpoint, and so fatal to any earthly success, I can but think that my ministry, often, alas, so far away, reached, if ever, the nearest to its own ideal, carried a ray of gospel light the most widely to hearts usually shut against it, and came, if at all, the nearest to his teachings who said: "Inasmuch as ye have done it unto the least of these my brethren, ye have done it unto me," and who himself on the cross, and as almost his last utterance for earth, spoke a word of kindness to a fellow criminal.

A third field my ministry has tried to cover is the practical use of scientific truth as an adjunct to the truths of religion. There is no other department of knowledge which in our day has had such wonderful development, no other which has given such a new and distinctive character to our nineteenth century civilization, no other which has had such tremendous bearings on every phase of thought as this of natural science, and, especially, of natural science as it is summed up and unified in the grand new teachings of evolution.

It is of no use to say that such a subject has no place in a Christian pulpit, and no message for an audience of common people hungering for the bread of life. It is the common people, as they did the gospel of old, who hear it gladly. There is no keeping it away from their minds; no darkening of church windows that can shut it out; no bars even of Presbyterian creeds which can prevent its coming in. It is in the very air they breathe; it is like all great movements of thought, something to which not a few great minds alone, but our race has come,

"Swayed by vaster ebbs and flows than can be known to you and me."

Believing in it most intensely as a part of God's revelation to-day, a vision not the less out of heaven because coming through the scriptures of rock and clod, and by the prophet tongues of brute and bird, I have not sought either on the one hand to put it in the place of the old revelation, or on the other to reconcile it with its mere formal letter, but have accepted it first in all its wholeness as scientific truth, and then used it as such to lengthen, broaden and fill out the old faith, as Jesus did his new gospel teachings to fulfil the old Mosaic law,— have tried to show how it has made the natural more full of miracle than the supernatural ever was; given in its long history of man's development a new conception of his worth and dignity; built on the great natural doctrine of the survival of the fittest, when the proper time came, the great religious doctrine of care for the unfittest; opened a new world for aspiration to mount up into; established

A MINISTER'S IDEAL

Christianity as a necessary stage in the unfolding of religious thought; and, most precious of all, brought Deity out of the far-away theological heavens where the Church had so long placed him to be this world's infinite, all pervading Presence,—

" Sent the shadow of himself, the Boundless, through the human soul,
Boundless inward in the atom, Boundless outward in the whole."

It is a use of the new truth, which, even as regards the Church itself, has seemed to me far more likely to prove for its ultimate advantage than any strengthening of it to resist its influence possibly could. Years ago when I was in Texas, a steamboat captain who had run his vessel on a trading trip two hundred miles up the Brazos River, had the water suddenly fall under it, as, in Texas, rivers are apt to do, and found himself caught fast on the flats. A great drought ensued and the vessel lay there for three years, the grass growing down to its keel, and the very alligators laughing at its fix. Then suddenly there came a terrible flood. The great deeps seemed to be broken up. Houses and barns built on the solid earth were washed away; other boats moored in the river swamped and sunk. What did this captain do? Crammed his boiler with oil and tar, cut his moorings, and with tiller in hand dashed down the rushing stream, making its very violence his friend, and in three days was on the broad sea with fifty fathoms of water under his keel, laughing at alligators and drouths. The world's church-ship starting years ago on a trip for souls along the stream of the old religion, has had here in our modern civilization its waters gradually go from under it, and finds itself hemmed in with the shoals of doubt. There has been a drouth for ages on its banks,— no showers of miracle, no rains of the supernatural, none at least it would let flow into its stream; and the ship in its fixedness has become to many an object of ridicule and scorn. Suddenly from up among the mountains there shoots down this great flood of scientific truth. Is it not equally wise for the church to do as the steamboat did, give itself, with steam and tiller, to the swelling floods, and let them bear it, as they will, to where, fearless of all drouths, it will have under its keel the fathoms of nature's infinite sea? And is it not indeed a worthy ambition for even the humblest of its crew, to help in using thus, what is likely to prove at last, religion's divinest gift?

And now, friends, turning from this ideal of a minister's and church's work, so full of grand possibilities, to what has been actually accomplished by us for its realization, how meager and imperfect, outwardly at least, the result is,— our beautiful church edifice, a little consecrated band within it, and here and there in the community at large, some soul, perhaps, stirred to a nobler life, but so far as the building of a large and prosperous society with a wide, visible influence on the world's affairs is concerned, what must honestly be acknowledged as almost nothing at all. How it might have been in the midst of more congenial surroundings and with less opposition on the part of some in our own ranks it is not needful now to consider, not certainly in any spirit of reproach against them. I take on myself the full responsibility for what has happened, both the holding up to you of the ideal promised land as an object to be started for out of the old Egypt, and the failing to bring you through the intervening wilderness to its shining shore. The fact is the vision has been too high for the viewer; the Canaan too far off and too glorious for the seeker. And it is to this cause, to its imperfect Moses, rather than to any opposing Ogs, Sihons, Hittites, and Jebusites that the coming short of it must be ascribed.

But meager as this outward result is, as compared with the ideal started for, I do not think we need look back on our efforts for it with one particle of regret or shame. To have struggled for a noble thing is in itself a success. As Lowell says:

> "Not failure but low aim is crime."

If our movement is a dead thing, it is dead on the field of honor. Whatever of weakness or mistake or want of shrewdness and tact may have been put into it, not one word or act or method have I ever sought to help it with that will not bear the fullest light even of religion's day. Prouder am I to have failed, if failure it is, in striving after such a church than I could be to have succeeded in building up after any meaner pattern the finest palace that wealth and fashion ever crammed.

> "'Tis not for heights of victory won,
>   But those we tried to gain,
> Will come our gracious Lord's well done,
>   And sweet effacing rain."

Defeat is not inconsistent with noble service, or lessening numbers with larger work. Victor Hugo tells the story in his "Legends of the Ages," that in one of the most decisive battles of modern Europe, a detachment of a hundred men was stationed in an old cemetery with orders to load and fire in one certain direction as fast as possible till night should come, and to hold the place at any cost. No position could apparently be humbler or less inspiring.

They could see no foe, all around them being thickest mist and smoke, get no encouragement from the result of their firing, the whole field being hid in darkness; and yet their place, though so humble, was swept repeatedly by the enemy's shot and shell, till every tomb had a dead body above it as well as one beneath its sod. Nevertheless obedient to orders and faithful to a soldier's grand ideal of duty, all day long out of ever thinning ranks they loaded and fired with what seemed to be an utter waste of ammunition, into what looked to be only the darkness. At last in the glimmering twilight a general rode up. "Who holds this redoubt?" An old sergeant limped forward. "Such and such a company of his majesty's regiment." "What!" exclaimed the officer, looking round, "How many of you are left?" "Myself, sire, wounded, and one man." "Report to-night at my tent and receive your promotion and your medals of honor," said the general, uncovering his head; "for know you, comrades, your unflinching fire all day long out of this old graveyard has raked the enemy's most cherished position, enabled our armies to win a glorious victory, and saved France!" So in the great battles of right and wrong, truth and error, on the broad field of the religious ages. It is the fidelity, pluck and perseverance of many a little band of men and women stationed, as you have been, in positions outwardly as obscure and humble as that old graveyard, and firing, as you have done, their whole lives long with what seems to be only a waste of devotion and into what looks to be only empty space, they, possibly, who at the falling of the last dim twilight will be found to have done the most to win the Lord's day and to save his kingdom.

> " So failure wins; the consequence
> Of loss becomes its recompense;
> And every wish for better things
> And undreamed beauty nearer brings."

Friends, it is in this faith and hope as to the final outcome of our church work, that I speak to you, one and all, my words of parting and farewell. If there have at times been opposition, misunderstanding and unfairness towards me from any, either here or in the community at large, I have been too much taken up with the beauty and grandeur of our work to have them awaken in me against their givers one particle of personal resentment,— have looked upon them as only the necessary friction that all undertakings a little ahead of their times have to encounter; and now in this closing hour, I wash even the remembrance of them from my mind, as at the close of day we

all do the stains of toil from our hands. And
you who have shared with me this grand vision,
worked with me so faithfully for its realization, and in many a dark night and hard struggle stood by me so unfaltering in its defense,
how can I thank you warmly enough for your
sympathy and support! It is hard every way
to break up the relation between us, glorified
to some of you by its association with loved
ones passed now from earth; hard most of all
to give up the joy and thrill of our comradeship
in struggling and suffering for a noble cause,
the sweetest, in some respects, that life has to
offer. But my interest and sympathy will be
with you and with your work as warmly in the
future as they have been in the past. Go on,
keeping still in sight the star which has so
long been our guide. May another and better
leader soon be found to conduct you from the
victory of failure to the sweeter, if not
grander, victory of success. Be assured that
the misunderstandings about us in the community, often among those we have tried the
hardest to befriend, will give place at last to
a knowledge of how broad and humanitarian,
how Christian, also, our aims have been. And
when the day of numbers, strength and popular
favor comes, as it surely will, and the church
we have dreamed of becomes the church you

have realized, all I ask is that you will remember kindly the one, nay, I ought rather to say the twain, who in your night of weakness were "not disobedient to its heavenly vision."

VI

THE HUMANITARIAN SIDE OF RELIGION

A FAREWELL SERMON, SHARON, 1904

He that loveth not his brother whom he hath seen, how can he love God whom he hath not seen? And this commandment have we from him, that he who loveth God love his brother also.—I John iv, 20, 21.

PARISHIONERS AND FRIENDS: Standing before you to-day for the last time in our relation as pastor and people, it is naturally not an occasion in which to set forth any new line of thought or form of duty. I want, rather, to gather up the threads of what I have been saying these four years of our intercourse into a single knot of truth that I can leave with you as a deepened impression,—want to speak again the one distinctive word that God has spoken to me as the leading word of our time, by which I would have you remember me when I have passed away beyond all speech. And that word is Man; that truth, the Humanitarian side of Religion.

There is a sense in which all religion is humanitarian. It is all meant, even its most theistic parts, not for angels, not for saints, especially, not for any select few recipients anywhere, but for men, all men. It appeals to our human nature; to what is our human nature not the less, because some of it is to its spiritual side. And all its virtues, all the faculties it calls into action, love, reverence, awe, adoration, as well as righteousness, sympathy, benevolence, helpfulness, are human virtues and human faculties.

There is a sense, also, in which all religion is theistic and spiritual. God is not a being who is widely separate from man and earth. All spirits are emanations of his spirit; all laws his laws; all goodness, doubly sweet in its human embodiments, the manifestation of his goodness; the finite love which bends over the cradle, a spark of the Infinite Love which bends over the universe. It is only by knowing man that we can know spirit and know God.

" No one could tell me where my soul might be:
  I searched for God, but God eluded me:
  I sought my brother out and found all three."

Humanitarian work is a form, sometimes the best form, of heavenly worship, even as the Bible says: " Pure ritual " — for that is what the word translated " religion " here means —

"pure ritual is to visit the fatherless and widows in their affliction and to keep one's self unspotted from the world." And everywhere, it is not the tools with which it is done, but the temper, that makes our toil divine; not Christ alone, but God in Christ, who says, "Inasmuch as ye have done it unto the least of the hungry and thirsty and sick and naked and imprisoned, ye have done it unto me."

But while these two sides of religion thus overlap each other in their full development, like north and south, east and west, humanitarianism is distinctively the side of it which begins with the relations, ethical and philanthropic, that man has with man, aiming at their improvement, and which reaches through them up to God, leaving to Theism the relations, doctrinal and devotional, which man has with Deity and which reach through him down to earth.

It is a religion whose starting-point is the relation man has with himself and with his own immediate family. A great deal of nonsense has been written about doing for self as necessarily the opposite of doing for humanity. Humanity is not a species of being separate from self, but is a species made up of selves,— its cult, at the start, not a religious quantity circumferenced by the race, but a religious quality centered in the individual; not a Mrs. Jellyby working for a Borioboola Gha in Central Africa to the neglect of herself and her own home, but a Mrs. Jellyby that as a vital part of its field includes herself and her belongings. It is only the full fountain which can make the full stream; only by knowing what the individual family is that there can be any meaning to the phrase, the family of man; only by a person's being strong and wise and good himself that he can help others to be strong and wise and good; and even to make for others a sacrifice of self that is of any value, there must first be a value of some kind stored up in the sacrificed self.

But how is a man thus to build up himself and his family? He cannot work on them directly, as he does on a house or a piece of furniture; he can do it only by working on something outside of himself and them. As all streams come from fountains, so all fountains in their turn come from streams. The body is made strong by acting on other bodies. To earn a living for himself and his own family a man must do something toward a living for other men and other families; to have humanitarianism within as a quality, must have a humanitarianism without that takes in the race. Reciprocity is the statesmanship of the soul, as it should be of the nation.

THE HUMANITARIAN SIDE 393

" There's not a blessing individuals find
But somehow leans and hearkens to mankind";

not a blessing that leans and hearkens to mankind that does not somehow the individual find, so beautifully do these two apparently contradictory parts of a humanitarian religion play into each other's hands.

Beyond self and family it is a religion which next reaches out into what is literally the neighborhood. Full of practical wisdom is the Old Testament injunction, Thou shalt love thy neighbor as thyself. Humanity, in its meaning of the race, is too large a thing for the mind at once to take in; love to man as a species what no heart, to begin with, is able to feel. But our neighbor,— he is a being we can see and know, he a part of humanity we are brought face to face with every day, he the one that without any contribution-box or missionary society we can help. And whatever he is in himself, Jew or Gentile, Catholic or Protestant, black or white, rich or poor, educated or ignorant, and, in its last stretch, saint or sinner, our religion on its humanitarian side should bring us into some sort of kindly relations with him,— a courteous greeting in the street, an exchange of visits now and then in the home, an avoidance, so far as possible, of all annoyance to him in the way of disagreeable sights

and sounds, and an acting to him the part of a
Good Samaritan when he falls among the
thieves of sickness, misfortune, and want.
The neighborhood is the Sunday-school room
of humanitarian religion, the distance between
its houses the base line of the triangulation in
the survey which is to take in the race; being
neighborly the opening chapter in the great
book of being humane.

It is a religion which finds for itself a large
field in the business world. It is not ashamed
to put on the merchant's coat, the mechanic's
blouse, the farmer's hat, the sailor's jacket;
and it considers it no desecration to make the
daybook and ledger a part of its sacred Scriptures. It does not quite include, not at least
to my conception of it, what is ordinarily expounded as Socialism. To be sure, it believes
in union, in partnership, in co-operation; but
it believes, also, in individualism, in competition, and to some extent in antagonism,— finds
these forces all at work in the human body, in
the starry skies, everywhere in nature as the
agents by which evolution is carried on and
progress brought about; and it sees no reason
why they should not be recognized as equally
helpful in the business world.

But it does not believe, any more than Socialism does, in any cut-throat competitions, or in any antagonisms that would destroy or maim or even weaken those engaged in them, whose efforts, however opposite, are honorably and honestly made. Its fundamental principle is that all business is itself normally a form of beneficence, a far better form of it than charity ever is, a form in which wages, salaries, prices, payments are but counters in the great world-game of mutual service. The articles in which it deals — significant name — are all goods, excluding, therefore, all shams, all speculations, all trades like liquor-selling which harm humanity. Its competitions are to see which party to them will do its best; its antagonisms, like the opposing muscles of the human body, those which help men forward, or of the jaws, which better bite off their food; its good bargains, bargains which are equally good for both sides; and commerce and the commercial spirit, in spite of their enormous evils, it believes in as the best missionaries God has on this earth to-day.

It has nothing to say against wealth, even excessive wealth, when it is honestly earned. If a man does society a million dollars' worth of service, it sees no reason why he should not have a million dollars' worth of reward. But if other men, laboring-men especially, have been partners with him in the service, then it holds that labor ought first of all to be a sharer with him in the returns.

But labor as well as capital has its humanitarian duties,— has no more right to be cut-throat or tyrannical or over-selfish than its antagonist has. The man who exacts four dollars a day for two dollars' worth of work is just as dishonest in principle as the one who takes four millions where only half of them are his due. Watered toil is as bad morally as watered stock. The Golden Rule is none too golden to be kept amid the dust and dirt of the factory. A form of faith as saintly in the kitchen as in the kirk is faithful service; and whatever question there may be about the theological value of good works, there is none anywhere about the humanitarian value of good work.

Passing on from the business world to what is known more distinctively as the social world, what does humanitarianism demand with regard to the different classes, sects, and races into which it is divided, and with regard to their relations with each other, often full of inequalities and bitterness? Not, certainly, any revolutionary action; not, on the one hand, that they should be utterly abolished and society reduced all to one dead level, or, on the

other, that there should be established any
forced and arbitrary equality of their rights
and intercourse. The social structure, with
all its enormous evils, is, as Herbert Spencer
has so admirably shown, one of the most beautiful and blessed of all the institutions humanity knows, its diversities of class, sect, and race
a part of that wonderful variety with which
nature everywhere, from flowery field to starry
sky, from elemental atoms to starry souls, is so
graciously filled, a variety which adds not only
to the world's esthetic charm, but is, also, absolutely essential for the doing of its varied
work.

" Order is Heaven's first law, and, this confessed,
  Some are and must be greater than the rest."

And to wipe out these diversities, make all
classes, all races, all religions, one class, one
race, one religion, even the best, would be as
bad socially as it would be physically — using
Paul's figure — to have the body all eye, all
ear, or even all brain.

No; what is needed is not revolution but reform, not the unity of sameness but the unity
of spirit, not equality of rank but equality of
opportunity, not that the members shall have
their treatment determined by the outward
badge of their class or race or religion, but
that they shall have it correspond with what

they are in themselves individually as human beings. Whether or not a man is " a white man " is to be answered not by whether or not he has a white skin, but by whether or not he has a white soul. It is here that the South makes its great mistake in the treatment of its colored citizens. To vary Pope's famous line a little,

" Honor and shame from no complexion rise."

If Booker Washington is inwardly good presidential company, there is no reason why Booker Washington should not sit outwardly at a presidential table. When Fred Douglass, one afternoon before the war, was walking down Broadway in New York, and everybody was shunning him, an officious individual, with a patronizing air, stepped up to him, exclaiming, " Here, Douglass, I am not ashamed to be seen walking with a nigger; come with me." " Indeed! " replied Douglass, drawing himself off, " and who may you be that a nigger shouldn't be ashamed to be seen walking with you? " There is no race, no religion, no class, that has a monopoly of personal worth. There are multitudes of black men that are more manly, more cultivated, more fitted for the best society, than multitudes of white men; multitudes of heathen who are more saintly, more humane, more fit for heaven than multitudes of Christians.

"What can ennoble sots, or slaves, or cowards?
Alas! not all the blood of all the Howards."

And such being the case, why should not each one be treated according to what he is, rather than according to what he is labeled,— the Guinea man ranked by his guinea worth, rather than by his Guinea stamp?

But this is not all. Humanitarianism has something to say about the treatment of the worst members, as well as the best ones, of its social classes,— about the sinful, the sick, the poor, the ignorant, the wronged, and the weak of our race,— believes in associating with them even more than with the best as a healer, helper, sympathizer, and friend,— would lift them up not by any outward arbitrary raising to a higher level, but by making them inwardly capable and fit to rise of themselves to any height. It beholds in every human being, beneath all the guises of ignorance, poverty, and sin, the splendor and the worth of an immortal soul. It finds its Christ located not on the throne of God, not amid the hills of Galilee alone, but in all the hungry and thirsty and naked and sick and imprisoned of earth.

Better still, it seeks to save men not only out

of sin and sickness and ignorance and wrong, but to save them from ever getting into them at first. While it carries at the bottom of its medicine-chest the pounds of cure, it carries at the top of it the ounces of prevention. It does not wait till the traveler has been assailed and left half dead, before going to his assistance, but wherever possible it thrashes the thieves before they have a chance to make the assault,— does not wait, if it can help it, till men are made drunkards before trying to make them sober, but would shut up the saloon first that tempts them to drink; and, better even than this, it aims in its highest ideal to have the road down to Jericho, and all the roads in Jericho, and all the roads of earth everywhere, so civilized and safe, and all the travelers on them so inwardly armed, that they can be trod without even the thought of thieves.

Turning now from the social world and its divisions to the political world and its different parts, who shall say that the same great humanitarian principles that apply to individuals and occupations and classes and races do not logically apply to kingdoms and nations and states and governments?

As regards patriotism, the narrower special love the citizen has for his country, love to man does not interfere with it, does not involve

THE HUMANITARIAN SIDE 401

the wiping out of political divisions, any more than it does with individual welfare and social distinctions. His country is a person's larger self,— is not a separate entity from humanity, but one of its members; and to love it and labor to build it up, the same as with his lesser self, is the necessary condition of enabling it to do its part for other countries and for the world at large.

How is it to be built up,— how the citizen show it his love? Of course in the case of a country a good deal of the work is to be done directly on itself. Its material interests are to be labored for, its institutions developed, its politics kept pure, its government supported, its liberties maintained, its conduct, when right, applauded, its conduct, when wrong, just as surely condemned, and, crowning all else, that without which wealth and institutions and government and liberties are all in vain, the manhood and womanhood of its citizens, the things which constitute them a worthy part of humanity, are to be unfolded.

But this alone is not enough. No nation ever reached its highest well-being by acting wholly on itself. Altruism is needed here for precisely the same reason, and it works on precisely the same principle, as in individual self-culture. It has to benefit other nations to get the highest benefit for itself — has to trade with them in goods, exchange with them ideas, share their discoveries in science, visit in their homes, get the stimulus which comes from competition with them in arts and manufactures,— have now and then a great World's Fair in which each shall show its best. And for this reason all tariffs, all custom-houses, all barriers of every kind to the freest intercourse are at once unpatriotic and unhumanitarian. No one nation can build up its own prosperity by tearing that of others down. To have profitable trade there must be money and goods and profit on both sides. And to have the great body of humanity all healthy, there must be, the same as with the physical body, the circulation of its life-blood without restriction to all its parts.

War waged in self-defense humanitarianism cannot, I suppose, wholly condemn. To be sure, all war, even defensive war, is hell. But there are different depths of hellishness even in hells; and tyranny, the loss of self-government, and the sight of homes ravaged and loved ones slain,— these are depths to it deeper than even the horrors of the battle-field.

"The sheathed blade may rust with darkest sin."

But humanitarianism does say that even defensive wars should be entered upon only when every possible expedient for peace has been exhausted; and all other wars, and all things that lead up to other wars, no matter under what pretense they are waged of extending over a people civilization, religion, good government, or even of opening a highway for the world's commerce,— all such wars it denounces as at once criminal aggressions and political blunders. Liberty, liberty to be themselves, liberty to work out their own destiny in their own way, is its watchword for all people and all lands. And arbitration, the gathering of all nations, the weak as well as strong, into the one great Parliament of Man, there to settle their differences and find their agreements,—

"All the full-brain, half-brain races led by armistice, love, and truth,"—

that is its crowning aim.

What is the basis of this humanitarian religion, what the root out of which all these duties and relations of human beings to each other finally grow?

It does indeed have the authority of Scripture. Jesus himself makes it explicitly one-half of all religion, illustrates alike its breadth and its depth with his parable of the Good Samaritan; and in the opening words of his prayer, left his followers of all races to use, "Our Father"; he has compelled them in the very act of recognizing the exalted filial relation they have with Deity to recognize the direct fraternal relation, "Our," that they have with each other.

But its real basis is deeper down than this. Christianity below all its splendid heights is most emphatically a natural religion,— does not rest merely on any written word, or bring its duties from any other world, or utter its sayings because as great sentiments they look and sound well. It builds always on our human nature, finds its Golden Rule by scraping away the dust from what was already in the soul, is a religion in the word's literal meaning of binding its recipients back to the great primal truths from which they had broken away; and the truth here on which its humanitarianism rests in the natural inborn unity and solidarity of our race, the fact that amid all their diversities and separations its parts are only the members of one larger human body,— mankind simply man written large.

It is a basis which is implied in the very wording of the Christian command, "Thou shalt love thy neighbor as thyself," a phrase legitimately meaning not merely as much as thyself, or in the same way as thyself, but as being a part of thyself. Man's separations are only on the outside. There are veins and arteries ramifying from land to land which pulse back and forth with a subtler blood than that of our individual flesh; muscles and nerves

THE HUMANITARIAN SIDE 405

reaching over mountains and dipping under seas, which bind nations together as limb to limb even when their armies are glaring at each other in the red light of battle-fields; nerves such as no anatomist has ever laid bare, along which peoples commune whose spoken words are to one another only as empty sounds.

The darker results of this oneness nature itself is continually reminding men of. The pestilence which springs up amid the filth and ignorance of some unknown village in far-off Asia has a part of its victims the next season in the heart of New York or Boston. The business depression which ever and anon breaks out in England or America makes its unticketed journey, independent of all railroads and steamships, and alike through the barred doors of tariffs and the open gates of free trade, completely around the globe. And sending our armies off ten thousand miles across the sea to torture Filipino patriots, and strike down Filipino liberties, the wave of violence started there recoils through seas of soul to fill our own land with murders and weaken the words that for a hundred years have declared our own freedom.

"For mankind are one in spirit, and an instinct bears along,
Round the earth's electric circle, the swift flash of right or wrong";

or, as the apostle Paul puts it, "Whether one member suffer, all the members suffer with it, or one member be honored, all the members rejoice with it."

The base of the humanitarian side of religion is simply the brighter and more developed side of this deep down, natural oneness. It takes what is often such a terrible thing in nature, our being linked for health or disease, joy or sorrow, liberty or tyranny with all, even the worst, of our race, and uses it as the foundation on which to build its temple of universal helpfulness and love. Are we bound up, it says, in one fate with our miserable neighbor? Then, instead of viewing him with hate and horror as tending to drag us down and make our fate one with his, let us, rather, view him with sympathy and assistance, so as to lift him up and make his fate one with ours. Confronted in nature with the alternative, Save or suffer — obey the "shalt" of love and live, or the "shalt" of law and die, it cordially chooses to save and live. With a divine alchemy it transmutes the base metal of fear as a motive power into the precious one of affection. And just as the man who loves his lesser self, if he has a sick stomach, or weak lung, or wounded arm, or even the humblest and most insignificant organ of his body diseased or suffering, will give it his special attention and aim to bring it

THE HUMANITARIAN SIDE

back to health, so man's love for his larger self, carried out, will lead him to give a like special care to all the like humblest and most insignificant parts of his larger race-self.

With its scope and basis thus defined, what is the duty of the Church with regard to this side of religion? Can there be any question that it ought to proclaim it as, at least, one-half of God's truth, and proclaim it not as an abstract principle merely, but in its direct application to the state of things in our own time?

Much indeed has been done in the past for its realization. Originally there was no recognition of it at all as any concern of religion. Enmity rather than love, killing and not saving, were for ages the supposed duty of man to all outside men; for ages even under Christianity the supposed duty of the churchman to all outside churches. It was a great day for religion when the word " humanity " came into its vocabulary, as great as it was for science when it got the word universe as a part of its speech. And since then, beyond question, wonderful has been the progress it has made both in the preaching of the Church and the practice of the world.

But, alas, with all that has been accomplished, how far is it from having reached either in breadth or depth the realization of its ideal! Look at the shortcomings of the individual man, at the wretchedness there often is in families, at the conflicts of labor and capital in the business world, at the ravages of intemperance in all classes of society, at the robbery and murder that are going on in our houses and streets, at the broad lines of separation that exist between the rich and the poor, at the self-seeking and wire-pulling and money-grafting of our politics, at the huge armies and navies that in the midst of our civilization are being prepared for war, at the strong races and nations that are trampling down the rights of the weak, at England holding even now in its homicidal arms the dead bodies of two strangled infant republics, at our own country, its hands yet red with the blood and torture of Filipino patriots; and without any pessimistic despair, but only recognizing things as they are, who shall say that "man's inhumanity to man" is all a thing of the past, and that the Church has not still a most imperative call to preach the humanitarian side of religion?

What though some of the issues before it are those of politics? Are politics to be set aside as a department of action that has nothing to do with morals, and under whose mantle corruption and crime are to hide safe from religion's condemning voice? When it is a nation

THE HUMANITARIAN SIDE 409

that is our neighbor, is the law of loving it as ourselves never to be spoken? When a political David has seized a poor State's one ewe lamb, is no church Nathan to go to him and say, " Thou art the man "? And when the traveler going down to Jericho is a whole people that thieves and robbers have wounded and left half dead, is no pulpit to cross over to him as a Good Samaritan with its healing oil and wine, no preacher to remonstrate with his countrymen beforehand against being the thieves and robbers who do the deed?

Of course, about all such new issues there will inevitably be a difference of opinion. Not everybody even of the Lord's army can march in the front ranks; and there may well be those who, before a step is taken, want to make sure it is one in advance. But, surely, in all issues where morals and religion are involved, the preacher, if fit for his place, leaving to others their secular side, ought always to lead off in at least presenting their higher claims, ought always, ahead of the practical, to keep waving the standard of the ideal.

This does not mean that even in moral issues the preacher is necessarily always right. He is liable, like all other men, to make mistakes,— leads off in many directions which prove to be aside from, and sometimes contrary to, the line in which God would lead. But this is true of all progress, is God's way of having men find out which is the right course. You have heard the story of the Arab captain with his troop of a hundred horsemen trying to cross at night an arm of the Red Sea, and losing the ridge shallow enough to take them over; how, after floundering about for a while, he gathered them all about him and started them off like the spokes of a wheel, in a hundred different directions, with orders for the one to shout who found the passable way. Ninety-nine of them got into deep water and failed, but one raised the required shout, and, following him, they all crossed in safety. That is what the great Captain of our salvation does with his men in finding the path of right for the world to take. He has them start off in different directions, some necessarily the wrong ones, and they fail. But among them some at least are sure to discover where real right lies, and, following it, humanity passes through seas of danger safely, from shore to shore. Who will say this is not better than standing still, or floundering aimlessly about? Who will say that the ninety-and-nine who fail do not contribute as much to finding the true course as the one who succeeds?

It is a duty, however, which belongs not to the preacher alone, but to the whole church. How otherwise than by carrying on its work a little further in the present can humanity make any return for the mighty work it has had done for it in the past? What is to be said of the man, inheriting the faith that has been gained for him by the toil and sacrifice of all the ages, — standing where he has to say

" By the light of burning heretics Christ's bleeding feet I track,
Toiling up new Calvaries ever with the cross that turns not back,—

who leaves the church as soon as the pulpit attempts to add

"One new word to that grand *Credo* which in prophet-hearts hath burned
Since the first man stood God-conquered with his face to heaven upturned"; —

what of the woman, breathing the humanitarian air which has been made sweet for her by the martyr-fires of uncounted Perpetuas and Blandinas, and dwelling in the safety that the pleadings and prayers of uncounted centuries have brought her to, who cannot stand the nervous strain of listening now and then to pleas for having the same blessings enlarged and passed on to other women and other lands? Is not the martyrdom of giving ear to a possible new truth a very small price to pay for the martyrdoms in which millions at the rack and the stake and on the battle-field have given their whole lives to secure to the hearer his now precious old truths?

But supposing such themes do empty the church somewhat for the passing hour, they are the only ones that can fill the church for the coming years. True of it in all their force are the words of Jesus, "Whosoever will save his life shall lose it, and whosoever will lose his life for my sake shall find it." Why are its doors so largely deserted now by the common people, a desertion that is complained of in all denominations far and wide? Is it not in part because the common people have lost their interest in the old problems of theology and in the concerns of another world, and have got the feeling that preachers are too timid to touch the great living problems of our own time and the concerns of this present earth? A while ago a gentleman, inquiring among the workingmen of our country why they did not attend religious services, and told by one of them it was because they did not like the subjects the ministers were preaching about, asked him what he would have them preach about? "About anything but heaven," was the reply; and undoubtedly he represented very largely the feeling of his class. There is no lack of interest in the earthly side of religion. Laborhalls are not deserted; political and reformatory meetings not thinly attended. And if the church is ever again to share humanity's numbers, it must get for itself the reputation of sharing humanity's work.

Does this mean that the church should give up the theistic and devotional side of religion to proclaim only its humanitarian side? Far from it. It means only that it should connect the two more closely together. It was not because the workingman disliked heaven that he did not want it preached about, but only because he had heard of it so much as a place wholly separate from earth. The work of the church should be like that of the great snow-mountains, so many of which I used to see on the western shore of our country,— Hood, Adams, Baker, St. Helen's, and Rainier. They rise up as pillars from earth into heaven. Through all the long winter months the clouds from far and wide bring to their royal brows the glittering diadems and the heaped-up treasures of the ice and snow. They catch the earliest beams of the morning, and around them linger and play, in rose and crimson and purple tints, the latest hues of eve, while all night long they hold communion with the shining stars and the immeasurable heights of spotless sky; and as the traveler comes into their presence, he can but bow down before them in profoundest awe as before the very altars, which indeed they are, of the Infinite God.

But this is only one part of their work. Out of their glittering peaks and their piled-up treasures of the ice and snow, out of the very things which so excite our awe and adoration, they send down through all the long summer months a thousand little rills, which flow through the meadows, make the grass green and the flowers fair, quench the thirst of beasts and cattle, turn the wheels of mills and factories, and at last, uniting together, form a mighty river, the Columbia, which bears on its bosom the commerce of a great city. And one part of this work they do just as faithfully and just as much in the spirit of its being their mission as they do the other.

So with the Christian church. It should indeed have its mounts of devotion, have its times when it towers up from earth and holds communion with God and the spirit-world and the everlasting mysteries. No religion is ever worth much for practical life which has never known what it is to lose itself in the ecstasy and mystery and inspiration of the spirit's realm. No soul is the one to come down and do the truest work for our common humanitarian world — even for its idiot boys, as Raphael has shown so well in his wonderful picture — that has not been transfigured and glorified and had its garments made shining white on the mountain-peaks of devotion. It should catch the first beams of each new truth from the great Sun of Righteousness that dawns over the earth, and be the brow around which linger and play all that is sweet and beautiful in the memories and associations of the older faiths. Yet all this is only a part of its work. Out of its hours of ecstasy and devotion, out of its new truths and its ancient memories, out of the very heights which excite most our awe and adoration, and where it holds communion closest with God and the spirit-world, it should send down its little rills of love and life into our common, every-day, human world, brightening up its homes, washing away the stains from its business, purifying its politics, lending its aid to the weary round of its shops and factories, filling the hearts of its adherents with kindness so that the very cattle they come in contact with from day to day will feel somehow in their dumb breasts that they have a Christian for a master, and bearing on its bosom of love the whole world's commerce nearer the eternal climes. Let the church do this work with the theistic and devotional side of its religion, use heaven to bless earth, and there need be no fear but that the workingman will want such a heaven preached to him, and that humanity everywhere will turn with fresh love to an institution from whose heights above there flow such streams into all its plains below.

Friends, it is this humanitarian side of religion that in the four years of my pastorate with you, and in all my ministry, I have tried to set forth,— in behalf of this, as well as for its own eternal worth, that I have tried to utilize its theistic and devotional side. I am sorry that all of you could not go with me, heart, hand, and hearing, in the work; glad that so many of you could do so, glad especially of those who, not able to go with me in their convictions, have given me not less cordially their presence and support.

If human errors and imperfections have mingled somewhat with my preaching other humanness; if at any time my words or spirit have seemed to you unduly harsh or needlessly wounding, all such I ask you to forgive and forget. One thing I can claim alike here and in all my ministry, that when the question of what to say has come up before me, I have never asked how it was going to affect my pocket or popularity or personal welfare in any way, but only whether it was the truth and a needed truth, and, this answered, have gone ahead and proclaimed it with all the clearness and force and love of which I was capable, believing with Tennyson,

> " Because right is right, to follow right
> Were wisdom, in the scorn of consequence,"—

THE HUMANITARIAN SIDE 417

at any rate, of consequence to one's self. And if ever it has been " one-sided preaching," the one side has always been the side of liberty, of progress, of the weak and oppressed, never the side of tyranny, of reaction, and of the strong oppressor; for I never yet have seen that wrong was in any danger of suffering wrong from lack of pleaders, even without religion's voice; and however confusedly the two may sometimes get mixed with each other, and whatever the party lines across which they may zigzag back and forth, I have always held with Browning that, everywhere,

"The right must be the right,
And other than the wrong, while Heaven endures."

Apart from its wider outlook, it is a pastorate, I am sure, which has not been wholly without those nearer human relations whose religious worth we all alike can recognize. Children in the Sunday-school and at the baptismal-font have been a part of humanity that we have unitedly served. We have known the jollity of happy social gatherings. Sorrow has come to our houses, and in the seats before me, where once sat the living forms of those we loved, there now sit their silent memories, forevermore our mutual friends. Sacred to me personally will its four years always be as the time when the one who in all my other pastorates has been my right-hand co-worker and adviser, and who held equally in her large soul all parts of religion, has dropped from my side. Never shall I forget the warm human sympathy, the ministry of comfort, that you all alike in those trying hours ministered back to me. I lay down my pastoral office with you to-day, but not my friendship and interest in your welfare, nor my purpose to help you in every desired way. I have learned while here to love your church, love the town, love the many noble individual specimens of humanity I have found in all the churches and all through the place; and my hope is that soon some other, perhaps younger, voice will be secured around which you of my own flock can all rally, and who, as cordially treated by the other pastors here as I have been, will lead you on yet further and better into being a useful, happy, and united church.

Turning now for a last loving look at the ideal my service with you has had in view, let me say in farewell that whatever you may have thought of the efforts for its realization while they were being carried on, I have no fears but that in the future the thing itself is what you will be proud more and more to have had labored for within your walls. There is a legend that when one of the great cathedrals of Europe was being built, an old man came along and

THE HUMANITARIAN SIDE 419

begged that he might be allowed to do some of its work. The architect respected the applicant's pious desire, but, fearing that his failing eyes and trembling hands might only mar what he regarded as the building's more important parts,— its sacred altar, stately columns, illumined windows, angel forms, and statue of the son of God,— gave him only the face of a man to carve high up among the shadows of the roof, where its imperfections, if any, would never be seen. The old man did lovingly what was thought to be his humble part; then, forced to lay down his tools as no longer needed, passed away, and for years the whole thing was forgotten. But one day, when the ascending sun was in the requisite position, a beam of light glancing through an illumined window, partly open, fell on the old man's work, revealing it as a thing of marvelous beauty. And thenceforward, as long as the cathedral stood, year after year on the day when the sun got round to lighting it up, crowds of people gathered within its doors to gaze thrilled and inspired, not on sacred altar and stately column and illumined window and figures of seraph and Saviour, but, as the divinest thing there, on the sweet human face carved by the loving hands of this nameless old man.

It is such an image, in that cathedral of God the nave and transept and majestic columns and sacred altar of which are the whole wide earth, whose features I have tried to carve — not alone, but as the humble member of a guild reaching through all churches and all sects; and, obscure and insignificant as the work may now seem, and soon as I, as one of its workmen, am to pass away and be forgotten, I have faith that in the coming years, when the sunlight of God shall have mounted higher up in the sky, its radiance will reveal its true character, and you will find that the divinest work done in this temple is humanitarian work, and its divinest product a redeemed and perfected man.